Contents

To the memory of Harry, my father.

Contributors

Peter Ratcliffe   Senior Lecturer in Sociology, University of Warwick, UK.

T. K. Oommen   Professor of Sociology, Jawaharlal Nehru University, New Delhi, India and President of International Sociological Association

Walter R. Allen   Professor of Sociology, University of California, Los Angeles, USA.

Christine Inglis   Director, Multicultural Centre, University of Sydney, Australia and Vice-President of Research Committee on Race, Minority and Ethnic Relations, International Sociological Association.

Rupert Taylor   Senior Lecturer, Department of Political Studies, University of the Witwatersrand, South Africa.

Radhika Coomaraswamy   Director, International Centre for Ethnic Studies, Colombo, Sri Lanka.

Ashok Kaul   Senior Lecturer in Sociology, Banares Hindu University, Varanasi, India.

L. Adele Jinadu   Professor of Political Science, University of Lagos, Nigeria and Electoral Commissioner, Government of Nigeria.

Devorah Kalekin-Fishman   Senior Lecturer in Education, University of Haifa, Israel.

Antonina Kłoskowska   Professor Emeritus, University of Warsaw, Poland and President, Polish Sociological Association.

Vasil Ziatdinov   Senior Researcher, Institute of Culture, Moscow, Russia.

Sviatoslav Grigoriev   Professor of Sociology, University of Altai, Russia.

Abbreviations and acronyms

AIAS   Australian Institute of Aboriginal Studies
AIMA   Australian Institute of Multicultural Affairs
ANC   African National Congress
ANU   Australian National University
ARC   Australian Research Council
ATSIC   Aboriginal and Torres Strait Islander Commission
CCCS   Centre for Contemporary Cultural Studies
CEBOS   Centre of Social Opinion Research
CPSU   Communist Party of the Soviet Union
CRE   Commission for Racial Equality
CRER   Centre for Research in Ethnic Relations
ESB   English-speaking background
FLS   Folk Legal System
GHS   General Household Survey
ICES   International Centre for Ethnic Studies
ISA   International Sociological Association
ISR   Institute for Social Research
LEA   Local Education Authority
LFS   Labour Force Survey
NDHS   National Dwelling and Housing Survey
NESB   Non English-speaking background
OPCS   Office of Population Census and Surveys
PSI   Policy Studies Institute
RLS   Religious Legal System
RUER   Research Unit on Ethnic Relations
SEG   Socio-Economic Group
SLS   State Legal System
SSRC   Social Science Research Council
TSSR   Tartar Soviet Socialist Republic
UNESCO   United Nations Educational, Scientific and Cultural Organization

Preface

In a sense this book was conceived at a meeting in New Delhi in August 1986. UNESCO had funded a three-day workshop linked to the International Sociological Association's XIth World Congress of Sociology to explore the links between theory, methods and substance in research on "race" and ethnic relations.

Marshall Murphree as convenor invited the author to represent western Europe at this meeting. I accepted the invitation but out of modesty declined the remit, preferring instead the rather more manageable task of evaluating the British research scene. A number of those whose work appears in the book were at this workshop; namely Walter Allen, Christine Inglis, Radhika Coomaraswamy and Adele Jinadu.

It soon became clear that we were moving into somewhat uncharted territory in that little consideration had been given in the literature to the interface between theory and research, and there had certainly been no systematic attempt to bring together scholars from around the world to engage in comparative work. With the fundamental political changes in Europe towards the end of the decade and the implications these had for our work, I decided to embark on the current project. Had I realized the impact this mammoth task would have on my life I might, in retrospect, have thought better of it!

I was sustained throughout by the generous support and encouragement of Marshall Murphree, and owe an enormous debt of gratitude to him. Without his help the book certainly would never have seen the light of day. I also received staunch support from Heribert Adam, who as President of the ISAs Research Committee on Race, Minority and Ethnic Relations from 1986 to 1990, both underscored the importance of the project and helped secure a grant from the ISA to assist in its progress.

As to financial support I am grateful both to UNESCO and the ISA for giving the work an early impetus. I could not have sustained the work ultimately, however, without sabbatical leave from my home institution, the University of Warwick, and a sizeable grant from their "Research and Innovations Fund".

The support from colleagues over many years is inestimable. It is somewhat invidious to select individuals for special mention, but one person has to be singled out. John Rex saved me from a career as a statistician and taught me the value of sociology. Despite our occasional differences, usually about soccer, he has remained immensely supportive by reinforcing my belief both in the importance of serious sociological work and the commitment to use this knowledge to address inequalities wrought by racism, apartheid and related cancers which continue to afflict the contemporary world.

Many others, too numerous to mention, both colleagues and students, have helped me clarify my ideas by discussion. Others have assisted in specific ways by commenting on drafts of various chapters; my sincere thanks go out here to Marian FitzGerald, David Mason, Karl Taeuber and Abebe Zegeye. I am also grateful to Peter Jackson and John Solomos for their constructive comments on an earlier, somewhat lengthier version of the book. None of the remaining errors and omissions are a reflection on their fastidiousness, of course; they are entirely my responsibility.

Thanks should go, last but certainly not least, to Mandy Broom and her colleagues in the Economics department at Warwick, for their sterling efforts in typing a large part of the manuscript, and battling against evil computer viruses in the process.

Peter Ratcliffe
July 1993.

Part One
CONCEPTUAL MATTERS

Chapter 1

Conceptualizing "race", ethnicity and nation: towards a comparative perspective

Peter Ratcliffe

Although the academic literature is replete with global theorizations of nations, nationalism and the ethnic origins of conflicting groups (Smith 1986, Gellner 1983, Anderson 1991, Hobsbawn 1990 – to mention but a few of the more prominent texts), with the exception of the works by Schermerhorn (1970) and Horowitz (1985) there have been few attempts to provide a systematic comparative analysis of social cleavages grounded in differences of "race", ethnicity and nation. While the present work cannot lay claim to providing a definitive account, it should at least provide the sound basis for such a venture.

It does so by assessing the salience of these three factors in very different societal contexts; "salience" being judged at many levels – material social inequalities, political action, policy debates, media and intellectual discourse, and so on. Its distinctiveness stems from the fact that the various chapters are written by scholars whose own origins (and workbases) lie in the societies about which they are writing. Their chapters also seek to reflect the nature of debates within these societies, rather than a selective reading of them dictated by the editor. In this way we would hope both to avoid the dangers of ethnocentrism, and to highlight the ways in which Western social science has influenced the ways in which issues are conceptualized.

The relevance of this work to the "world community" need hardly be stated. As Horowitz wrote in relation to one of our pivotal concepts: "Ethnicity has fought and bled and burned its way into public and scholarly consciousness" (1985: xi). And as we approach the end of 1993 much uncertainty surrounds the future of the "nations" of the former Soviet Union, "ethnic cleansing" is routinely employed as a euphemism for the carnage in what was Yugoslavia, and neo-Nazis in the unified Germany make a mockery of claims that "racism" and "fascism" have been buried along with Hitler.

Fully recognizing that "class", religious, linguistic and gender divisions are also an important feature of much conflict, the book aims to address three central questions. First, it seeks to explain the emergence of contemporary conflict by analyzing the historical entrenchment of enmities. The crux of the matter may be, for example, the imposition of slavery or colonial rule, migratory movements, the division of territory following war, and/or the systematic political oppression of certain groups.

Secondly, the book is concerned to uncover the ways in which collective enmities are created, manipulated and reproduced at different historical junctures. For example, how do differing modes of discourse at the level of the polity, media and academe impact on social relations between groups? The final, and interlinking, theme is a critical evaluation of the ways in which social scientists have theorized structural inequalities and conflict within particular societies; and the vexed question of how the resulting theorizations feed into the substantive research agenda.

Because of the complexity of the issues involved the present chapter aims to do rather more than simply indicate the scope of the volume. As the substantive essays may at one level be seen as "raw data", it needs to provide a framework for a comparative analysis. This means spelling out the central ideas which link the various contributions.

The first section discusses the key concepts of "race", ethnicity and nation, and provides the basis for the central orienting principle of the book. As section two explains, chapters are essentially divided on the basis of the relative salience of "race" on the one hand, and "ethnicity and nation" on the other. Except for a few concluding remarks in the final section, the remainder of the chapter is devoted to an analysis of those societies (a) where "race"-thinking dominates debates, and (b) where conflict/inequalities are principally seen as based on "ethnic" or "national" divisions (or both, in the event of struggles grounded in "ethno-nationalism").

"Race", ethnicity and nation: a conceptual minefield

"Race"

As Ratcliffe (in this volume) discusses in some detail the controversy surrounding the analytical status of the term "race" there is no need to rehearse the arguments here. Suffice it to say that the rejection of its "scientific status" and concerns as to the potential dangers of its retention in academic discourse have led many to discard it. The convention adopted in the present work will be to place it in inverted commas, unless its use is regarded as unproblematic within a particular society, e.g. the USA. "Local" conventions will be observed both as a way of reflecting existing discourse and of highlighting differences which are invariably of theoretical and substantive significance.

To exclude it altogether would be to deny its presence in contemporary debates. And for two reasons it is also important for our argument:
   a) we aim to assess the centrality of "race"-thinking, at different levels of discourse, to contemporary forms of social conflict, and
   b) there is a need to address the reasons for its presence or absence in the various spheres of debate. In particular we need to ask why it is that in some societies an explicit denial of the existential status of the term, does not necessarily imply a rejection of its essential content.

Take, for example, the case of Israel. As is argued by Kalekin-Fishman (in this volume), an essentially "racial" classification of groups by the State is accompanied by a total denial of "race" as an issue; the latter being intimately associated in the "public mind" with the holocaust. Balibar (1991b: 53) goes further in arguing that:

> . . . the State of Israel, faced with an internal and an external enemy and the impossible gamble of forging an "Israeli nation" developed a powerful racism directed both against the "Eastern" Jews (called "Blacks") and the Palestinians, who were driven out of their lands and colonized.

This highlights very effectively both the agentiveness of the process that is usually labelled "racialization", and its location within a specific mode and level of discourse. It also suggests a link both between racialization and racism, and between state racism and the process of "nation-building".

But, what exactly is "racism"? A few writers have argued that it has been used so loosely, to represent a host of things from beliefs to individual actions to state policies that, along with "race" it should be rejected. Most would argue simply for a greater level of clarity, and would agree with Rex's view, expressed as early as 1970, that the key element is the existence of "deterministic belief systems". Racism is present in situations where:

4

> . . . the inequalities and differentiation inherent in a social structure are related to physical and cultural criteria of an ascriptive kind and are rationalized in terms of deterministic belief systems, of which the most usual in recent years has made reference to biological science. (Rex 1970: 39)

As we saw above, the absence of "race"-thinking, at whatever level of discourse, does not imply that the *ideational content* of the concept (even when narrowly perceived as biological) is absent. This much was clear in the case of Israel, where "blackness" as a supposed phenotypical characteristic (i.e. skin colour) was equated with evil, mirroring the linguistic imagery stemming from centuries of Western expansion and the exploitation of African peoples.

This linking of biology with "deterministic belief systems" in the absence of an explicitly racialized discourse also appears in the chapter by Ziatdinov and Grigoriev (see chapter 12). Scientific and political debates in the former Soviet Union eschewed "race" terminology but nonetheless characterized Tartars, for example, as a warlike, dangerous and backward people who possessed quite distinctive, and exclusive, "Mongoloid" features. Popular discourse among Russians also displays concern about the possibility that "in every Russian flows at least one drop of Tartar blood" (p. 245).

Presumably then, if it is the case that "race"-thinking can exist without a complementary "racialized discourse", then so too can racism. The crux of the argument rests on the element of the Rex definition which conceives of forms of "race" conflict in which "deterministic belief systems" do not take an explicitly biological form. Balibar talks, for example, of a "new" racism which is a "racism without races". It is a racism, he argues:

> whose dominant theme is not biological heredity but the insurmountability of cultural differences, a racism which, at first sight, does not postulate the superiority of certain groups or peoples in relation to others but "only" the harmfulness of abolishing frontiers, the incompatibility of life-styles and traditions. (1991a: 21)

He follows Taguieff in labelling this as "differentialist racism".

There are undoubtedly widely varying conceptualizations of "race" and racism, arguably different strains of racism impacting on the various communities within particular societies, and different discriminatory practices, and associated modes of discourse, within various levels of a polity (polity here being interpreted in the widest sense to encompass all institutional settings, from central and local government to academe, business, commerce, the media, and so on). It is possible therefore to speak of "state racism", "institutional(ized) racism" within organizations, "media racism", and also (some would argue) "academic racism" (cf. Essed 1987).

Despite the potential dangers of using the same term in such different contexts, and despite the problems with "race", both will be retained as pivotal concepts in the current volume. However, they are not presented uncritically, nor are they seen as representing ideas which were, or are, necessarily distinct *in essence* from (say) nationalism and ethnicity.

Ethnicity

Picking up the obvious implication of the previous remark, it is clear that in both "popular" and academic discourse much confusion surrounds the concept of ethnicity. At one level ethnicity and ethnic imagery are represented simply as synonymous with, or appropriate euphemisms for, "race". Thus, in Britain, there is a coyness in the public policy domain about explicit reference to "racial" groups (despite the existence of the 1976 *Race* Relations Act and its monitoring body, the Commission for *Racial* Equality). Reference is usually made instead to the "*ethnic* minorities" or "minority *ethnic* communities". In the USA on the other hand, as Allen (chapter 3) shows, "race" inequalities are explicitly discussed, if not successfully addressed. And, as we have already seen, in some societies such as Germany and Israel, memories of the holocaust result in a blanket avoidance of the term "race".

The significance of ethnicity lies in its salience for group consciousness and collective action. But, if it is not simply a surrogate for "race" what is it? A comprehensive definition from Bulmer (1986: 54) and quoted by Ratcliffe (in this volume) includes "common ancestry", "memories of a shared past" and aspects of group identity based on "kinship, religion, language, shared territory, nationality or physical appearance". The advantage of such a conceptualization is that it encompasses most of the issues around which human societies have organized and struggled for centuries. But there are at least four fundamental problems.

First, because of its very comprehensiveness and flexibility it opens the door to the creation or nomination of an almost limitless number of "ethnic groups" without regard to the significance of the delineating factors.

Secondly, and of more significance, however, is the fact that if applied

6

uncritically it presents a view of ethnicity that is inherently both static and uniform. As Horowitz (1985: 4) says, "shifting contexts make ethnicity now more, now less prominent. The international environment plays a part in its emergence and remission". Although primordial ties are a key element of "ethnic consciousness" these are not fixed in a deterministic sense, no more than perceptions of them have a cognitive commonality. Ethnic formations at particular historical junctures retain an element of fluidity, and are subject to fractionalization on the basis of other factors such as class and gender.

The third area of concern relates to the question of "situational ethnicity". Not only do ethnic consciousness and the attendant social relations change over time, they also cannot correctly be seen as invariant with respect to social context.

Finally, there is a sense in which ethnicity, ethnic identity and possibly also "nation", are in reality elusive. It could be argued, for example, that one's identity is not only situationally variant, but is also a repository for, and partly a function of, exogenous contemporary factors, both material and ideological. It is in essence an "imagined" and/or "fictional" creation.

Nation

. . . it is an imagined political community – and imagined as both inherently limited and sovereign.

This for Anderson (1991: 6) is the essence of "nation". Further,

It is *imagined* because the members of even the smallest nation will never know most of their fellow-members, meet them, or even hear of them, yet in the minds of each lives the image of their communion. (ibid.: 6)

Nation is thereby seen as an anthropological entity, and the key question is that of how the ideological framework underpinning this feeling of commonality emerges and takes hold.

This in itself raises a series of interesting comparative questions, in that the mode of development can be seen as associated with particular political and socio-cultural relations at often quite specific historical junctures; for example, the domination or oppression of peoples, the political vulnerability of a state, the aspirations to hegemony of an ethno-cultural elite, and so on.

But the "awareness" of a distinct national identity clearly *in itself* does not lead to the development of nationalist movements. One needs to ask a second series of comparative questions about the ways in which communal identity is mobilized, and the necessary and sufficient conditions for this mobilization to take place (at the same time avoiding the pitfalls of a crude historicism). Thus, in the current Balkan conflict there are specific questions about mobilization around the concept of a "Greater Serbia" and comparative questions with (say) the forms of ethno-nationalism discussed by Kaul later in this volume.

The final set of issues are in some ways the most germane to the theme of this book. These relate to the links between the presence of a national identity, the development of nationalist movements, and the resort to racist or "ethnicist" ideologies. Useful here is the counterpoint of two central concepts by Adam (1990) in his article "Exclusive Nationalism versus Inclusive Patriotism". It reminds us that nationalist movements are clearly not *by definition* mono-ethnic or mono-"racial", nor do they necessarily appeal to such a narrow consciousness. Furthermore, as well as noting the significance of ethnic fluidity and situational ethnicity, Adam also reminds us that "solidarity and antagonism live side by side" and "despite its emphasis on unity a nationalist movement or ethnie is rarely monolithic" (ibid.: 577).

Oommen (in chapter 2 below) gives a detailed and systematic analysis of the relations between "nation", "ethnie" and claims to territory; necessarily a key element of much inter-group conflict. In doing so he implicitly disputes Anderson's idea of "nations" as "imagined communities".

The salience of "race", ethnicity and nation

The title of this section provides a major pointer to the central theme of the book, and to its organization. In spelling out the meanings attached to our key concepts, albeit briefly due to the usual constraints of space, it has been suggested that the relative salience of the three concepts varies markedly between societies, the reasons being of considerable social and political significance, in addition to being of sociological interest. The key questions appear on the surface to relate to the historical bases of conflict, the experience of oppression and suppression at different historical junctures, and the management of actual, or potential, conflict within contemporary social formations; but contemporary discourse may seek to suppress the "essential nature" of social cleavages, in the light of historical sensitivities. Thus, as we saw earlier, given recent memories of the holocaust, in present-day Germany and Israel both "race"-thinking and the labelling of conflict as due to racist activity, are explicitly avoided.

An interesting and much broader question relates to whether certain societies, or types of society, are in a sense predisposed to develop modes of discourse which reflect historical realities. Is it correct to argue, for example, as Murphree (1988: 20) does by implication, that the salience of "race" is greatest "in Anglo-Saxon societies"? Could one perhaps broaden the base of this generalization to encompass European or Western societies in general on the basis of their involvement in the exploitation of "black" labour via colonization, slavery and indenture? Mason (1986: 5) goes further by questioning the linkage between the historical "facts" and the notion of primordialism by asking:

> Are those forms of human behaviour associated with the racist beliefs and practices characteristic of the history of 19th and 20th-century Europe and its offshoots unique, and hence explicable in terms of some aspect of that history, or are they merely one form taken by a primordial ethnocentrism?

Whatever view one takes of the links between primordialism and the racialization of social relations in recent European history, it is clear that "race"-thinking and the development of scientific racism in the 19th century were central features of the cultural map, indeed "world-view", of these particular societies. In the final analysis it is essentially the imprint of these paradigms on contemporary social relations which concerns us.

In examining the relationship between academic theorizations of "race", ethnicity and nation and the associated research agenda in different societies, the book will aim to stimulate the development of scholarly work which adopts a systematic (internationally) comparative framework. Chapter 2 does this by providing further clarification both of state, nation and ethnie, and of closely related concepts such as the "nation-state". Oommen suggests that concepts emerge within particular historical contexts, but need to transcend them in order to possess scientific utility. Much confusion, he argues, stems from their different usage by scholars. "Nation" and "state" are treated as if coterminous by some writers, thereby denying the reality of multinational states. This is seen to some extent as a problem peculiar to "Western social science" in that the nation-state is more appropriate to Western societies than elsewhere. But it can be argued that even here the (mono)nation-state is something of a misnomer. One only has to

9

think of the UK and the distinct "nations" of Scots and Welsh with their own national territory.

More provocative, however, are (a) his theoretical separation of religion and nation, and (b) his definition of ethnicity. As to the first of these, he argues (p. 35) that:

> The unfortunate but persisting tendency to define religious collectivities as nations has not only perpetuated conceptual confusion but also human misery.

This provokes one to reflect on the debates in the UK as to whether Sikhs constituted a distinct nation and were as such protected by the "Race Relations" legislation. It also provides an interesting backdrop to the ethnonationalist struggles discussed by Kaul in chapter 8; struggles moreover that appear on the face of it to have religious cleavages at their very epicentre.

As to ethnicity, Oommen defines this (p. 39) as "a product of conquest, colonization and immigration and the consequent disengagement between culture and territory". Now, while this appears to negate the possibility of a positive ethnicity, for example ethnicity as a culture of resistance, this is not totally so. Elsewhere he recognizes the presence of "instrumental ethnicity" and argues that in conjunction with "symbolic ethnicity" it provides the necessary, but not sufficient, conditions for the transformation from "ethnie" to "nation". Where some scholars would take issue with him is over the apparent fixity of these categories, in that it could be suggested that material deprivation set against a historical experience of oppression can produce quite distinct cultural forms, and not simply "the anxiety to preserve one's cultural identity" (p. 39).

What Oommen's essay provides, however, is a highly insightful analysis of the multitude of ways in which the state–nation–ethnie nexus exists in different societal contexts. There is also a dynamism in the account because of his insistence on a *processual* approach. Taken in conjunction with the earlier part of the present chapter, where we stressed the potential significance of other key factors such as "race", class and gender, we have a powerful framework for a serious comparative analysis of social relations in "multiracial", polyethnic societies.

10

The "race" paradigm: a Western obsession?

The second section of the book looks at a group of societies where the dominant analytical approaches see "race", or a "racialization process", as the key to understanding social inequalities and conflict between groups. All, significantly perhaps given our earlier discussion, are European societies or are controlled politically and economically by Europeans, whether in a majority, as in the USA and Australia, or a minority as in South Africa.

Walter Allen's paper presents a comprehensive account of the historical experience of Black Americans in US society. It also shows how central to social relations the question of phenotypical difference is. "Race", represented by skin colour, became part of everyday discourse with the advent of slavery; and de jure "Jim Crow" segregation ensured that following abolition "the nigger knew his [sic] place". Social distinctions were so marked that some theorists such as Lloyd Warner likened them to those of caste.

The key question which Allen addresses is that of whether the salience of "race" has declined in recent decades; in other words whether other factors such as class, gender or economic status are more adequate predictors of life chances and social standing in contemporary America. His answer is that although some prominent writers, such as William Julius Wilson, have suggested this to be the case, the empirical evidence does not support the thesis. While not denying that the position of African American men had changed markedly since the Second World War, he produces data which show that, controlling for educational attainment, they still lag significantly behind their white counterparts. Black women had on the whole fared rather better but there were still major gender differentials overall. Looking also at data on residential segregation the general situation suggested a clear bifurcation; with a burgeoning Black elite accompanied by the continuation of a massive "black underclass" locked into urban poverty and squalor.

Questions of cultural and ethnic specificity are also of great significance both academically and politically, as are studies which illuminate the relative positions of the so-called "hyphenated Americans", e.g. those of Mexican, Native (Indian) and "Asian" origin. But the overarching paradigm is that of "race". The general political concern is that of the ongoing effects of racism, effects that remain despite the undoubted economic progress and social mobility of many.

11

Insofar as Africa can be seen as a "common territory" under Oommen's definition, and insofar as a common consciousness has evolved, African Americans may be conceived of as constituting a nation rather than an ethnie. Aspirations to statehood is a different matter. Certainly at the highpoint of the Black Power movement in the 1960s, there were those who sought a separate state within the current territory of the US. And some Pan-Africanists saw a return to Africa as an ideal. (Indeed some groups of African American intellectuals have recently proposed dropping "American" from the identity label.) For most of America's Black population, however, the reality of everyday life is that of a marginalized, racialized minority.

For Australia's Aboriginal population the gains in terms of social mobility have been considerably less impressive than those of the average African American. What there is by way of bifurcation relates in this case not to the "black" population but to the world of the academic and policy-maker. As Inglis demonstrates, the factor which distinguishes the Australian literature from that in the UK, USA and South Africa is that there is a complete disjuncture between accounts relating to the Aboriginal population and those concerned with the "ethnic minorities", i.e. the rest of the non-indigenous population.

Rather than representing imported labour as in the USA, of course, Aboriginal peoples have an obvious moral and legal claim to the lands of their ancestors. Though marginalized, and almost exterminated by violence and disease during the early period of colonial settlement, they are in a very real sense a submerged nation with deep primordial attachments. Early anthropological studies served to reify and underscore their marginality by treating them as a "zoo"; as a people with interesting, exotic cultural practices worthy of dissection, description and subsequent transmission to the wider academic community. In this way a form of insidious racism was institutionalized within intellectual discourse.

In addition, as Inglis explains, immigration policy was concerned historically with reinforcing the "European" character of its population. It was therefore exclusivist in "racial" terms, and resisted in particular the importation of labour from south-east Asia. When the restrictions were no longer tenable, the government adopted a policy of assimilation, albeit one which specifically excluded the Aboriginal population. Inglis describes research into "visibility" as a "no-go area", meaning that phenotype-based racism, while implicitly sanctioned by the State by virtue of its approach to immigration and evidenced by everyday discourse and practices, was nevertheless to be denied exposure through empirical research.

Inglis sees the research agenda as not only avoiding structural inequality within Australian society, but also of avoiding the whole question of the relations between marginalized groups (in particular Aboriginals and "part-Aboriginals") and the rest of society. As in the UK, multiculturalism followed assimilation as the official goal of state policy. But by focusing on cultural difference and (more narrowly) linguistic competence, it was effectively a facade behind which social inequalities could remain unresearched, unrecognized in official circles, and therefore unchallenged.

South Africa, on the other hand, has since 1948 imposed a system of rigid de jure "racial" separation, with differential relations to the polity on the part of the various officially designated groups. And whereas the Aboriginal population of Australia has won significant concessions from the state via affirmative action programmes and the like, progress in South Africa, despite the release of Nelson Mandela and the unbanning of the African National Congress (ANC), has been slow and faltering. Pressure from the (largely Afrikaner) extreme Right and the Conservative Party has even succeeded at times in stalling talks on power sharing between the ANC and the government of de Klerk. But the catalyst for the breakdown has been the involvement of state forces in stoking up internecine strife between the ANC and the largely Zulu-based Inkatha movement.

All of this is well known. Furthermore, there have been volumes written on the sociology of South African society. The debates between M. G. Smith, Leo Kuper, John Rex and Harold Wolpe on the various Marxian and Pluralist paradigms are familiar academic terrain (see, for example, Smith & Kuper 1969, Kuper 1974, Rex 1971, 1973, Wolpe 1986). Rupert Taylor builds on this literature, and also an earlier paper (Taylor 1991) in which he addressed one of the key issues in contemporary South Africa, namely the attempt to diffuse the political opposition to a "racial" hegemony by manipulating ethnic differentiation and "tribalized" social relations. As in Nigeria, as we shall see shortly, the past intrudes on the present through the reproduction of colonial tribal policy. It also raises intriguing comparative questions in that one aspect of racialization in western societies is the cementing of ascribed differences between groups.

Taylor criticizes writers in the Marxian tradition for failing to engage successfully with the idea of "race" (by seeing it essentially as an example of "false consciousness"). The liberal mainstream tradition within academe is in turn berated for maintaining the "race" paradigm and thereby reifying "racial" divisions. Taylor argues that multiracialism, as adopted by many "black" (or predominantly "black") groups, including the ANC, imposes a false theoretical problematic and invokes an unacceptable political agenda for the future. "Non-Racialism" is proposed as the solution to both errors.

Ratcliffe focuses on the debates which dominate the British literature, namely the position of "racialized" minorities. The essay reflects the concern with nomenclature, and shows how these concerns have political implications going far beyond the usual academic quest for conceptual clarity. It illustrates how inequalities based on "race", class and gender have been theorized, and stresses that "race" in one form or another is conventionally the principal orienting variable for empirical and theoretical research.

However, it must be said that there are those who dissent from the current orthodoxy. In a recent scathing attack on prominent sections of academe and the "race industry" (most notably the Commission for Racial Equality) Ballard (1992) argued that there should be a much greater emphasis on ethnic differentiation and the positive achievements of some individuals in the face of widespread discrimination. He is undoubtedly correct in suggesting that some writers have distorted the position of "black" communities by slipping into a "victim-oriented" approach. On the other hand, it is a mistake (a) to suggest that the majority have done so, and (b) to deny that the racialization of discourse, and associated discriminatory acts, are the major problems facing minorities, irrespective of class and gender considerations. Also, as implied earlier, there is often an imperceptibly thin line between racism and "ethnicism" (cf. Taguieff's "differentialist racism").

As Oommen argues, Britain's "black" communities could be conceived of as ethnies, who display certain elements of a common identity but lack a moral or legal claim (whether primordial or otherwise) to land, and thence to statehood. We are talking, of course, about those who were in the main drawn to Britain from the ex-colonies, and it is these countries which represent the locus of national identity for many, irrespective of citizenship or putative nationality. The "national question" which Ratcliffe does not address for reasons of space is that concerning the Welsh, Scots and Irish. This would clearly demand a detailed historical analysis of colonial relations and their links to contemporary debates; for example, aspirations to statehood.

But what of the dominance of "race"-thinking in the four societies considered in this section? Is it a peculiar obsession; is it indeed evidence of a primordial ethnocentrism, as Mason asks? Certainly it relates to populations that are perceived to be physically distinct, and the politically dominant segments of these societies are descendants of those who colonized and enslaved the subjugated ethnies/nations and at the same time developed pseudo-scientific theories that suggested a hierarchy of "fitness"/abilities. A primordial ethnocentrism clearly implies, as Mason (1986: 5-6) suggests, a "naturalness" and determinism which would be extremely difficult to justify on moral grounds, and impossible to establish scientifically. Few would deny, however, that racism is deeply embedded, if in very different ways, in each of the four societies. Each has a long history involving the suppression of rights; African Americans as imported slaves, Australian Aboriginals as a subject of genocide leading to near extinction, South African "blacks" as a colonized minority subjected to various forms of unfree labour, and African-Caribbeans and South Asians in Britain, imported as migrant labour but the descendants of enslaved and colonized peoples.

Finally it should be emphasized once again that beyond this dominant form of discourse and oppressive material reality, are questions of ethnic differentiation and conflict. We now turn to societies in which an explicit reference to "race" plays little part in dominant debates. The important question now is whether this results from very different forms of social relations, a genuine lack of significance given to physical differentiation, or, as suggested earlier, an official denial of racism and "race"-based inequalities because of historical and/or political sensitivities.

Ethnicity, nation and ethno-nationalism

The first two chapters in this section relate to aspects of South Asian society. In so doing they provide an interesting comparison with Oommen's analysis, in particular his conceptualization of aspirations to "nation" status and his perception of religion as an "irrelevant variable" in ethno-nationalist struggles. Both Coomaraswamy (on Sri Lanka) and Kaul (on Punjab and Kashmir) are concerned to provide an understanding of bloody and protracted ethnic conflict. Both also see that one cannot successfully do that without a clear understanding of the impact and legacy of British colonial rule. The hidden hand of "racial" exploitation must also be revealed in so far as economic and political relations between the "developed" core and the "developing" periphery also bear the ideological imprint of these earlier epochs.

In rather the same way as Blauner (1971) berated sociologists in the USA for being caught out by the explosion of "racial" violence in their cities in the late 1960s, Coomaraswamy asks:

> Why is it that well-developed research communities in Sri Lanka and India did not predict or devise concepts to understand the nature and degree of Sri Lanka's ethnic conflict or India's regional violence? Why were they so unprepared that when the conflict finally became intractable, there was no literature to offer a satisfactory explanation of the phenomenon, no empirical evidence on which to begin further exploration and very few conceptual insights into the historical roots of the violent social upheavals which were taking place? (p. 147)

Her answer involves a complex web made up of three central strands; nationalist ideology, intellectual biases and the reproduction of historical accounts as commonsense ideology. As to the first of these it is argued that since independence the research agenda has focused heavily on "economic aspects of development" and "the creation of a nationalist ideology". In other words the demands of minority groups such as the Tamils have been marginalized; nationalist ideology imposing a trans-ethnic consciousness.

Intellectual bias stems from the dominance of historical accounts, heavily influenced by the Oxford tradition, which chronicle ancient ethnic conflicts and determine rights. Ethnic studies, she argues, are largely undertaken by anthropologists and are regarded as marginal or even "obscurantist" by the political Left, on the grounds that they prioritize "ethnicity" at the expense of class. Others see the emphasis on ethnicity as divisive and as presenting a threat to the development of a strong coherent nationalist ideology. Rather as Margaret Thatcher, in her rôle as British Prime Minister in the 1980s, denied the salience of "racial" inequality, so the Sri Lankan government adopted an ostrich-like posture to the Tamil issue.

Coomaraswamy sees the third issue as particularly important. Especially since independence the "facts of history", which form a key part of the school curriculum and are central to contemporary debates, have been used to bolster the overarching nationalist ideology, thereby denying legitimacy to the Tamil cause. Major research bodies such the Marga Institute have researched every dimension of social and economic inequality except that which relates to ethnicity. Tamils are likened by Coomaraswamy to the Muslims in India, in that they are customarily characterized as the "invader" or "outsider", and their claims to nation status and separate statehood are denied on the basis of "historical land rights". Some have even gone as far as to suggest that the difference between the Tamil Hindu and the Sinhala Buddhist is one of "race", and have thereby justified the former's inferior status.

Ashok Kaul in his paper seeks to uncover the roots of what he calls ethno-nationalism. As in the case of Sri Lanka he argues that one cannot understand ethnic, religious and political rivalries without a thorough appreciation of the distortions to Indian society wrought by "colonial social engineering", both during British occupation and through the imposition of partition. He explains why the latter in particular was bound to spark bloody conflict.

But the major focus of the chapter is the more recent communal strife in Punjab and Kashmir. Western commentators have tended to suggest that religious bigotry and nationalist movements grounded in one or other form of religious fundamentalism were at the root of the "problems". Oommen, as noted earlier, argues that although religious ties are clearly central to cultural and ethnic identity, their *objective* relevance to national struggles is more questionable – hence his reference to the invoking of "irrelevant variables". Kaul makes a similar point in suggesting that the Akali Dal party in the 1970s was behind the *creation* of a "new religious symbolism" geared to demonstrate that "the Sikhs were a different, and distinct, nation" (p. 170). He then goes on to argue that more "overtly extremist organizations . . . marginalized the political parties and waged a war against the state calling for a separate nation of Khalistan" the implication being that the new "symbolism" was constructed with political ends in mind and was subverted by those with a broader agenda.

The key issue is seen as uneven development set against a historical background where "cultural integration did not precede political unification" and where "the imbalances of the 'old society' and the rationale behind the 'new (nation-)state' created structural inconsistencies" (p. 175). Religion and caste are seen as having been highjacked by small regional parties in order to garner support, and this "communalization of politics" has in turn led to a shift in the power structure of the country. Kaul's analysis ultimately leads him to suggest by way of conclusion that what is needed is a separation of religion from the polity, essentially by its confinement to the "private domain" (realizing of course that such a policy is considerably easier to propose than to deliver).

Another country subjected to British colonial rule was Nigeria. And once again, as is clear from Jinadu's contribution, this had a major impact not just on social relations but also on the nature of intellectual debates. During the colonial period most academic research on ethnic relations was undertaken by social and cultural anthropologists. Their work, argues Jinadu, was never sufficiently divorced from the ethos of colonialism, indeed "much of this was useful in facilitating colonial rule" (p. 183). Research Units such as the West African Institute of Social Research at the University College, Ibadan, were "geared to facilitating colonial administration and social control" (p. 183). Jinadu goes even further, however, by pointing to a form of academic colonialism, where research units were set up in Britain with the express remit of studying "native" peoples in the colonies.

What this implies, of course, is that the supposedly "scientific" process of data gathering was contaminated with a form of racism. The "cartographic studies of individual ethnic groups" produced a rigid "tribalized" image of Nigerian society which rather than illuminating the true nature of social relations instead drew a veil over it by treating communities as discrete and incompatible entities. What Jinadu's paper demonstrates is the inability of Western social science to grasp Nigeria's reality. Ethnocentrism led to a situation where theories grounded in the experiences of US cities were "tested out" there: and when the agenda moved on to study the process of "modernization" researchers imposed the value position that this process and the maintenance of ethnic identity were essentially incompatible. The assumption, in Jinadu's words, was that detribalization "is a sine qua non for the political integration of the new nations of Africa", the logic being that "modernization would increasingly make ethnicity fall into desuetude . . . " (p. 184).

In arguing forcibly that this thesis is fundamentally flawed, he proposes, along with Nnoli (1978), that ethnicity should be located within colonial racism. He also proposes a materialist theoretical framework which reflects the centrality of class relations. Thus, "the politicization of ethnicity or rather the ethnicization of politics in Nigeria is related to the process of class formation and class political behaviour" (p. 187). Ethnicity is therefore something which can be manipulated to serve certain class interests and thereby promote particular political goals. And ethnic relations are at least partially rooted in colonial racism and post-colonial ideas about, and state policies on, modernism and urbanism.

One key issue to come out of Jinadu's paper is the impact of Western concepts and theoretical models on non-Western societies; pointing in essence to a form of "academic colonialism". Devorah Kalekin-Fishman's essay on Israel also displays all the hallmarks of Western, and in particular US, social scientific ideas. Conceptualizations of ethnicity and ethnic relations are firmly rooted in the Parsonian tradition, and official sources espouse the image of a plural society conforming to the "best" traditions of a modern Western democratic state.

Much emphasis is placed on the concept of "belonging". The State was conceived as a "homeland" for the Jewish nation, and migrating to Israel is therefore seen as "returning home" and is portrayed as a positive act, hence the use of the metaphor of "ascension". Of note here is an interesting contrast with the use of "Mother Country", which in popular discourse in the 1950s provided a rationale for the migration of labour from the Caribbean to Britain. In this case the colonial power was clearly offering no more than marginal "ethnie" status to migrants (cf. chapter 6). Jewish migrants to Israel were accorded "nation" status, but were effectively seen by the State as in reality two nations. Jews were recorded in the Statistical Yearbook as originating from "Europe–America" or "Asia–Africa" and these labels are seen to carry with them clear status connotations as well as an ideological content variously interpreted as "Western/non-Western", "North/South", "First World/Third World" or, more contentiously, the phenotype dichotomy "White/Black".

As was noted earlier, the paper makes it clear that "the category of 'race' in this phenotypical sense is never used *officially*" (p. 201, emphasis added). Furthermore, "in academic research . . . the possible impact of 'colour' on social processes is a non-subject" (p. 201). Against the background of the holocaust such an "oversight" is clearly understandable, but it is clear that "race" and the racialization of groups, both Jewish and non-Jewish, is an important issue. As Kalekin-Fishman (p. 202) says:

> Popular discourse departs from official terminology . . . to disclose quasi-racist sentiments and attitudes; in it "colour" is shorthand for the conflation of morality, class and ethnicity. Those of European background frequently talk about the members of non-Western communities (Jews as well as Arabs) as "black" . . . these groups are characterized by negative personality traits, such as irresponsibility (mirroring forms of racialized discourse in, for example, the UK and USA).

So there is resort to the form of "commonsense racist ideology" outlined by Lawrence (1982), and the denial of the claim to statehood by the Palestinian nation can be seen to carry with it "racial" overtones.

In Poland both "race" and "national relations" belong to the realm of "sensitive" issues (Kloskowska, in this volume: p. 220), the first for historical reasons once again linked to the holocaust, the second clearly a function of Poland's subjection to Soviet hegemony up to the late 1980s; and perhaps rather more indirectly to the long and complex history of struggles over territorial integrity. She argues that some (minority) cultures were regarded as "mere regional variations of the national culture" and as such were "positively evaluated" (p. 221). Others by implication were not. But even in the former case it is clear that this "positive evaluation" did nothing to assuage the national aspirations of these minority groups. As to the intellectual climate under Soviet influence it is suggested (p. 233) that:

> . . . empirical studies of national problems aroused political suspicions in so far as they threatened to make explicit unfavourable social attitudes toward the eastern neighbour. So it was easier to write about the new nationalisms in Africa . . . than about the Polish scene.

As to the issue of "race" there appears to be little discussion in Polish sociology. Kloskowska suggests that a major reason is the fact "that 'real' inter-racial contacts were very scarce" (p. 230) in the post-war period. But this implicitly prioritizes skin colour. It could be argued that the Jewish minority continues to be subjected to a process of racialization. Many were treated so badly that they either left Poland or relinquished their religious identity. To those who would expect these old ideas to wither away in the new era of "democracy", one has only to point to the recent national elections where some politicians and newspapers went to great lengths to "expose" the *true identity* of rivals who had undergone conversion from Judaism during the Soviet period (in many cases twenty or thirty years earlier). Irrespective of the rarity of these cases the very fact that the arguments were expected to strike a chord within the consciousness of the "true" Polish nation suggests a continuing deep-seated antipathy.

Further, in discussing earlier periods of Polish nationalism, Kloskowska draws significant parallels with the American Deep South when she says (p. 222) that:

> The nationalistic attitudes of the Polish majority towards the eastern minorities could be likened to those of "traditionally minded" white Americans from the South to the Negroes; the latter being tolerated (and even liked) so long as they knew, and kept "their place" . . .

One of the most significant issues addressed in the chapter relates to different types of nationalism. Her discussion of "defensive" as against "acquisitive" nationalism recalls debates in the Western literature as to the viability of the concept of "black" or "reverse" racism. Once again the pivotal factor is the nature and structure of power relations. Hence a nationalism that provides a bulwark against an external aggressor (or potential aggressor?) might be seen as morally justifiable, but not a nationalism that invokes an expansionist ideology. But the key question, of course, as ever, is that of the rectitude of a particular cause. The basis of nationhood after all turns on the issue of whether there is, or can be, such a thing as an unambiguous (objective?) moral, historical and/or legal claim to land.

In the final essay, land rights and the acquisition of nation status are the central issues. Ziatdinov and Grigoriev focus on the position of Tartars within what was until recently the Soviet Union. Not surprisingly the initial questions concern history, culture, language and, crucially, the "traditional" territory of the Tartars. The greater emphasis (than in other chapters) on historical detail is vital, since it reveals a considerable blurring of detail and some confusion among historians as to the precise identity of the Tartar nation. This stems essentially from the apparent misappropriation, or misallocation, of the name "Tartar" in the 13th century.

The moral of this historical narrative is the difficulty with the whole notion of "primordialism" when applied to human collectivities. Ethnic, cultural and religious struggles produce ongoing social transformations, with the intermixing of formerly distinct populations (hence, of course, one of the key flaws in the claims to scientific status of the concept of "race"). However, the writers do present a strong defence of the rights of present day Tartars, and produce recent empirical evidence that suggest that a certain common consciousness, and common will, exists.

The central argument of the paper concerns the process of Russification; the attempt to impose a common culture and language on the many nations and ethnies within the borders of the former Soviet Union. In examining in particular the relations between Russians and Tartars it demonstrates the resistance of the latter to any attempt to eradicate their language, literature and cultural traditions. With the dispersal of Tartars throughout the vast area of the USSR (and even beyond) some acculturation had undoubtedly taken place, but Ziatdinov and Grigoriev suggest that recent migration to the "traditional" home of Tartar culture may well halt or even reverse this trend.

So here we have a nation with aspirations to statehood; a real possibility given the scale and speed of political change in the region. Claims to land remain modest, and necessarily so given the vast tracts of Central Asia settled by their ancestors. But vital questions remain as to such things as

21

the resolution of potential conflicts over political rights, the rule of law, and the control of economic interests under devolved power.

Concluding remarks:
towards a comparative perspective

The principal aim of this chapter has been to clarify some of the key concepts and to demonstrate their uses in the context of particular societies. It also aimed to suggest ways in which the substantive material in the remaining chapters can be used to generate a series of important comparative questions. Global theorization is still a long way off if by that one means an overarching fusion of the dialectical linkages between these social cleavages and the material bases of the various societies. Indeed it may be that such a search proves illusory.

What follows does, however, represent a major contribution to such debates; in two senses. First, it provides an analysis of the way in which social scientists have conceptualized the relationship between "race", ethnicity and nation on the one hand, and such issues as class, gender and religion on the other. The chapters by Oommen, Taylor and Ratcliffe are particularly relevant here. The latter essay in particular discusses the attempts of Western theorists to apply a variety of Marxian, neo-Marxian, Weberian, Pluralist and other paradigms to this task. Although substantively focused on Britain, it is suggested that the arguments have a much broader salience; with the important caveat that ethnocentrism and cultural imperialism have at times led to accounts which distorted both the *construction* of social reality and the *nature* of that reality (cf. the chapters by Jinadu, Coomaraswamy, Kalekin-Fishman and Taylor).

The second major contribution of the volume is the historical analysis of the material social forces which give potency to "race"-, ethnic- and nation-thinking. Central here are the institutions of slavery (and other forms of "unfree" labour), colonialism (and other forms of expansionism), and labour migration. The subjugation of peoples, "ethnic cleansing" and the denial of equal rights within a given polity are typically rationalized in terms of historically entrenched enmities based on one or other form of identity, whether "real" or "imagined", self-generated or ascriptive in nature.

The key elements of a thoroughgoing comparative analysis would be migration and power (economic, political, and military). Each of the societies covered by this volume have undergone major changes in "racial", ethnic and national composition as a result of being subjected to, or subjecting others to, some form of colonial regime involving the control and/ or subjugation of some population segment(s). Changes over time in the balance of power have then led to transformations in (say) ethnic hierarchies and invoked major population movements, whether within the bounds of the existing state or beyond it. These migratory movements then in turn impact on the structure of social relations in the new area(s) of settlement, and may or may not, as Oommen argues in the following chapter, lead to conflict over territory and/or their status as nation or ethnie.

Migratory movements involve very different levels of coercion or voluntarism. Accepting the argument that no migration can be interpreted as "voluntary" in an absolute sense, we need to add an extra dimension in a comparative schema. Returning to the "Mother Country" (Britain) on the part of the descendants of slaves in the Caribbean, or ex-colonial subjects in South Asia, is very different from the "ascension" of Jews to their "Mother Country" (Israel). In the latter case, and to a lesser extent that of European migration in response to the Australian government's "populate or perish" edict, "nation-building" was the political project. On offer was a national identity and membership of a superordinate group, in the one case with respect to Arabs and Palestinians, the other with respect to Aboriginals and to a lesser extent the "Non-English Speaking Populations". Britain as "Mother Country" was an entirely different matter. "She" turned to her ex-colonial subjects as an economically necessary evil, offering (irrespective of formal citizenship rights) second class status as members of an ethnie, a "minority ethnic group". Jewish migrants and the new Australians by and large "belonged"; the new (predominantly Black) Britons did not, except in a grudging sense.

For other groups statehood, the formal realization of nation status, was to be fought or at least strived for. Thus the migration of Tartars, in the wake of the collapse of communism and the Soviet Empire, is seen as part of a process of ethnogenesis and a reclamation of territorial integrity (as represented by Tartarstan). Many Sikhs, as noted by Kaul, see their future in terms of the nation of Khalistan. Struggles for land rights by the Aboriginal population of Australia is widely interpreted as a demand for nation status from a people subjected to more than a century of (internal) colonialism, leading at one point, as Inglis argues, to their virtual extinction.

The title of this chapter implied a tentative attempt at a comparative framework: it would be somewhat foolhardy to suggest that we have progressed much beyond this. A thoroughgoing systematic comparative analysis of conflicts based on "race", ethnicity and nation in our 10 societies would represent a daunting task. The above analysis pinpoints the central issues, however, and the comparisons both of key elements of social conflict and the marshalling of varying forms and levels of discourse should provide a sound basis for future explicitly comparative work.

References

Adam, H. 1990. Exclusive nationalism versus inclusive patriotism: state ideologies for divided societies. *Innovation* 3 (4), 56–87.

Anderson, B. 1991. *Imagined communities*. London: Verso.

Balibar, E. 1991a. Is there a "neo-racism"?. In *Race, nation, class: ambiguous identities*, E. Balibar & I. Wallerstein (eds), 17–28. London: Verso.

Balibar, E. 1991b. Racism and nationalism, ibid. 37–67.

Ballard, R. 1992. New clothes for the Emperor? The conceptual nakedness of the race relations industry in Britain. *New Community* 8 (3), 481–92.

Blauner, R. 1972. *Racial oppression in America*. New York: Harper & Row.

Bulmer, M. 1986. Race and ethnicity. In *Key variables in social investigation*. R. G. Burgess (ed.) London: Routledge & Kegan Paul.

Essed, P. 1987. *Academic racism: common sense in the social sciences*. (Working Paper 5) Amsterdam: Centre for Race and Ethnic Studies.

Gellner, E. 1983. *Nations and nationalism*. Oxford: Basil Blackwell.

Hobsbawm, E. 1990. *Nations and nationalism since 1780*. Cambridge: Cambridge University Press.

Horowitz, D. L. 1985. *Ethnic groups in conflict*. Berkeley & Los Angeles: University of California Press.

Kuper, L. 1974. *Race, class and power*. London: Duckworth.

Lawrence, E. 1982. Just plain common sense: the "roots" of racism. In *The Empire Strikes Back: Race and Racism in 70s Britain*. CCCS, 47–94. London: Hutchinson.

Mason, D. 1986. Introduction. Controversies and continuities in race and ethnic relations theory. In *Theories of race and ethnic relations*, J. Rex & D. Mason (eds), 1–19. Cambridge: Cambridge University Press.

Murphree, M. W. (ed.) 1988. *Linkages between methodology, research and theory in race and ethnic studies*. Centre for Applied Social Sciences, University of Zimbabwe.

Nnoli, O. 1978. *Ethnic politics in Nigeria*. Enugu: Fourth Dimension.

Rex, J. A. 1970. The concept of race in sociological theory. In *Race and racial-*

ism, S. Zubaida (ed.), 35-55. London: Tavistock.

Rex, J. A. 1971. The plural society: The South African case. *Race* **XII** (4), 401-13.

Rex, J. A. 1973. The Plural Society - The South African case. In *Race, colonialism and the city* J. Rex, 269-83, London: Routledge & Kegan Paul.

Schermerhorn, R. 1970. *Comparative ethnic relations*. New York: Random House.

Smith, A. 1986. *The ethnic origins of nations*. Oxford: Basil Blackwell.

Smith, M. G. & L. Kuper 1969. *Pluralism in Africa*. Berkeley & Los Angeles: University of California Press.

Taylor, R. 1991. The myth of ethnic division: township conflict on the Reef. *Race and Class* **33** (2): 1-14.

Wolpe, H. 1986. Class concepts, class struggle and racism. In *Theories of race and ethnic relations*, J. Rex & D. Mason (eds), 110-30. Cambridge: Cambridge University Press.

Chapter 2

State, nation and ethnie:
the processual linkages

T. K. Oommen

Concepts in social science are formulated on the basis of specific historical experiences, but unless they transcend their empirical contexts they are
of limited utility. One of the tasks of social science is to establish links
between concepts and theories vis-a-vis a variety of empirical situations
in order to establish their plausibility and test their validity. I propose to
undertake this task with reference to three concepts, namely state, nation
and ethnie. As a prelude to this, it is necessary to deal, albeit briefly, with
the senses in which the three concepts are employed in contemporary social
science. I must make it clear that my intention is not to attempt an analysis of the "state-of-the-art" but to indicate how the content and career of
these concepts have been tempered by the empirical contexts from which
they emanated, and the need to transcend the same.

Conceptual clarifications

In contemporary Western social science theory a state is defined as an entity
(a) endowed with political sovereignty over a clearly defined territorial
area, (b) having a monopoly on the use of legitimate force, and (c) con-
sisting of citizens with terminal loyalty. A series of empirical situations
is assumed to be in existence for such a definition to be operative. For
example, if a "people" do not have their own territory in which to lead
settled lives, they are defined as being "stateless". Yet, it is well known
that settled agriculture (the starting point of settled life) is a relatively recent
phenomenon in the long span of human history.

Similarly, the notion of citizenship, that is, membership in a state with full political rights, the most universal expression of which is franchise, is a phenomenon of 20th century Europe. It was only in 1919, after the First World War, that citizenship was accepted in principle in Europe; and it became a "sacred" right everywhere in Europe only as recently as the 1940s. This "contemporization" of human social reality by a "retreat into the present", to recall the evocative phrase of Elias (1989) creates an abysmal wedge between the past and the present.

The notion of monopoly on the use of *legitimate* force does not take into account that a wide variety of structures – kingdoms, empires, city-states, republics and federations – are covered by the notion of state. Even the Greek city-state, widely acknowledged for its "direct democracy", did not permit the participation of slaves and plebeians in the decision-making process. Empires and kingdoms had subjects but not citizens. The history of ex-colonial societies is replete with instances of protest against the illegitimacy of the colonial state. The expression "state terrorism" is frequently invoked today to describe the activities of authoritarian states: that is to say, except in the case of truly democratic states, the attribute of legitimate force is a misnomer. The problematique of the Weberian definition (see Gerth & Mills 1948) lies in completely ignoring the question "Who is exercising force?" and in focusing exclusively on "What is the state?".

The terminal loyalty of a citizen to the state,

(a) implies the co-terminality between state and nation,
(b) makes a mockery of the very Western notion of the autonomy of, and division of labour between, church and state, and
(c) pursuantly, presupposes a hierarchy of loyalty with primacy to the state.

Yet, as a citizen of a multi-religious and multilingual state-society, one may have several terminal loyalties, each of which, having different contexts, need not necessarily be mutually contradictory. Thus for example, one may have one's terminal loyalty, in the religious context, to the ecclesiastical authority that has jurisdiction over co-religionists distributed over several states, but this need not necessarily be in conflict with one's terminal loyalty to the state as a citizen. Therefore, it is tenable to conceptualize the co-existence of a series of terminal loyalties each of which has a different context or content.

It is useful to recall here the empirical contexts that seem to have influenced the definition of a state in the West. Basing his argument on the west European experience Gellner (1983) claimed that language is the fulcrum on which nations (he uses states and nations as interchangeable entities) are built. This is so because, according to him, unless there exists a common communication medium industrial societies cannot be sustained. However, this argument cannot be accepted in the light of empirical facts, even for Europe itself, since, at the time he was writing, there were 73 nations but only 24 states (Smith 1983). Apart from this inconsistency between empirical reality and its conceptualization, there are several other flaws in the argument. First, a common communication medium is necessary not only for an industrial society but for any society; the very existence of a society implies this, even though the nature and intensity of communication may vary within societies. Secondly, it is clearly the case that several nations can and do co-exist in the territorial area of one state (e.g. the UK, India), but Gellner's argument denies the very possibility of multilingual, and by implication, multinational states. Thirdly, if we pursue the argument to its logical conclusion it would mean that

(a) multinational states would/should break-up into mono-national states and/or

(b) the dominant language, which invariably means the language of the dominant nation in the state, will have to be imposed on other nations within that state.

To expose the untenability of Gellner's argument let me cite the Indian case. According to Indian census data more than 1500 languages are spoken in India. Of these at least 105 have 10,000 or more speakers and 12 have 10,000,000 or more speakers (see Oommen 1990). There is no language spoken or understood by the entire Indian population. Hindi with its numerous dialects is the most widely dispersed language in India, but is spoken by only 38 per cent of its population. Gellner may in turn argue that India is not a nation, but can we deny that it is a state? Further, to "build" an Indian "nation" of the Gellnerian type several nations and the language of millions of people would have to be destroyed! That is, to qualify for the appellation "state/nation" India should either split herself into several units or impose the same language on a population that comprises one-sixth of humanity. Indeed, the Indian state/nation survives precisely because of its policy of multilingualism. Essentially, the point is that Gellner's argument and conceptualization are based on extremely limited empirical experience; the result being that they are invalid for multinational states, of which there are numerous cases.

There is another feature of a state, namely a common legal system, that is believed to be a universal attribute. Once again, this description fits only culturally homogenous and uni-religious state societies. In the case of multi-religious and culturally plural societies three different types of legal systems, operating at different levels and contexts, co-exist. The State Legal System (SLS) applies uniformly to all citizens: but if the population is drawn from different religious faiths and if the state has not yet evolved and implemented a Uniform Civil Code, several Religious Legal Systems (RLS) would co-exist. While SLS is applied to fellow citizens, RLS is subscribed to by co-religionists distributed over several states. Thirdly, Folk Legal Systems (FLS) exist and are often recognized, if not always administered, by the state. Thus, there are FLS both in the reservations of Native Americans and in certain tribal areas in India. The three legal systems often co-exist, therefore, and are applicable to different sets of persons within the state-society in different permutations and combinations. To put it succinctly, cultural diversity begets and sustains legal pluralism. Ignoring this fact (or this possibility), it is often argued that a uniform State Legal System, universally applicable to all citizens, is a distinguishing mark of the modern state, a position that smacks of empirical naïvete and conceptual myopia or even claustrophobia.

If the relatively simple and more recent notion of "state" has defied clear definition, applicable to the various empirical situations, it is hardly surprising, perhaps, that the concept of "nation" which has a longer career and is rather more complex, presents even greater problems.

In its classical Latin sense, "nasci" meant a tribal-ethnic group, a people born in the same place and territory. Nation as a community of citizens, that is, a political entity, is a creation of the French Revolution; and having followed the maxim, "one-nation, one-state", nation has in Europe become at once both a cultural and a political entity. Small wonder then, that a nation is defined as " . . . a people, a folk, held together by some or all of such more or less immutable characteristics as common descent, territory, history, language, religion, way of life, or other attributes that members of the group have from birth onward" (Petersen 1975: 181) as well as " . . . a community of sentiment which would adequately manifest itself in a state of its own; hence a nation is a community which normally tends to produce a state of its own" (Weber, in Gerth & Mills 1948: 176). Thus, it came to be believed that it is not only natural for a nation to have a state but also necessary for a nation to have its own state so that its cultural identity is maintained and protected.

While in the above sense nation represents the people of a country without distinction of rank, there are at least a few who use the terms to denote class. Thus Disraeli (1926: 67) referred to

> . . . two nations between whom there is no intercourse and no sympa-
> thy; who are ignorant of each other's habits, thoughts and feelings, as
> if they were dwellers in different zones, or inhabitants of different plan-
> ets; who are formed by different breeding, are fed by different food, are
> ordered by different manners and are not governed by the same laws,
> the rich and the poor.

Similarly, Marx refers to "the division of the French nation into two
nations, the nation of owners and the nation of workers" (Marx 1977: 144).
Responses to such descriptions have been made by many, as for example,
by Gramsci who equates the national with the popular to avoid the nation-
people hiatus. However, one of the reasons why nation-based inequality
and oppression are ignored in much of Western analyses may be that the
empirical situation does not appear to warrant it; most Western states being
seen as uni-national. However, the issue of dominant nations oppressing
and exploiting the weak and subordinate nations is germane to all multinational states in the East and the West.

Given the trajectory of Western history – the advocacy of intense and
terminal loyalty to one's nation-state, the maxim "one-nation, one-state",
the Crusades, the World Wars, Nazi horrors, not to mention slavery and
colonialism – nationalism is perceived both as a positive and a negative
force. These views are clearly articulated by J. S. Mill and Lord Acton.
Mill (cited in Smith 1983: 9) unambiguously endorsed the doctrine of
national self-determination.

> It is, in general, a necessary condition for free institutions that the
> boundaries of government should coincide in the main with those of na-
> tionality: where the sentiment of nationality exists in any force, there
> is a prima facie case for uniting all the members of the nationality un-
> der the same government, and a government to themselves apart. This
> is merely saying that the question of government ought to be decided by
> the governed.

In contrast, in his essay on Nationality Lord Acton (ibid.: 9) wrote: "Nationality does not aim at either liberty or prosperity, both of which it sac-
rifices to the imperative necessity of making the nation the mould and
measure of the state. Its course will be marked with material as well as
moral ruin . . . "

In the voluminous writings on nation and nationalism both connotations

– positive and negative – frequently surface; but it would be correct to say that the connotations change depending upon the historicity of context. Thus nationalism has been viewed as a positive force in the ex-colonial countries in the context of anti-imperialism struggles. But should any of the constituent units of the multinational colony assert that it is a separate nation and mobilize its national sentiment after the attainment of freedom, the rest of the constituents, particularly the dominant nation, would invariably dispute the claim and instantly condemn the mobilization as being "anti-national".

It is untenable to follow the Latin sense of the term nation, which refers to a tribal-ethnic group, in the contemporary world. Before the French Revolution, the polities were either small (tribes, peasant village, caste councils, city-states) or large (empires, federations, universal churches). Today the tendency is to establish viable polities. There are only around 230 states in the contemporary world. But in Africa alone there are about 6000 tribes and in South Asia over 600. Not only are many of these tribes too small in size to constitute viable states, they may not always have a marked cultural distinctiveness either. Further, if the political dimension is taken into account many are either "stateless" societies and/or are incorporated into larger polities. Therefore, it is better to follow Coleman's (1958: 423-4) definition of tribe here: "The tribe is the largest social group defined primarily in terms of kinship, and is normally an aggregate of clans, intermediate to nationality".

Even if a tribe is not a nation, the possibility of some tribes becoming nations should not be ruled out. However, to invoke the term nation to refer to class is not helpful to our analysis and need not be pursued here. This leaves us with two definitions by Peterson and Weber. The problematic attribute in the list of characteristics invoked by Peterson in defining "nation", is religion. In this context one should provide answers to two questions: "What are the irreducible minimum conditions for that entity to exist, and whether or not the removal of one of the attributes would endanger the existence of that entity?".

I suggest that there are only *two* basic prerequisites for a nation to exist: common territory and communication. Religion is not a pre-requisite for a nation to emerge or exist; the fact that religion is often invoked to mobilize people into collective actions in the context of nation-formation should not mislead us into accepting it as an attribute of nation. This is so because,

(a) secular ideologies have also been used for the same purpose,

31

(b) there are many multi-religious nations,

(c) one can think of a nation of agnostics or atheists, and

(d) there is no necessary linkage between religion and territory.

The unfortunate but persisting tendency to define religious collectivities as nations has not only perpetuated conceptual confusion but human misery.

The only difficulty in the Weberian definition is an unwarranted assumption, namely, "a nation is a community which normally tends to produce a state of its own". Perhaps the reverse would be true if a nation is not subjected to discrimination, exploitation and oppression by another nation; that is, a nation tends to produce its state when it faces abnormal situations. Thus, but for the Tamils, none of the numerous *major* nations that constitute the Indian state have articulated any desire to produce their own states. The tendency to secede is confined to smaller nations located on inter-state borders, some of which face the threat of extinction because of the steps taken by the central state authority in the name of "national security". However, this is not to suggest that relatively larger nations in a multinational state would simply acquiesce. Quite the contrary, not only do they have the power to resist the domination, they also usually demand, and are successful in securing, a certain level of political autonomy within a federal system.

Given the ideological preference in the West, not only have state and nation been used interchangeably, they have also been seen as coterminus in much Western social science theory. Bauman's astute observation ought to be recalled here in full:

> Sociology, as it came of age in the bosom of Western civilisation and as we know it today, is endemically national-based. It does not recognize a totality broader than a politically organized nation: the term "society", as used by well-nigh all sociologists regardless of their school loyalties, is, for all practical purposes, a name for an entity identical in size and composition with the nation-state (1973: 42–3).

Further,

> . . . with hardly any exception, all the concepts and analytical tools currently employed by social scientists are geared to a view of the human world in which the most voluminous totality is a "society", a notion equivalent for all practical purposes, to the concept of the "nation-state". (ibid.: 78)

This predicament and vision are also largely shared by conventional Marxian theory; but two assumptions – the dispensability of state and the centrality of class and (an empirical fact) multinational socialist states – prompted Marxists to reassess and amend their analysis. It was felt that the state would wither away as it was essentially an instrument of the dominant class. Similarly, since the proletariat does not have any "fatherland", and "nationalism" represents a form of false consciousness, the possibility of each nation aspiring to constitute its own state was not taken seriously. But the struggle of dominated nations against imperialism was recognized and given respectability, and the possibility of "nationalities" coexisting in the same state during the transitional period was conceded.

Nationalities are nations without states – nations that failed to establish their own states (Worsley 1984: 247–8). In this mode of conceptualization "nationality" is a consolation prize for a nation that has not realized its aspiration of becoming a state. The prediction is that the nation would aspire to achieve its goal as and when it acquires the requisite striking power. However, as I have noted above, this is not supported by empirical evidence; there are numerous nations that have never staked a claim to statehood, though they have opted for a separate administration within a federal system. The notion of nationality unfolds an ambivalence in conceptualization because it shares the assumption that nations without states are untenable.

To conclude, if nations in Europe are essentially cultural entities that tend to establish their own states, then, in the colonized parts of the world as well as in the ex-colonial countries, nations are viewed as political units. Further, most of the "new nations" are also culturally plural. Thus African nations have emerged through the incorporation of many tribes who spoke different languages or dialects and followed different religious faiths. While "race" is the most salient common feature, even this criterion is not universal, as exemplified in the case of South Africa which is a multi-"racial" state. In Asia, almost all nations are multi-religious and multilingual. In the case of Latin America, the populations of particular nations are multi-"racial", multilingual, multi-religious or all of these. In North America and Australia "national" populations are constituted predominantly by migrants from Europe who spoke different languages and who belonged to different religious denominations. Understandably, the connotation of the term nation and the background of the national population vary across continents. With the possible exception of parts of western Europe, "nation-states" are on the whole culturally heterogeneous.

33

The point to be noted is that it is the historicity of context that invests meanings on concepts. The "people" of the USA did not have a pre-existent "nation" (in the European sense) to latch on to their nationalism and yet American nationalism led to the formation of a state. On the other hand, "nations" may not always clamour for their own sovereign states, as borne out by the experience of India.

The nationalist movements of ex-colonial countries were explicitly political and oriented towards state building. These movements had been geared to transform colonies into states and subjects into citizens, but at the height of the struggle against imperialism it was often forgotten that colonies were multinational entities. The primary objective of the anti-imperialist struggle was to liberate the colonies from the political yoke of a "sovereign" power and establish self-government. Understandably, but unfortunately, nations and states came to be treated by many intellectuals as synonymous entities creating enormous conceptual confusion. Thus, in the case of Europe, as noted earlier, nation (a cultural entity) co-exists with state (a political entity) and the hyphenated term nation-state is viable. However, in most other cases the use of the latter term is ill-conceived.

"Ethnie" is a French word referring to a people who share a common culture and life-style but do not occupy their ancestral territory, that is, homeland. However, it is the term "ethnicity" that one frequently encounters in social science and popular writings. An ethnic group is characterized in terms of a multiplicity of attributes – religion, sect, caste, region, language, descent, race, colour, culture, and so on. These attributes, singly or in different combinations, are invoked to define ethnic groups and ethnicity but one rarely sees any specification of the crucial variable(s). This can only perpetuate analytical anomie.

Ethnicity in its original sense refers to common descent, the largest ethnic group being a tribe. In this sense, an ethnic group is relatively small, shares a common culture and traces descent to a common ancestor. However, in today's world, societies and groups are not insulated by descent and kinship. They are constantly exposed to alien influences through migration and colonization as well as through "institutions" such as the mass media. This changing context has also invested a new meaning to ethnicity. In Africa a tribe in its homeland, that is, its original village, is not referred to as an ethnic group. It is a term used to refer to the uprooted, the migrant segment of the tribe in urban settlements.

The terms "ethnic" and "ethnicity" are perhaps most favoured in the USA and western Europe, as they arguably should be, in that they convey crucial elements of the social scene there; the USA for example, is a conglomeration of varieties of people "uprooted" or "dislodged" from different nations. However, despite their wide currency it could be argued that the concepts best suited to describing the overall situation in Europe are nation (and nationality), given the strong attachment of the populations to their homelands. This is equally true of Asian countries. Most Asian states contain several nations, and the process of state formation is not yet complete and stable largely because of their multinational composition. Therefore, to assert one's identity in national terms is to signify danger for the state! The national identity is often de-legitimized to uphold the integrity of the state (Oommen 1986: 107–28). Further, assertions of identity based on religion, language, region, tribe, and so on, are viewed as "communal", "parochial" and even "anti-national".

I have hinted above that the hyphenated term "nation-state" stems from the limited West European experience. Hyphenated terms such as "ethno-nationalism" have been coined more recently by some (e.g. Richmond 1987: 3–18) to refer to nationalism based on primordial loyalties. Similarly, Worsley writes:

> Nationalism is also a form of ethnicity but it is a special form. It is the institutionalisation of one particular ethnic identity by attaching it to the state. Ethnic groups do not necessarily act together except when they have special interests to secure. When those interests are to obtain a state of its own (or part of a state) the group becomes a nationality. (1984: 247)

This conceptualization also suffers from several difficulties. First, it attributes a specificity to ethnic groups that is common to all groups. No group action, whatever the basis of the group formation, takes place unless the group has a special interest to secure. Secondly, it shares with other conceptualizations the false assumption that the linkage between nation and state is axiomatic. Thirdly, while it recognizes instrumental ethnicity, it denies symbolic ethnicity. It seems to me that it is the combination of instrumental ethnicity emanating out of material deprivation and symbolic ethnicity based on the anxiety to preserve one's cultural identity that gives birth to the motive force for state formation. Deprivations emanating out of inequality or denial of identity will not in themselves lead to the crystallization of the demand for a separate state. Such a demand is plausible only if the ethnic group can constitute itself into a nation, the pre-requisites of which are common territory and language.

35

To make sense of the prevailing confusion we need to conceptualize ethnicity as an interactional, as distinct from an attributional, notion; that is, ethnicity is a product of conquest, colonization and immigration and the consequent disengagement between culture and territory. It is the transformation of the "outs" into the "ins" which leads to the process of ethnies becoming nations.

Concepts and reality

If people having the same descent, history and language lived in their ancestral territory, issues of ethnicity would not arise. But in the last five hundred years, largely because of slavery, colonialism and the migrations that accompanied or followed them, the situation has drastically changed. One may identify three variants here. First, the colonial masters withdrew after nearly two centuries of occupation of foreign territory in response to nationalist movements, as in the case of Asia and Africa. Secondly, both the migrants and natives co-exist in varying proportions, as in the case of Latin America and, to a certain extent, Australia. Thirdly, the native population are exterminated and/or completely marginalized, as in the case of North America. The present concern is not to discuss the specificities of these situations but simply to suggest that state–nation–ethnie linkages manifest themselves in different ways.

In those situations where the native populations were small in size (due to sparsely populated territory) and/or weak (because of economic and technological factors) the colonial migrants established their legal claim over the territory first through war and suppression, but subsequently staking a moral claim over the area as their homeland. For example, to strengthen their claim, immigrants to America exterminated and marginalized the native nations first, then fought the American War of Independence to cut the umbilical cord between the British empire and the American colony.

Yet, a certain amount of ambivalence continued to exist as the first few generations of European immigrants to America searched for their home in Europe. The phenomenon of "hyphenated Americans" is a manifestation of this ambivalence. On the other hand, the trajectory of experience and status passage of later immigrants to the USA is quite different: immigrant workers/students (an occupational status), acquisition of citizenship (membership in polity), struggle for rights and privileges as an ethnic group (interest articulation), and adoption/acceptance of the USA as homeland (becoming nationals). While the first two phases call for only individual actions, the latter two entail collective actions and identities. Admittedly, the linkages between ethnie, nation and state differ in the case of the initial colonizing migrants and that of the later (employment seeking) migrants.

In contrast, in Asia and Africa the colonial state was replaced by the national state; the populations involved had been for centuries the native inhabitants of the territory. The "nation" was simply a label used to refer to the territory of the colonial state whether it was maintained as one entity or broken into segments; whether directly administered or indirectly controlled. What emerged from the anti-colonial struggles in Asia and Africa were states and not nations. And yet, the new entity was instantly labelled, and believed to be, a nation or at least a nation-in-the-making. It is this erroneous labelling of states as nations that is at the root of a large number of problems experienced by the "new nations" of Asia and Africa.

Discrimination, oppression and exploitation, objectively experienced and/or subjectively perceived, emerge in situations of disjuncture between state, nation and ethnie. One can identify at least six empirical situations:

1. Vivisection of a nation into two or more segments and assigning them to different states. The classic case is that of the Kurds, numbering 20 million, being apportioned between Iran, Iraq and Turkey. The Nagas and Mizos of India afford other examples. This is true of numerous nations, particularly subaltern peoples, situated on interstate borders; usually their bifurcation is created for reasons of "state-craft" and deemed necessary in the light of "national security".

2. Division of national territory across two or more states invoking religion as the basis of nation and state formation. In this process, common history, descent, collective experience and memory, common culture and lifestyle become relegated to the background, or even disowned, and competing claims for the national territory may be made by two different states. In this process every effort is made to construct alternate visions of collective memory and history. The Israeli–Palestinian and Sri Lankan cases are instances of this type, involving ongoing struggles. The creation of two Punjabs, two Bengals and two Irelands can be considered as cases where the overarching state sees the issues as having been "settled" and the problems "solved".

3. Colonization of a territory by a distinct and distant alien people resulting in the extermination and/or marginalization of the native nations. There are at least four variants of this:

37

(a) a situation where the colonizers did not physically liquidate the native people, although they enslaved, exploited and marginalized them. In the wake of the anti-colonial movements of the 20th century, the native peoples have launched and continue their struggle, not so much to drive out the alien colonizer but to establish a just society in which both the native population and the "immigrants" can have a dignified co-existence. The most outstanding case of this type is South Africa.

(b) A situation where the immigrant population has established its hegemony and yet the native population is not entirely without a voice and continues to work towards re-empowerment. The case of Australia comes to mind here.

(c) A situation where the initial migrants have established unequivocal dominance, the local nations are virtually decimated but due to immigration policy, a wide variety of ethnic groups co-exist. Thus in the United States, a polyethnic state, a hierarchy of ethnic layers is formed: White Anglo-Saxon Protestants, Asian-Americans, Hispanics, Native-Americans, Blacks, and so on (see Oommen 1989: 279-307).

(d) A situation in which the migrants enter with low status (e.g. indentured labour) but settle down and eventually claim the territory as their adopted homeland. But the claim is not conceded by the native population, who attempt in turn to establish their hegemony over the alien elements. The case of Fiji fits this characterization.

4. Internal colonization of the territory or homeland of a weak/minority nation by the dominant nation, usually sponsored by the state, leading to conflicts between nations and ethnies. This is usually done to render irrelevant the moral and legal claims of a nation over its homeland (in which it has a clear majority). Examples of this are Tibet in China, Tamil territory in Sri Lanka, and the Chittagong Hill Tract inhabited by Buddhist tribals in Bangladesh. Sometimes internal colonization is sponsored by the state in order to control the local situation; the well-known case of Russians being assigned to different Republics in the old Soviet Union exemplifies this.

5. Apportioning a nation between different administrative units within the same state. This is illustrated by the case of Armenians in the USSR (prior to its demise at the end of 1991) and that of Bhils, Santals, Gonds etc. in India, each of whom number a few million. Through this act of vivisection the possibility of a nation aspiring to an exclusive administrative unit within the state is attenuated, leading to culturocide as each of the segments assigned to different administrative units are compelled

to undergo a process of acculturation vis-a-vis different dominant groups (see Oommen 1990).

6. Discrimination against ethnies by the state and the dominant nation in the context of economic opportunities, civil rights and political privileges even though they have been residents of the territory for decades, or even centuries. The treatment of ethnies in several European countries illustrates this tendency. The discrimination becomes particularly acute when the ethnies belong to different phenotypical, religious or language groups.

In the light of these empirical situations the following points may be made:

1. Whatever may be the definition of state, nation and ethnicity there seems to be an implicit expectation that these should coalesce. Where they do not, discrimination, exploitation and even oppression of weak/small nations and ethnies are likely to ensue; a process then legitimated in the name of "national interests".

2. Once the geographical boundary of a state is fixed, irrespective of the circumstances that led to the incorporation of the different units and ignoring the irrelevance of the rationale, the state – the political elite and the cultural mainstream (the dominant nation) – would invariably disapprove of, even ruthlessly suppress, any of the constituents who wish to opt out of the state. Even those who advocate the doctrine of self-determination are no exception to this.

3. There is an innate tendency on the part of the dominant nation/ethnie to establish hegemony over the smaller/weaker nations and ethnies. The hegemony of the dominant collectivity is defined (by itself) as nationalism. The weaker/smaller nations and ethnies are encouraged to become assimilated. If they do not fall in line, their resistance is labelled as parochial, chauvinistic and anti-national.

4. The weaker/smaller nations and ethnies tend to preserve the purity of their culture, and strive to maintain their identity even when these may not be viable propositions. In trying to pursue their objectives these collectivities may exaggerate their disadvantages and deprivations.

5. Given the above scenario, nations and ethnies tend to believe that their material interests can be protected, and cultural identity maintained, only if they have a state (or an administrative unit) of their own.

It will be clear by now that any effort to define the concepts of ethnie, nation and state by a set of fixed attributes will not help us to come to grips with empirical reality. On the other hand, if one views them processually the possibility of attaining clarity and establishing isomorphism between concepts and reality would be high. To explicate this let us briefly examine the situation in South Asia.

An empirical example: South Asia

From very early times migrants from different parts of the world have come to South Asia and made it their home. While the alien elements are not altogether absent among Christians and Muslims, an overwhelming majority of them are converts from local castes and tribes. Therefore, notwithstanding the persistent tendency among a section of Hindus, particularly in north India, to perceive Christians and Muslims as "aliens", those within the latter categories views themselves as natives and nationals. In contrast, the Jews, the Zoroastrians and the Baha'is, who migrated to India from their ancestral homeland in the Persian Gulf, remained ethnies although they became citizens of India. The date of entry of the Jews into India cannot be fixed with accuracy. They have remained a small group, not exceeding 26,000 even at their peak in the 1940s, and have retained their ethnic identity as (say) Bene Israel, Baghdadi or Palestinian (Schermerhorn 1978). The majority of the Jews left for Israel in the wake of the Zionist movement, although they were not subjected to persecution in India; a clear indication of the Jews having remained a migrant community (in India).

The Zoroastrians came to India in the 18th century and made India their "home". Although more than 75 per cent of the world's Zoroastrians live in India, their number does not exceed 100,000. Having settled mainly in urban Bombay they could not develop an identity with any specific territory in India. Notwithstanding their intense involvement in the anti-colonial struggle, producing leaders of "national" stature, and contributing substantially to the economic development of India, they remain socially and culturally insulated. These two factors, as well as an inadequate identification with any part of Indian territory and socio-cultural insularity, render them an ethnie, despite their being loyal citizens of the India state.

A handful of Baha'is came to India relatively recently (a little over a century ago), but a phenomenal increase in their number (400,000) occurred around the 1960s through mass conversions (Garlington 1977). The fact that an overwhelming majority of Baha'is are converts from local castes in the Malwa region of central India, imparts an instant nativity to them. They firmly identify themselves with Malwa as their homeland and speak the local language; that is, there is a basic difference between Baha'is who migrated to India and those Indians who embraced the faith. The point I am making is that religion is largely irrelevant to the development of nationality; all three religious groups - Jews, Zoroastrians and Baha'is - are "foreign" collectivities. It is their mode of incorporation which determines whether they remain ethnies or become nationals. The point can be further reinforced by reference to the cases of Sindhi Hindu and Sikh migrants to India in the wake of partition.

The Sindhi Hindus came to India as "refugees" in the wake of partition, and were dispersed into a large number of urban centres. Sindhi is spoken by two million people and is accorded official recognition as one of the country's major languages (out of over 15,000 in total) by including it in the VIII Schedule of the Indian Constitution. Despite this, given the absence of a common territory over which they can lay any claim, the Sindhis remain an ethnie: there is not a "state", "region" or district which the Sindhis consider as their homeland. In contrast, the Punjabi Hindu and Sikh refugees who settled in east Punjab considered that region to be their homeland, staked their claim to administer or govern that territory, and thereby became a nation. Subsequently, invoking an "irrelevant variable" (namely, religion) the Sikhs began to claim parts of Punjab as their homeland, a process which led to the creation of two administrative units - Punjabi Suba and Haryana. (Significantly, the official basis of the division is claimed to be language.)

This is equally true of the other South Asian states. For example, those Muslims who migrated to Pakistan in the wake of partition, the Mohajirins, are treated as outsiders (i.e. ethnies) by the nationals (i.e. linguistic groups with a territorial base). The Hindi-speaking Muslims, usually referred to as Bihari Muslims (of Bangladesh) were declared aliens soon after the break-up of Pakistan, and even Pakistan is unwilling to accommodate them. The Tamil-speaking community of Sri Lanka asserts its cultural identity, identifies a specific part of the country as its homeland and believes that its future can be secure only in a Tamil state; but the dominant Singhala-speaking community rejects this argument and the Sri Lankan state has not even conceded a separate administrative unit for the Tamils. The Tamils define themselves as a nation and stake their claim to establish a state on that basis but the Sri Lankan state and the cultural mainstream treat them as an ethnie.

Clearly the situation in India is more vexatious given her stupendous size, staggering diversity and state policy. Establishing administrative units based on language and tribe provides legal recognition and moral legitimacy to those who inhabit their ancestral territory. In all the languages of South Asia the concept of *desh* (homeland) exists. These entities and the newly created administrative units are often at variance. This rupture between legal and moral entities (homeland) is at the root of a lot of dissensus. To complicate matters, the principle of single citizenship enshrined in the Indian Constitution provides for all the citizens of India the right to live and work in any part of the country irrespective of their national or ethnic origin. This lack of congruity between citizenship and nationality gives birth to the emergence of "insiders" and "outsiders"; the former being nations and the latter ethnies. The ideology of "the sons of the soil" and frequent mobilizations to assert primacy within the territory which the collectivity defines as its homeland, is essentially a conflict between nations and ethnies. The fact that such conflicts are visible and virulent when the collectivities involved are distinct in physical and/or religious terms point to the possibility of objectively irrelevant variables assuming saliency.

The distinction between nations and ethnies can also be explicated by referring to the processes involved in the status shift experienced by, or accorded to, migrants of Indian origin living outside India. It is estimated that some twelve million persons of "Indian origin" live outside India (Jain 1989); they may fall into four categories. First, there are those who succeeded in claiming the territory to which they migrated and adopted as their new homeland, as in countries like Nepal, Mauritius, Trinidad, Surinam, Malaysia or Singapore. In such cases the migrants have become nationals. Secondly, there are those cases in which the claim has been made but not yet fully conceded or is contested, as in the case of the Sri Lankan Tamils or Fiji Indians. These remain ethnies but retain high hopes of becoming nationals. Thirdly, we have the situations in which migrants have become residents and citizens but do not as yet claim the country as their homeland, for example, "Indians" in Great Britain or the USA. Finally, there are migrants who are neither citizens nor aspire to settle down in the country into which they have migrated because such prospects do not exist. The most telling example here is that of the nearly one million Indian workers in the Middle East. It is clear that the four categories from ethnie to national status depend upon a combination of factors: size, concentration in a given territory, economic standing, political clout, assertion of cultural identity, and so on. In the absence of these conditions assimilation would constitute a means to the same end.

It is instructive to recall here that 98 per cent of the inhabitants of Sri

Lanka are migrants from India. The native nations of the island are all marginalized and the largest surviving collectivity, the Veddas, constitute just one per cent of the population. The fact that both Singhala-Buddhists and Tamil-Hindus accept their own common Indian origin does not help: while the former have succeeded in establishing their "national hegemony" the latter are still striving to get their claim as nationals accepted. In the case of Fiji, although the people of Indian origin constitute 52 per cent of the population and are economically affluent, they have not yet fully succeeded in gaining acceptance as nationals. In contrast, people of Indian origin in Mauritius (69 per cent) and Surinam (38 per cent) seem to have succeeded in graduating from the status of ethnie to that of nation. The point is, the size of the population as such is not a critical variable in the status shift. This is clear when we note that 54 per cent of the population in Bahrain, 51 per cent in the United Arab Emirates and 45 per cent in Quatar are of Indian origin. And yet, they are neither citizens of these countries nor are they nationals; they remain mere migrants. The very possibility of transforming their status from migrant/resident to ethnie and then to national and citizen is blocked by state policy. Thus it is clear that the state can be either a facilitator or an obstacle in the process of transformation of a migrant collectivity to the status of an ethnie and from an ethnie into that of a nation.

Towards a reformulation

From the data presented one can clearly discern the linkages between ethnie, nation and state. However, ignoring the processual dimension, erroneous conceptualizations have been made regarding the three empirical entities which may be designated as the statist, the nationalist and the ethnicist perspectives. The statist views everything from the perspective of state-craft and state-building. But the legitimacy of the state is dependent not only on what it does but also on who holds power and authority. To circumvent this difficulty state actions are simply labelled as actions taken in the interests of the nation. By this sleight of hand state and nation are treated as coterminous, a move which yields high pay-offs to the managers of the state because, if the state as an institution comes to be perceived as partisan, an illegitimate and even oppressive nation is instantly invested with legitimacy. Indeed, it often becomes a sacrosanct entity, since nation is taken to be the totality of the people, unlike the state which represents and upholds the interests only of a section of the people, be it on the basis of class, gender, religion or political persuasion.

Precisely because the statists tend to hijack the nation in the interests of a section of the people, the nationalists, particularly from those nations who suffer discrimination between state and nation, tend to *demonize* both the state (insofar as it is a captive of the dominant nation) and the cultural mainstream (if it displays hegemonic tendencies). The nationalist is convinced that each nation has its own genius and ought to have its own state; this being seen as a pre-requisite for the maintenance of its cultural identity. Yet historical experience and empirical reality contradict these assumptions. It is not the case that all nations aspire to exclusive states; several nations can co-exist within the same state yet realize their separate potential. Conversely, there are several instances of one nation being divided into several states without blocking national creativity. The state-nation coterminality is not an empirical fact but a distorted vision or an ideological preference. To view everything from a nationalist perspective is to produce hegemony and chauvinism.

If the nationalist insists on the uniqueness of the nation, the ethnicist is committed to the preservation of the cultural purity of the ethnie. The ethnicist invariably forgets that all cultures have both assets and liabilities and hence it is *not* desirable to preserve *all* aspects of cultures. In any case, the notion of cultural purity is a myth, and even if it did exist, cultures could not be preserved in their pristine purity in a fast changing world. Further, to preserve cultures certain pre-requisites need to be met, namely minimum size, physical concentration and constant interaction. It may be recalled here that in the name of cultural purity groups have indulged, not infrequently, in racism, slavery, untouchability, female infanticide, and so on. Thus, there may be a very thin dividing line between state terrorism, nationalist fascism and cultural relativism.

The point I want to reaffirm is that all three perspectives – statist, nationalist and ethnicist – have substantial negative connotations when viewed from the humanist perspective, and a solution is sought by wishing away state-nation, state-ethnie and nation-ethnie ruptures. Instead, it is necessary to unambiguously recognize both the specificities and linkages between them.

To recapitulate, an ethnie is a collectivity that shares a common life-style and language but does not live in its homeland. Ethnicity, then, is a product of *dissociation* between territory and culture. If an ethnie aspires towards, and is successful in, establishing its moral claim over the territory to which it has migrated and with which it identifies as its homeland, it becomes a nation. A nation, therefore, is a collectivity which has moral claim over the territory it inhabits; it is the fusion of territory and culture which gives birth to nationhood: but as I have indicated earlier not all elements of a culture are "relevant" or "necessary". If language is a necessary ingredient for constituting a nation, religion is an irrelevant one. This is not a statement of personal preference or belief but one of empirical necessity.

A nation need not aspire to establish a legal claim over the territory on which it has a moral claim; if it does, and succeeds, it becomes a nation-state. What binds the people of a state together is common citizenship. It is a legal community. The coincidental coterminality of a legal collectivity and a cultural community should not be taken as a necessity. To do so is to jeopardize even the conceptual possibility of multinational and poly-ethnic states.

The process conceived here is not unilinear. Just as an ethnie can transform into a nation and a state, the reverse process is plausible and often occurs in practice. State policies often lead to the ethnification of nations; people of persecuted nations migrate to distant territories, either within or across the state boundaries. Whether or not they remain ethnies or become nations at their point of arrival would depend upon the existential conditions that await them, or in which they choose to live. If the state can dismantle nations it can also facilitate the transformation of ethnies into nations by assisting the settlement of migrants of the same background in a contiguous territory. Further, the possibility of a migrant population becoming citizens (that is members of a polity), without becoming nationals, of becoming members of a cultural community, or of being denied the possibility of becoming either citizens or nationals, are all empirically plausible. The point to be noted is this: the moment one conceptualizes the state–nation–ethnie linkage processually one succeeds in establishing substantial correspondence between empirical facts and conceptual tools, the first and necessary step towards the construction of a viable, authentic theory.

References

Bauman, Z. 1973. *Culture as praxis*. London: Routledge & Kegan Paul.
Coleman, J. S. 1958. *Nigeria: background to nationalism*. Berkeley & Los An-

geles: University of California Press.

Disraeli, B. 1926. *Sybil or The two nations*. London: Oxford University Press (The World Classics No. 291.)

Elias, N. 1989. The retreat of sociologists in the present. *Theory, Culture and Society* **4**, 2/3, 223–48.

Garlington, W. 1977. The Baha'i faith in Malwa. In *Religion in South Asia*, G. A. Oddie (ed.), 101–18. New Delhi, Manohar.

Gellner, E. 1983. *Nations and nationalism*. Oxford: Basil Blackwell.

Gerth, H. & C. W. Mills (eds) 1948. *From Max Weber: essays in sociology*. London: Routledge & Kegan Paul.

Jain, P. C. 1989. Indians abroad: a current population estimate. *Economic and Political Weekly* **17** (8), 299–304.

Marx, K. 1977. *Collected Works*, vol. 7. Moscow: Progress.

Oommen, T. K. 1986. Social movements and nation-state in India: towards a relegitimization of cultural nationalism. *Journal of Social and Economic Studies* **3** (2), 107–29.

Oommen, T. K. 1989. Ethnicity, immigration and cultural pluralism: India and United States of America. In *Cross-national research in sociology*, M. L. Kohn (ed.), 279–305. Newbury Park: Sage Publications.

Oommen, T. K. 1990. *State and society in India: studies in nation-building*. New Delhi: Sage Publications.

Petersen, W. 1975. On the subnations of western Europe. In *Ethnicity: theory and experience*, N. Glazer & D. P. Moynihan (eds), 177–208. Cambridge, Mass.: Harvard University Press.

Richmond, A. H. 1987. Ethnic nationalism: social science paradigms. *International Social Science Journal*, 39 (1), 3–18.

Schermerhorn, R. A. 1978. *Ethnic plurality in India*. Tucson: University of Arizona Press.

Smith, A. D. 1983. *Theories of nationalism*, 2nd edn. London: Duckworth.

Worsley, P. 1984. *The three worlds: culture and world development*. Chicago: Chicago University Press.

Part Two
THE SALIENCE OF "RACE"

Chapter 3

The dilemma persists: race, class and inequality in American life

Walter R. Allen

The past forty-five years have been momentous in the history of black America. In 1945, the majority of black Americans experienced life under the severest of restrictions, imposed by a racial caste system. In much of the country, blacks could not attend the same schools, eat at the same restaurants or stay at the same hotels as whites. Black Americans were also denied opportunities in education and employment and, in southern states, their voting rights. They lagged far behind whites in terms of earnings, health status and occupational achievement. However, 1954 brought a critical shift in their legal status, a shift many thought equal in importance to the Emancipation Proclamation. On 17 May 1954, the Supreme Court declared racial segregation in the public schools to be illegal. This epic decision provided yet another beacon of promise in the long history of struggle, offering black Americans the prospect of a new future filled with much greater opportunities.

Three decades later, a great transition had occurred in the political, economic and social fortunes of African Americans. In 1984, black America saw its first viable candidate for the presidency of the United States. In relatively short succession, black Americans also saw the first black Miss America and the first US black in space. These firsts were the culmination of steadily increasing black access to the society at large. Blacks were visible as directors of large foundations, as mayors of major urban centres, as superstars of the stage, screen and playing fields and as owners of thriving business enterprises. A black man even ascended to the post of Chairman of the Joint Chiefs of Staff, the highest military position in the nation. The social and economic tides of black America had indeed shifted, ushering in a level of prosperity and accomplishment previously unrivalled in the history of this country.

This chapter describes significant demographic patterns and trends which illustrate the advances of many black Americans from 1950 to the late 1980s. But, we also examine trends from this period which indicate a deterioration in the socio-economic circumstances and life chances of a significant portion of the black population. These two contrasting realities in the black community represent profound counterpoints for attempts to assess the changing status of black Americans. At one extreme is an emerging black elite. At the other is a black underclass mired in poverty and possibly at risk of permanent exclusion from full participation in the wider society.

These two contrasting trends in the status of black Americans have been at the centre of provocative debates about economics and race for more than a decade (Sowell 1975, Wilson 1978, Willie 1979, Marable 1983, Farley 1984, Fusfeld & Bates 1984, Murray 1984). The debate can be summarized by the following questions:

1. To what extent has the relative social and economic position of blacks in America improved since the Civil Rights Movement of the 1960s and the Black Liberation Struggle of the 1970s?
2. To what extent have social and economic cleavages among black Americans become even wider than hitherto?
3. To what extent has the government's obligation to provide equal opportunities to black Americans been fulfilled?

Three questions, therefore, orient the contemporary debate over race and economics in black America. Has there been substantial economic progress? Has this economic progress been widely distributed across the black community? What is the proper rôle for government to play now and in the future?

This chapter explores these issues, setting in the process three goals. First, we review the literature on race and economics as factors in the lives of black Americans. Secondly, we provide a brief empirical synopsis of important social and economic developments among black Americans from 1950 to 1980, by summarizing census data that compare income distributions, occupational classifications, educational attainment and family organization for blacks and whites. The final aim is to generate further study of the race–economics nexus by indicating directions for future research.

Economics and race in the black community: origins of the debate

Social scientists writing about African Americans have long debated the relative importance of economics and race. *The Philadelphia negro: a social study*, which represents the first sociological study in this area, was devoted to an examination of how racial identity and economic status jointly shaped the realities of blacks living in Philadelphia in the late 19th century (DuBois 1967). In painstaking detail, DuBois sought first to show how a system of race discrimination imposed severe limits on the educational attainments, occupations, housing, family organization and quality of life experienced by the 9000 blacks living in the city's fifth ward, and second, to document the factors, usually economic, educational and cultural in nature, which explained differences among blacks.

His conclusion was that the health status, illiteracy rates, crime patterns, housing and family life of blacks were conditioned not only by race discrimination but also, and especially, by economics. Indeed DuBois, in concluding that the denial of economic opportunities was at the centre of the problems experienced by blacks, says "There is no doubt that in Philadelphia the centre and kernel of the Negro problem so far as the white people are concerned is the narrow opportunities afforded Negroes for earning a decent living" (ibid: 394).

E. Franklin Frazier conducted a series of investigations during the 1930s that once again focused on the relationship between race and economics. In the first, a 1931 study of black family life in Chicago, Frazier examined the hypothesis that "family disorganization among Negroes was an aspect of the selective and segregative process of the urban community" (Frazier 1964: 416). He argued that clear-cut economic differences existed within Chicago's black population. These were so significant and distinctive that Frazier used them to partition the black community into five well defined socio-economic zones. As one moved outward from the black community's centre (the most economically depressed zone), the overall social and economic standing of the black community improved. At the same time, the overall quality of life experienced by blacks improved.

In 1937, Frazier replicated his Chicago study in *Negro Harlem: An Ecological Study*. Once again, he sought empirical support for his theory of how economics and race combined to influence the lives of African Americans. The data supported the view of black community life as internally differentiated. Economic status was granted primary importance as the cause of these divisions. Thus, in New York as in Chicago, his data showed the link between economic status in the black community and the observed levels of marital instability, illegitimacy and crime. The prevalence of such problems declined in direct proportion to the increases in a neighbourhood's overall socio-economic standing.

Two other seminal works on the interaction of race and economics in black America were published during the 1930s, focusing this time on the "southern experience". In *Shadow of the Plantation*, Charles Johnson conducted an intensive study of over 2400 blacks living in rural Macon County, Alabama (Johnson 1934). The stated purpose of his research was to understand the customs and institutions of Negro peasants as representatives of an authentic folk culture. After detailing family life, social relations, religious beliefs, health status and education patterns, Johnson concluded,

> It has been impossible to escape the force of tradition, as represented in the customs established under the institution of slavery and adhered to by the white population in their relation to the Negroes, and by the Negroes in relation to themselves (ibid.: 208).

Under the enduring influence of a plantation economy, rural southern blacks were characterized by great cultural isolation, high rates of illiteracy, low social mobility and limited opportunities for schooling. Due to the twin historical forces of economic and racial subjugation, the life circumstances and life chances of blacks in Johnson's study were greatly restricted. Where rural blacks in other areas of the South were able to avoid or temper negative conditions in their lives, it was because they possessed greater economic resources. To demonstrate this point, Johnson compared rural blacks in Gibson County, Tennessee to those of Macon County, Alabama.

> In Gibson County there is greater and longer-range migration, a more pronounced interest in education, more property ownership, and more clearly recognizable affectional ties within families . . . Differences in customs follow closely these statistical differences, and suggest very clearly the different standards and codes under which the two types of rural areas operate (ibid.: 211).

Deep South: a social anthropological study of caste and class described economics and race in a small southern city located in the heart of the "Black Belt" (Davis et al. 1941). The city was a trade centre for surrounding cotton counties which were 80 per cent black; over 50 per cent of the city's population was also black. Thus, in many respects, this city represented a mid-way point between the northern urban and southern rural settings. The researchers, a black married couple and a white married couple (all were trained social anthropologists), lived in "Old City" for two years observing the system of race and economic relations.

The researchers concluded that life in "Old City" was directed by an elaborate set of rules based on racial and economic group membership. Of the two, race far exceeded economics in defining the boundaries of life:

> The "caste line" defines a social gulf across which Negroes may not pass, either through marriage or those other intimacies which "Old City" calls "social equality". A ritual reminder is omnipresent in all relationships that there are two separate castes – a superordinate white group and a subordinate Negro group" (ibid.: 59).

Since race discrimination was located in the context of the total society, race influenced – and was influenced by – other factors in the society. The researchers concluded that "One of the most important factors in modifying caste behaviour is the class structure of both the Negro and white castes".

Shortly after publication of *Deep South*, another important study of race and class appeared. This book, *Black metropolis: a study of negro life in a northern city* (Drake & Cayton 1945), provided an assessment of black community life and how these factors influenced the personalities and institutions of blacks in Chicago. It reveals important, and marked, differences between the lives of black Americans living in a large, northern city and those in a small southern city. Nevertheless, there was a disturbing consistency across these two settings. Despite more plentiful economic, educational and political opportunities in the North,

> . . . the *type* of status relations controlling Negroes and whites remains the same and continues to keep the Negro in an inferior and restricted position. He cannot climb into the higher group although he can climb higher in his own group (ibid.: 781).

The second major study of the broader historical and theoretical questions underlying the interaction of economics and race was *Caste, class and race* by Oliver Cox. In an attempt to clarify the concepts of his title, Cox based his analysis on black–white relations in the United States. Like the others before him, he found a close correspondence between race and economics. However, he is more explicit as to the roots of this correspondence, seeing racial antipathy as a key instrument in the perpetuation of an exploitative economic system. Cox (1948: 534) argues,

> . . . Negroes must learn that their interest is primarily bound up with that of the white common people in a struggle for power and not essentially in a climb for social status.

Finally, two major studies from the 1940s looked at questions of race and economics among black Americans in broader relief. Gunnar Myrdal's *An American dilemma: the negro problem and modern democracy* was first published in 1944. This study was the most detailed and all-encompassing ever done on black Americans. Myrdal concluded that the chronic economic underdevelopment of black Americans resulted from an established tradition of subordinate relations with whites. Myrdal observed,

> There is a cultural and institutional tradition that white people exploit Negroes . . . Within this framework of adverse tradition, the Negro in every generation has had a most disadvantageous start. Discrimination against Negroes is thus rooted in this tradition of economic exploitation. (Myrdal 1962: 208)

Race and economics in contemporary America: has the significance of race declined?

The Civil Rights Movement in many ways constituted a watershed in the history of black Americans (Morris 1984), since this mass-based social movement was an important stage in changing black–white relations. The myriad of strategies employed during the Movement included mass civil disobedience, court litigation, economic boycotts, urban rebellion, voter registration, and mobilization of the mass media – to name but a few. Concerted political action during the Civil Rights Movement resulted in the enactment of new legislation and the issuance of Presidential Executive Orders, and changed public opinion such that the social status of black Americans was drastically redefined.

It is important to stress that, in many respects, this Movement represented the culmination of trends set in motion by the Emancipation Proclamation and earlier events in American History. Thus, the changes evident by 1980 in the social, political and economic status of African Americans were products of factors both contemporary and historical. William J. Wilson's argument to this effect spurred lively debate over the relationship of race and economics in contemporary America.

In *The declining significance of race*, Wilson argued that "Race relations in America have undergone fundamental changes in recent years, so much so that now the life chances of individual blacks have more to do with their economic class position than with their day-to-day encounters with whites" (Wilson 1978: 1). According to Wilson, traditional patterns of interaction between blacks and whites, characterized by systematic racial oppression, had been fundamentally altered. This had come about because of changes in the system of production; that is, structural shifts in the national economy. More specifically, Wilson argued that, with the shift from a plantation-based or pre-industrial economy to a manufacturing-based or industrialized economy, the relation of blacks to the national economy and to whites was fundamentally changed.

Wilson goes on to argue that "as race declined in importance in the economic sector, the Negro class structure became more differentiated and black life chances became increasingly a consequence of class affiliation" (ibid.: 153). Once the artificial cap on black social mobility, represented by strict segregation, was removed, greater income, occupational and educational differentiation was observed within the black community. Two countervailing trends resulted. Black Americans with resources or "access to the means of production", as Wilson puts it, experienced unprecedented job opportunities and upward social mobility. At the same time, those who lacked education and job skills experienced soaring unemployment levels, declining labour force participation rates, increasing confinement to low-wage occupations and a growing reliance on welfare. This in turn was argued to be attributable, in part, to those structural changes in the economy which eliminated many jobs in agriculture and manufacturing once filled by blacks.

In 1978, C. Eric Lincoln presented an essay "The new black estate" at the University of Mississippi's Symposium on Southern History which supported Wilson's basic assertions. Lincoln suggested that the Supreme Court ruling outlawing segregation in the nation's schools was both the impetus for further change and a reflection of changes that had already occurred in the black American identity and the diversification of the black community. Lincoln saw the emergence of a sizeable black middle class as a positive sign. The old caste system had finally been broken; economics rather than race was now the primary factor in the lives of black Americans. But he noted troubling developments as a consequence of this change.

. . . for the black masses appear to be in a steady decline even as the black elite search for their niche in the American dream. The gulf widens; the old bonds are ravelling under the tension of new opportunities, new privileges, new interests, and new horizons for some. (Lincoln 1978: 28)

Among many voices raised to contest Wilson's thesis of "a declining significance of race" was that of Charles V. Willie. In *The caste and class controversy*, he brought together numerous critiques of Wilson's book (Willie 1979). They rejected its central premise that economic class group, more so than racial identity, explains the limited mobility opportunities of poor blacks. Thus, Robert Hill cautioned against overstatements of the actual economic gains of blacks in the 1960s and 1970s; Thomas Pettigrew pointed to the persistence of significant race differences within class groups; and Dorothy Newman implicated the international flight of capital and industry in the creation of a black underclass in the USA. Of all the critics, Willie was most explicit in his rejection of the Wilson thesis. Instead, he suggests

. . . that the significance of race is increasing and that it is increasing especially for middle-class blacks who, because of school desegration and affirmative action and other integration programmes, are coming into direct contact with whites for the first time for extended interaction (ibid.: 157).

Wilson's thesis is also criticized by Oliver & Glick (1982) who call it the "new orthodoxy on black mobility". This doctrine assumes that:
1. occupational opportunities and social mobility increased dramatically for blacks in the 1960s,
2. any remaining race discrimination in securing jobs or social mobility is an artifact of past, rather than present, forces and social policy, rather than race or other group characteristics.

These authors conclude:

The ultimate error of the new orthodoxy is its failure to acknowledge that the gains made by blacks during the 1960s came in an atypical era. It was an era which witnessed the greatest effort at government intervention in US history, an era of economic abundance and social and political turmoil (ibid.: 522).

They also criticize the tendency to overstate black gains, the persistence of drastic black–white differences in occupational equality and the clear instability of much of the black progress.

Sharon Collins's critique of Wilson's position argues that the demand for black middle-class workers was largely created by federal government programmes. Moreover, she sees the black middle-class workforce as concentrated in segregated areas of the labour market. As a disproportionately public-sector workforce, blacks "are most likely to be found in federal, state, and local government functions that legitimize and subsidize black underclass dependency. Blacks employed in the private sector continue to be concentrated in economically underdeveloped areas, or in intermediary positions" (Collins 1983: 379). The end result is instability in black employment opportunities and limited social mobility even among the middle and upper classes.

In criticizing Wilson's thesis, Farley poses the question of whether the social and economic gulf between blacks and whites has indeed narrowed (Farley 1984). The data show a considerable reduction in differentials in educational attainment, and the occupational status and earnings of employed workers. There was little improvement, however, in relative unemployment rates or in rates of labour force participation. Progress in the areas of school integration, family income, poverty and residential segregation was, at best, mixed. Adopting what he refers to as the "optimistic view", Farley concludes that racial differences on key indicators of social and economic status will continue to diminish in the future.

In a later study, Farley & Bianchi specifically addressed the question of social class polarization among blacks. Here, as in the earlier study, he concludes that the premise of polarization in the black community is doubtful. The pattern is not one where "a growing share of all income is obtained by the rich" (Farley & Bianchi 1985: 25). On the other hand, the relative employability of blacks with limited education is worsening compared to better-educated blacks – and for that matter compared to less-educated whites.

The comparative status of black and white Americans

Our review of the race and economics debate reveals points of agreement and disagreement. There is agreement that race relations in the United States have changed in fundamental ways since 1945. They have evolved from a strictly enforced caste system, characterized by the absolute, unequivocal subordination of blacks into a system of power relations between the races that is influenced by colour, social characteristics and economic status. The issue for debate, therefore, is not whether race relations in the USA have changed. Rather, the questions to be resolved concern the extent of this change and how it was achieved.

In the section which follows we address a more empirical question, namely "How have the social and economic characteristics of black Americans changed since 1950?" The assessment of these changes will be limited to a summary of selected socio-economic trends. More detailed and systematic examinations of their social and economic progress are contained in Reid (1982) and Farley & Allen (1987). Data for this assessment are drawn from the 1980 Census 5 per cent sample of US households. From the roughly 14 million households included in this national sample, a subsample of 450,000 households was selected for analysis. The sampling ratios used were as follows: blacks, 1 in 100; whites, Hispanics, Asians and others, 1 in 1000.

Black life in the USA has been characterized by an existence on the periphery. Blacks found themselves denied the most fundamental human rights: indeed, the Supreme Court's decisions proclaimed at one point that blacks possessed "no rights which whites are bound to respect". The result of these severe restrictions has been a pattern of systematic underdevelopment. Although blacks have largely been freed from the most oppressive aspects of the machinery which insured their underdevelopment, the legacy of this early era remains. It is apparent in the persistent deprivations of blacks, relative to whites, in educational attainment, occupational distribution, patterns of employment, income levels and geographic location. Continuing patterns of discrimination merge with accumulated disadvantages to sustain black deprivation.

The standard of living experienced by blacks serves to illustrate the persistent disadvantage. In 1950 black males had incomes averaging 54 per cent of those for white men; by 1984 this ratio had changed only minimally (the black male average rising to 60 per cent). Young black males, the cohort that we might expect to have benefited most from the society's recent apparent commitment to equality of opportunity, fared slightly better – but they too lagged significantly behind their white peers. In 1983, young black males with Bachelor's degrees had incomes averaging 75 per cent of the comparable white figure, and young black high school graduates had incomes equivalent to 68 per cent of their white peers. Black male earnings gained on those of whites in relative, but not absolute terms. Thus, black men continue to suffer a 10 to 15 per cent earnings deprivation relative to white men with comparable demographic and labour force characteristics.

57

Since the Second World War, the unemployment rate for black men has consistently been more or less twice that for white men. This race disadvantage persists at all educational levels, across the entire age range and in all regions. Although black men have made tremendous strides relative to their earlier occupational distributions, when a sizeable proportion were concentrated in agriculture, they continue to lag behind whites. By 1980 black representation in the more prestigious occupational categories reached the levels that characterized the white male labour force thirty years earlier.

Black women have almost attained parity with white women in terms of employment levels and earnings. In 1950, they earned on average only 45 per cent of the figure for whites; by 1984 they were earning 89 cents for every dollar earned by white women. Indeed, in many educational and occupational categories they actually earned more than white women with comparable qualifications. These gains are impressive; but they must be kept in perspective. Women as a whole continued to lag significantly behind men in terms of personal earnings. As of 1983, black female college graduates earned 77 cents for every dollar earned by black men with Bachelor's degrees, and the equivalent figure for black high school graduates was 65 per cent. In the same year, the earnings ratios of white females to those of their male peers were 50 per cent for college graduates and 40 per cent for high school graduates. Further, it is important to be reminded that when compared to white women black women more often work full-time and have higher unemployment rates.

Black women have also made significant strides occupationally. In 1940, 60 per cent were concentrated in the domestic service category, but by 1980 this proportion had declined to 7 per cent. Black women were swiftly closing the gap in occupational distribution with their white peers. Nevertheless, the occupational distribution for black women in 1980 was quite similar to that attained by white women three decades earlier. Black women continued to experience rates of unemployment significantly higher than those of white women, a difference which was consistent across age, education, occupation and regional categories. For the most part, the country's labour force continues to be segmented by gender. In 1980, as was true in 1940, black and white women were concentrated in certain female-stereotyped occupations. More often than not, these "pink collar" occupations were of lower prestige, paid lower salaries and offered fewer opportunities for upward mobility.

Selective comparisons reveal other important differences between blacks and whites. We see a dramatic shift in patterns of household composition and family structure among blacks. From 1940 to the present, the proportion of husband/wife-headed households among blacks declined from 77 to 61 per cent; the proportion of female-headed households increased over the same period from 17 to 35 per cent. The proportion of children under age 18 residing with both parents dropped from 75 per cent in 1969 to 50 per cent in 1984. This tremendous shift in black family patterns parallels the steady decline in black male employment and labour force participation rates since 1950.

Blacks and whites continue to be differentiated by geographical location. Despite the massive migrations since 1900 which took African Americans from rural to urban areas and from the South to the Midwest, West and North, their lives remain to a large extent separate from mainstream white society. In fact, of all ethnic/racial groups in this society – including recent migrants – African Americans are the group most residentially segregated from whites. To eliminate the geographical isolation of blacks in the 16 largest metropolitan areas in 1960, 81 per cent of blacks (or whites) would have needed to relocate to different neighbourhoods. To accomplish this same end in 1980, twenty years later, 77 per cent of whites (or blacks) would have to be relocated. African Americans with annual earnings in excess of $50,000 were as segregated from whites in 1980 as those with earnings below $5000 a year (79 as against 76 per cent). Similarly, black college graduates were as segregated from whites in housing as were blacks with less than a high school education (71 as against 76 per cent). In the USA today, as was true 50 years ago, residential areas continue to be starkly delineated by race, and segregation by race in where people live and where their children attend school is therefore the rule rather than the exception.

The dilemma: economics and colour in America

We have briefly examined the nexus of race and economics in contemporary black America. We began by reviewing the historical research record, and then considered selected demographic patterns for the years 1950 to 1980. The contemporary debate over "the declining significance of race" provided an orienting framework throughout. We asked the question, "What is the relative power of economics and colour in the lives of African Americans?"

Early studies demonstrate the undeniable power of race over the lives

59

of African Americans. Caste barriers in American society once defined the least white person as more important than the greatest black person. While the force of this prescription was, to an extent, modifiable by related social factors (e.g. region, occupational class, education, biological lineage), the essential elements of our race-based caste system remained intact. It is critical to note, however, the importance attributed to economic factors in such calculations. For, even when slavery (the purest expression of this country's caste system) was at its height, Free Negroes of economic means were able to use their resources to buffer the effects of the caste system on their lives (Fields 1985).

The racial caste system has had a very heavy economic emphasis since its inception (Fusfeld & Bates 1984, Marable 1983). The system's origins, definitions and justifications were related to this country's efforts to develop its agricultural, industrial and economic capacity. Blacks were instrumental in this equation, first as a seemingly limitless supply of slave labour, then as a source of inexpensive rural agrarian peonage and urban proletarian labour, and finally as a reserve labour force in the post-industrial setting. The historical redefinition of the racial caste system has placed greater emphasis on economic factors – there is consensus on this point. Disagreement persists, however, on the extent to which race played a part in the emergence and concretization of economic inequalities.

The empirical record presents a picture of substantial progress by *some* African Americans since 1950. There have been significant improvements for blacks in selected social and economic arenas. The legal basis of segregation and race discrimination has been all but eliminated. Relative to the Second World War era, African Americans have increased their earnings power, their educational attainment, and their occupational status. Blacks, continue, however, to lag significantly behind whites on measures of overall social and economic well-being. But of even more pressing concern is the group of African Americans who lag significantly behind not only whites, but also other blacks.

The so-called black "underclass" represents the subgroup of black Americans characterized by: chronic unemployment, lack of real opportunities to succeed, prospects of intergenerational poverty and angry despair (Glasgow 1980). In this sense, the underclass is trapped. Denial of opportunity and resources sentences them to life on society's periphery. The process that culminated in the creation and maintenance of a black underclass is broad, complex and historical, having to do with the transformation of the economic base and with changes in the significance of race. Therefore, simplistic explanations are problematic. It is not sufficient to attribute sole causality for current patterns to racism, or capitalism, or government social policy or individual values: all had a part to play.

The black chronically poor are thus a reflection of the interplay between race, class,and gender within a post-industrial society; a post-industrial society, one should add, predicated on the assumption that vast social and economic inequality is acceptable. A political economy perspective is useful, therefore, because it recognizes the complex interconnections between these social forces. This perspective also challenges economic inequality on moral grounds. As has been argued:

> Today's urban racial ghettos are the result of the same forces that created modern America, and one of the byproducts of American affluence is a ghettoized racial underclass . . . Racism is more than a psychological problem of whites; it has roots in white-black economic relationships. Poverty is not simply the result of poor education skills and work habits of the poor. It is one outcome of the structure and functioning of the economy (Fusfeld & Bates 1984: xiii–xiv).

Approaching the question of "caste or class" from a political economy perspective elevates the debate and offers a persuasive analysis of the problem. Many commentators have addressed the system of historical, economic, social and political factors that account for the persistence of racial inequality in the US (e.g. Carmichael & Hamilton 1967, Allen 1969, Baron 1969, Tabb 1970, Swan 1981, Fusfeld & Bates 1984). These scholars describe a system which oppresses the overwhelming majority of black Americans, a system that limits their choices and futures, largely because they are of African ancestry. In the past, race definitely loomed large as the basis of this oppression. Equally certain is the fact that race is not without substantial significance in the present.

> Given the fundamental racism of American society, what we find is that even though racial exploitation is no longer an essential element in terms of sustaining a sector of a ruling class, racial dominance has become so socially diffused that it has become an inextricable part of the mediating process through which much of the basic economic and political controls for the whole society are exercised. In other words, the mechanisms for subjugating black people have become interlaced with the complex of mechanisms by which power is exercised over both white and black (Baron 1969: 171).

Although social scientists have seen fit to debate the significance of race in the lives of black Americans, black people themselves display little confusion over this point. Data from ethnographic research (Gwaltney 1980) and from survey research (Hatchett 1982) are consistent; African Americans continue to see race as a significant factor. More often than not, respondents cite race discrimination as a primary basis for the denial of equal education, employment and housing opportunities for themselves personally, and for black people generally.

American sociology has been slow to move beyond an emphasis on individual psychology and behaviour in the examination of racial inequality. The current debate over "caste and class" in black America offers an opportunity for expanding our horizons, for engaging in the joint consideration of systematic, structural and individual factors as determinants of black life chances. It is ironic to note in this connection the long history of speculations about the emergence of an underclass in modern society. Marx foresaw the creation and perpetuation of a "lumpen proletariat" in post-industrial societies; Cox anticipated a future for blacks as "exploited and exploitable workers, . . . more highly urbanized than any other native-born population group in the country'"(Cox 1948: xxxiii), and C. Wright Mills concluded, "The bottom of this society is politically fragmented, and even as a passive fact, increasingly powerless; at the bottom there is emerging a mass society" (Mills 1956: 324). The challenge confronting the discipline is to develop more complex theory and conceptualizations of the nexus between race and economics in America. Early formulations must be merged with rigorous empirical methods in an attempt to better understand how economics influence race and how race influences economics in the post-industrial United States.

Research agenda for the study of
race and class in America

The comprehensive study of racial stratification requires the development of more sophisticated models. Such models need to incorporate a focus on macro- or societal-level factors (e.g. economic relations, social history), middle-range or institutional-level factors (e.g. labour force participation, family structure) and micro- or individual-level factors (e.g. attitudes, behavioural patterns). The myriad of variables and their complex interrelationships suggest that research should employ a multi-method approach, involving the collation of data from official statistics, social surveys, and field studies.

Resisting the temptation to define an agenda as ambitious as the 100-year research plan for the study of black life and culture outlined by DuBois during his years at Atlanta University (DuBois 1967: 205–35), certain key issues must nevertheless be addressed. First, at the macro-level, there are questions

(a) as to the US involvement in the International Division of Labour with its "North-South" component,

(b) as to the racial division of labour *within* the US, given the radical shift towards a post-industrial structure, and

(c) as to the continued salience of the ideology of racial stratification.

Secondly, in the realm of "middle-range" theorization, there are pressing institutional issues. These relate to contemporary racial stratification in the spheres of health, welfare, education and housing services; and also to the struggle towards emancipation for the "black underclass", and (upward) occupational mobility. The need for *action-research* into self-help, and other black-run, community organizations leads to the third, and final, area of the agenda – micro-level issues. There is an urgent need here for emancipatory research focusing on motivation, self-concept and cultural values, as negative racial stereotyping has been seen to combine with institutionalized discriminatory behaviour to reduce self-esteem.

Racial stratification in America: the great divide

Following a wide-ranging study of factors contributing to the urban rebellions of the 1960s, President Johnson's Commission on Civil Disorders (also known as the Kerner Commission) concluded that "our nation is moving toward two societies, one black, one white – separate and unequal". Our findings have validated this conclusion to a great extent. After detailed analysis of statistical data, we have shown that, for the majority of African Americans, life continues to be experienced as "separate and unequal".

The next logical step is to ask, "Through what combination of circumstances and factors did this socio-economic underdevelopment of African Americans originate and how has it been perpetuated?" Of course, the answers to these questions are as varied as the individuals who offer them; "slavery", "lack of motivation", "capitalism", "poor family values", "racism", and "systematic oppression" to name but a few. While each explanation triggers an accompanying theory of black underdevelopment, none is completely satisfying. For, rather than resulting solely from economic relationships or socio-psychological attitudes or historical conditions, racial inequalities have been shaped by all of these.

No convincing explanation of contemporary inequalities can afford to ignore the awesome impact of chattel slavery on individuals, and on this country's institutions. By the same token, it is impossible to study race relations without probing the psychological depths of racist thinking in this society. Similarly, to understand race in America is to understand the place of black deprivation in an economic system based on industrial capitalism and private ownership.

Elements of the African American experience, culture and character combine with racial discrimination and stratification and with elements of the Euro-American experience, culture and character to account for the persistent racial inequalities. However, to suggest that black Americans bear the major responsibility for their own plight is to ignore history and to deny the reality of racism and the associated machinery of racial discrimination and racial oppression.

Charles Johnson and Robert Park, writing about the bloody race riot in Chicago in 1919, observed:

> It is important for our white citizens always to remember that the Negroes alone of all our immigrants came to America against their will by the special compelling invitation of the whites; that the institution of slavery was introduced, expanded, and maintained in the United States by the white people and for their own benefit; and that they likewise created the conditions that followed emancipation (Chicago Commission on Race Relations 1922: xxiii).

Throughout history, when opportunities for black advancement opened, they moved swiftly to take them, often at great personal risk and sacrifice. The historical record also reveals America's discomfort with sustained black progress, particularly when this progress results in any sizeable diminution in the economic supremacy of whites. Thus, the pattern has consistently been one where "windows of opportunity" were promptly closed just as black gains began to produce significant reductions in economic disparities. Historical examples of this pattern reveal surges of black progress, followed by significant reductions, as the dominant white group mobilized "to turn back the clock", in order to protect their advantage. Obvious examples here are the periods spanned by Reconstruction and the modern Civil Rights Movement. In both eras whites were threatened by black advances and reacted with repressive strategies calculated to restore and protect white dominance.

Blacks and whites in this country are inextricably connected and implicated in one another's lives. Their lives are bound by relationships that are economic, social, cultural, psychological – and biological. Blacks have contributed mightily to the country's economic development (Carmichael & Hamilton 1967, Allen 1969, Fusfeld & Bates 1984: 136–54). Much of what is considered to be American in language, literature, music and scientific discoveries represents the contributions – more often than not unacknowledged – of black people (Dillard 1973, Brawley 1937, Miller 1971, Franklin 1980, Manning 1983). African Americans have played, and continue to play, a significant rôle in the building of US society.

The challenge which confronts the country today is that of achieving true equality between blacks and whites, and indeed between all those of different ethnic, religious or national origins. Its future rests on the ability to become more inclusive than exclusive, more open than closed and more egalitarian than elitist. History will judge us on the extent to which the inspirational ideals articulated by the American Constitution found expression in real life day-to-day affairs.

References

Allen, R. L. 1969. *Black awakening in capitalist America: an analytical history.* New York: Anchor Books.

Allen, W. R. & R. Farley 1986. The shifting social and economic tides of Black America, 1950–1980. *Annual Review of Sociology* 12, 277–306.

Ball-Rokeach, S. J. & J. F. Short, Jr. 1985. Collective violence: the redress of grievance and public policy. In *American violence and public policy: an update of the National Commission on the Causes of the Prevention of Violence.* New Haven: Yale University Press.

Baron, H. M. 1969. *The web of urban racism.* New Jersey: Prentice Hall.

Brawley, B. 1937. *The negro genius: a new appraisal of the achievement of the American negro in literature and the fine arts.* New York: Dod Mead.

Carmichael, S. & C. V. Hamilton 1967. *Black power: the politics of liberation in America.* New York: Vintage.

Chicago Commission on Race Relations 1922. *The negro in Chicago: a study of race relations and race riot.* Chicago: University of Chicago Press.

Clarke, K. B. & K. C. Harris 1985. What do Blacks really want? *Ebony* **XL** (January), 108-15.

Collins, S. 1983. The making of the Black middle class. *Social Problems* **30** (April), 369-81.

Cox, O. C. 1948. *Caste, class and race: a study in social dynamics*. New York: Doubleday.

Davis, A., B. Gardner, M. Gardner 1941. *Deep South: a social anthropological study of caste and class*. Chicago: University of Chicago Press.

Dillard, J. L. 1973. *Black English: its history and usage in the United States*. New York: Alfred A. Knopf.

Drake, St C. & H. Cayton 1945. *Black metropolis: a study of negro life in a northern city*. New York: Harcourt Brace.

DuBois, W. E. B. 1967. *The Philadelphia negro: a social study*. New York: Schocken.

Farley, R. 1984. *Blacks and whites: narrowing the gap?* Cambridge, Mass: Harvard University Press.

Farley, R. 1985. Social class polarization: is it occurring among blacks? *Research in Race and Ethnic Relations* **4**, 1-31.

Farley, R. & W. Allen 1987. *The color line and the quality of life: the problem of the twentieth century*. New York: Russel Sage Foundation. (Paperback edition, New York: Oxford University Press, 1989).

Fields, B. J. 1985. *Slavery and freedom on the middle grounds: Maryland during the nineteenth century*. New Haven, Connecticut: Yale University Press.

Franklin, J. H. 1980. *From slavery to freedom: a history of negro Americans*. New York: Alfred A. Knopf.

Frazier, E. F. 1937. Negro Harlem: an ecological study. *American Journal of Sociology* **43**, 72-88.

Frazier, E. F. 1964. The negro family in Chicago. In *Contributions to urban sociology*, E. W. Burgess & D. J. Bogue (eds), 404-18. Chicago: University of Chicago Press.

Fusfeld, D. & T. Bates 1984. *The political economy of the urban ghetto*. Carbondale: Southern Illinois University Press.

Glasgow, D. 1980. *The black underclass: poverty, unemployment and entrapment of ghetto youth*. San Francisco: Jossey-Bass.

Gwaltney, J. L. 1980. *Drylongro: a self-portrait of black America*. New York: Vintage.

Hatchett, S. 1982. *Black racial attitude change in Detroit, 1968-1976*. PhD thesis: Department of Sociology, University of Michigan, Ann Arbor, Michigan.

Hatchett, S. 1983. *Black Americans surveyed: two unique ISR studies explore the experience and perspectives of black America*. University of Michigan, Ann Arbor: Institute for Social Research Newsletter (Spring/Summer): 3-7.

Hill, R. 1981. *Economic policies and black progress: myths and realities*. Washington, DC: National Urban League, Research Department.

Johnson, C. S. 1934. *Shadow of the plantation*. Chicago: University of Chicago Press.

Ladner, J. 1971. *Tomorrow's tomorrow: the black woman*. Garden City, NY: Doubleday.

Manning, K. 1983. *Black Apollo of science: the life of Enerest Everett Just*. New York: Oxford University Press.

Marable, M. 1983. *How capitalism underdeveloped black America: problems in race, political economy and society*. Boston: South End.

Miller, R. (ed.) 1971. *Black American literature: 1760–present*. Beverly Hills, CA: Glencoe Press.

Mills, C. W. 1956. *Power elite*. New York: Oxford University Press.

Morris, A. 1984. *The origins of the Civil Rights Movement: black communities organise for change*. New York: Free Press.

Murray, C. 1984. *Losing ground: American social policy 1950–1980*. New York: Basic Books.

Myrdal, G. 1962. *An American dilemma: the negro problem and modern democracy*, vols. I, II. New York: Pantheon (original published 1944).

Oberschall, A. 1973. *Social conflict and social movement*. Englewood Cliffs, NJ: Prentice Hall.

Oliver, M. & M. Glick 1982. An analysis of the new orthodoxy on black mobility. *Social Problems* **29** (June), 511–23.

Rainwater, L. 1970. *Behind the ghetto walls: black families in a federal slum*. Chicago: Aldine.

Reid, J. 1982. Black America in the 1980s. *Population Bulletin* **37** (4), 1–38.

Sidran, B. 1971. *Black talk*. New York: Da Capo Press.

Smith, J. & F. Welch 1986. *Closing the gap: forty years of economic progress for blacks*. Santa Monica, CA: Rand Corporation.

Sowell, T. 1975. *Race and economics*. New York: McKay.

Swan, L. A. 1981. *Survival and progress: the Afro-American experience*. Westport, Conn: Greenwood.

Tabb, W. 1970. *The political economy of the urban ghetto*. New York: Norton.

Willie, C. V. 1979. *The caste and class controversy*. Bayside, NY: General Hall.

Wilson, W. J. 1978. *The declining significance of race: blacks and changing American institutions*. Chicago: University of Chicago Press.

Wilson, W. J. 1985. Cycles of deprivation and the underclass debate. *Social Service Review* (December), 541–9.

Chapter 4

Race and ethnic relations in Australia: theory, methods and substance

Christine Inglis

Introduction

Rather than simply summarize the substantial literature on race and ethnicity in Australia (see Inglis 1986a) this chapter focuses specifically on the linkages between methodology, theorization and the research process. Central to this will be a reflection on the bifurcation between research on Aboriginal as against non-Aboriginal groups. It will be seen to highlight differences in disciplinary origins, theoretical perspectives and policy orientations. In particular, it will become clear that whereas research on the Aboriginal population reflects methodological homogeneity the literature on non-Aboriginal groups displays a considerable diversity both of theoretical paradigms and empirical processes.

The social context of Australian research on race and ethnic relations

Research traditions do not develop in isolation and an understanding of these two Australian traditions must begin with an examination of the social context within which they have developed. Three distinct, though at times interacting, levels may be characterized as the societal, the institutional, and the interpersonal.

The societal level

Government policies have been developed in the context of increasing ethnic diversity. Permanent European settlement began with the British in

1788 and began a process in which the indigenous Aboriginal population came to be dominated and overwhelmed by the increasing number of immigrants. From a population estimated at over 300,000 in 1788, by 1891 their numbers had declined to around 111,000 (Price 1979: A96). Indeed, contemporary discourse represented them as "a dying race". The present Aboriginal population, though displaying all the outward signs of a highly disadvantaged minority, now comprises over one per cent of Australia's population and includes individuals from many diverse linguistic and cultural backgrounds experiencing highly varied patterns of contact with the larger society (Australia 1985: 29–30).

During the 19th century Australia's immigrant population continued to expand. The gold rushes in particular generated a significant influx of Chinese and others of non-British background. However, because of their transitory intentions or the discrimination they experienced (or a combination of both) their stay was often temporary and they had little direct rôle in the formulation of the major social and political institutions. By 1947 Australia's population of 7.5 million was still predominantly Anglo-Celtic[1] with over 90 per cent originating from the United Kingdom or Ireland. The present population of nearly 17 million comprises 22 per cent who were born overseas and approximately 40 per cent who either arrived after 1947 or are the Australian-born children of these migrants.

More significant than the numerical growth in the population is the ethnic diversity of migrants. Of the post-war arrivals nearly two-thirds are from outside the United Kingdom and Ireland. As a result, nearly one-quarter of the Australian population is now from non-British and, often, non-English speaking backgrounds. Those arriving since the 1970s are now more likely to be of "Asian" than European origin.[2] Thus contemporary patterns of race and ethnic relations represent a fusion of the earlier "settler colonialism" with a situation where ethnically diverse settler groups are, individually and collectively, minorities within the larger Anglo-Celtic society.

In this context, boundary maintenance and rôle ascription become both important indicators of patterns of social relations and a key element of researchers' constructs of these relations. In Australia, the terms "migrant" and "immigrant" are used interchangeably to refer to all those born overseas. But colloquial discourse reveals disagreement, confusion and lack of clarity. Thus individuals of British or English-speaking background (ESB) frequently lose the "migrant" appellation whereas the non-ESB (or NESB) do not. The use of the term "migrant" in this context carries with it connotations both of social disadvantage and of "outsider".

The omission from studies of "migrants" of those from English-speaking countries is sometimes an unconscious reflection of popular usage but usually indicates a focus on social disadvantage. The continuing significance of "migrant" background (including the Australian-born) led during the 1970s to the colloquial use of the term "ethnic"; the principal subgroup being "Asian". Official policy has been ambivalent in that reference to "ethno-specific" services and programmes typically means those for members of specific NESB groups. But, lest it be thought that government policy is positively discriminatory to "ethnics", official usage also stresses that all Australians have an "ethnic background". It is in this form that policy discourse comes closest to the way Australian researchers use the term "ethnic group"; namely to refer to groups linked by common heritage, and usually language and/or religion.

While "race" is widely used colloquially, academic researchers involved in non-Aboriginal studies eschew use of the term since the significance of physical "visibility" is treated as problematic and not assumed to be the determining factor in inter-group relations.

Since the mid-1980s official government terminology has shifted from "migrant" to "NESB"; with policies intended to encompass second or later generations of settlers. As a result much recent research has focused on "NESBs" either as a single category or as a conflation of a number of diverse groups. Official statistics are frequently organized into NESB and ESB based on the language status attributed to the country of birth of either the migrant or, for Australian-born, his/her parents.[3] Less commonly, language actually spoken may be used as the basis of allocation.

The differentiation of the Aboriginal population as the "visible" minority is indicative of the continuation of two distinct patterns of "ethnic" and "race" relations within the one society. These are associated with differences in government policy strategies which can only in part be explained by the far greater social disadvantage experienced by the Aboriginal population (Inglis 1986b). The legal embodiment of this distinction was the Australian Constitution which, until a referendum change in 1967, excluded Aborigines from legal equality with the rest of the population.

Although never expressed as clearly as in the post-1947 period, the dominant theme underlying immigration policy from the 19th century was "assimilation". As migrants were required, and expected, to assimilate into Australian society, preference was given to groups perceived as culturally compatible; thus minimizing the need for "special provisions".

In contrast, Aboriginal policy has shifted over time; from assimilation to segregation to preserve the "dying race" (in the late 19th century), and back to assimilation (in the late 1930s) in response to their numerical increase. But despite policy changes the extensive geographical segregation of Aboriginal groups continued.

By the late 1960s both policies of assimilation were under attack. In the case of Aborigines the pressures from international organizations, such as the United Nations, and the indigenous Aboriginal protest movements culminated in the success of the 1967 referendum, which gave the Aboriginal population full citizenship rights. By the early 1970s the present policy of "self-determination" was being developed. A contentious issue here became the definition of "Aboriginal" in that it governed eligibility for the various special services and programmes geared to reducing disadvantage. The government's official definition emphasizes the three elements of descent, self-identity, and acceptance as an Aboriginal by the Aboriginal community. There is undoubtedly a process of "ethnogenesis" involving the development of a pan-Aboriginal identity around the common elements of culture, land rights and, most recently, deaths in custody.

With non-Aboriginal groups also, assimilation as a policy proved unacceptable. Both academic research and the day-to-day experiences of teachers, nurses and social workers highlighted the absence of assimilation. These, together with demands for "ethnic rights" and power, convinced the government to change direction. After a brief period of "integration", the current policy of "multiculturalism" was adopted. Drawing on the Canadian model developed slightly earlier, it is premised on the existence of cultural diversity. But this diversity is seen exclusively in terms of ethnicity, with class and gender issues ignored (Foster & Stockley 1984). Because of this the focus on cultural maintenance has been increasingly complemented by an emphasis on achieving greater equity and facilitating participation in the larger society. At the same time the policy's scope has been extended from migrants to all Australians, with Aborigines being explicitly included within the policy. This is a sensitive issue as many feel that their identification as an "ethnic group" undermines their status as original inhabitants – a First Nation – (Jennett 1987: 67).

A common feature of "multiculturalism" and "self-determination" is the government's greatly increased contacts with those seen as representatives of their respective ethnic groups. In 1990 the Commonwealth Government set up the Aboriginal and Torres Strait Islander Commission (ATSIC) with over 780 elected Regional Councillors and 17 Elected Commissioners.

71

Contacts with non-Aboriginal groups occur through less formal lobby groups such as the Federation of Ethnic Communities Councils.

Data from research is also critical for policy formation. Two agencies which sponsor such research are the Office of Multicultural Affairs in the Department of Prime Minister and Cabinet (from 1987), and the Bureau of Immigration Research set up two years later within the Department of Immigration, Local Government and Ethnic Affairs. Although the latter has a more narrowly defined rôle there is considerable overlap and potential tension between the two agencies, given that their futures are ultimately dependent on political support for their work. The significance here is that funding possibilities draw "institutional" interest and inevitably influence the direction of the latter's research agenda.

The institutional level

Two of the most important factors influencing theory development are a researcher's institutional location and sources of funding. The last twenty years have witnessed major changes in both, and especially so in research on race and ethnicity. Rather than research being confined to universities it is now increasingly located in specialist government-funded research institutes, government departments, private consultancy firms, and non-governmental community agencies.

These locational shifts have also been accompanied by major changes in the funding environment. As sources of support for "pure" research have declined, so more researchers have been compelled to bid for funds earmarked for policy-driven projects concerned with "multiculturalism" and "self-determination", and especially so in non-Aboriginal research. With recent contractions in university research funds the major (potential) source of support for "pure" research is the Australian Research Council (ARC), and in practice little money goes to studies of race/ethnicity.

An alternative source of funding for work on Aboriginal issues is the Australian Institute of Aboriginal Studies (AIAS). Providing a variety of grants for approved academic projects, AIAS is one of two special purpose government-sponsored institutes (the other being the Australian Institute of Multicultural Affairs set up in 1979). But AIMA came to be perceived as a highly partisan vehicle of the ruling political party, and was ultimately closed down in 1986. Although AIAS avoided such extreme criticism it, too, was the subject of a special inquiry in the early 1980s. This led to a demand for it to reflect more effectively the needs and concerns of Aborigines, a change in orientation now reflected in the participation of Aborigines in specifying research priorities as well as in vetting and approving specific researchers and research proposals. In the absence of sufficiently organized and institutionalized community expression non-Aboriginal ethnic groups have yet to reach such a position; though significantly the case was strongly articulated by NESB women's groups at a 1992 Bureau of Immigration Research Conference on "Women and Migration".

To conclude, the key point is that at both national and state levels different departments and agencies deal with Aboriginal and non-Aboriginal affairs. The bifurcation of both policy and research then has a "knock-on" effect at the individual, interpersonal level.

Interpersonal level

This intellectual bifurcation means that one has almost two separate research traditions. Those writing about Aboriginal issues rarely discuss relations with other "ethnic/racial" groups, and vice versa. This division has major theoretical and methodological implications as we shall see later in the chapter. In many ways it concerns the nature of, and relations between, sociology and allied disciplines such as anthropology, and perhaps in particular the late development of the former as a distinct discipline in Australia.

Austin (1984) argues that there are four distinct research paradigms in the literature: Marxian, Weberian, Stratificationist (concerned with social mobility), and Regional/Community Studies. Significantly, however, there is seen to be a high level of academic "balkanization", evidenced by a lack of cross-fertilization. How these relate to divisions in Aboriginal/non-Aboriginal research traditions is the key question for the remainder of the chapter.

Research focusing on Aborigines

Anthropological research on the Aboriginal population began in the 19th century. Ethnographic work, premised on the functionalist model of closed systems, focused on their physiological characteristics, culture and social institutions, e.g. kinship, religion and language. As "'traditional' pre-industrial peoples" their study was seen as the sole preserve of anthropologists (Austin 1984: 100). Relations between Aborigines and European society were not studied and, due largely to an essentialist view of culture, nor were urban or part-Aboriginal groups.

Over the last twenty years, and despite major changes in the social situation of Aborigines, the basic research agenda and methodology have changed little. On the other hand, consultancy research does not always involve extended fieldwork and tends to highlight policy concerns such as land rights, compensation and development programmes.

Within this traditional ethnographic framework, however, one detects a greater immediacy, a theoretical emphasis on human agency, and the presence of an actor's individual choice reflecting the changed context of the researcher's rôle (Myers 1986: 139, Sullivan 1986: 18). A more negative assessment is that the theoretical emphasis on traditional culture has continued, and this has produced a critique of Aboriginal responses to change as indicative of lack of adaptation, erosion or even cultural "loss" (Cowlishaw 1986a: 8).

A project sponsored in the early 1960s by the Social Science Research Council under the direction of Charles Rowley marked a watershed in that it broke with anthropological "tradition". Here the focus was on contacts between Aborigines and non-Aborigines. The research team, many of whom by training were not anthropologists, drew on historical, statistical and primary research to construct a telling account of structures underpinning the widespread exploitation and social disadvantage of the Aboriginal population (Rowley 1970, 1971a, 1971b). At the same time the studies illustrated the diversity of experiences of Aborigines, including those of part-Aboriginal descent.

Despite the significance of the research as a major influence in attracting public support for changes in Aboriginal policy it is not widely referred to in anthropological literature (for reasons already stated). An exception is work generated by its alleged under-theorization of "exploitation". Thus Hartwig (1978: 122-4) proposed an "internal colonialism" model which incorporated an analysis of class relations both within and between the Aboriginal and European populations (see also, Jennett 1987). And Beckett, starting with the concept of internal colonialism, developed a model of "welfare colonialism" (1988) in which he examines the rôle of the State in conditioning these relations. The non-determinism of the model and the marked sense of Aboriginal agency and power has led Morris (1989), within a Foucaultian framework, to argue that resistance was an important element in the response of the Dhan-gadi Aborigines to European settlement and domination.

This theme of resistance has been underscored by recent archival research by both European and Aboriginal scholars. This shows that Aboriginal groups waged a continuing and to some extent effective resistance to European settlement (e.g. Reynolds 1989, Langton 1988). An important component of this historical reappraisal has been the work of feminist scholars on the position of Aboriginal women in both pre-and post-colonial Australia; thus introducing vital new perspectives into the previous, male-centred, view of Aboriginal society. Supplementing historical and ethnographic data, researchers are also turning to Aboriginal writing as a means of examining women's experiences (Larbalestier 1991).

An issue which many of the feminist writers are addressing is the nature and construction of Aboriginal women's identity in relation to both Aboriginal and European society. This is part of a broader focus on ethnogenesis and the development of a pan-Aboriginal political identity noted earlier. Beckett (1988: 13) argues that it is wrong to see "Aboriginality" as largely a reactive ethnicity (to State "racialization", i.e. the State's construction of "Aboriginality"). Instead, he suggests that this "construct" has attained a degree of autonomy. Its content has been defined essentially in exclusivist and oppositional terms, i.e. in terms of the uniqueness of Aboriginal culture and its incompatibility with "European" society and institutions. Often there is an uncritical, tacit acceptance of the Aboriginal view that the gaining of land rights will be the key to solving disadvantage. But as Keefe (1988: 74) notes, these characteristics of "Aboriginality-as-persistence" equate with attempts by government advisers and officials to specify the characteristics of "Aboriginality" (and they share a cultural essentialism).

Only recently have researchers begun to examine the relations between identity construction, the political ideology of "Aboriginality", and European society (Cowlishaw 1986b, Jordan 1984, Keefe 1988). Keefe's work, based on neo-Marxian theories, focuses on the concept of "resistance", and the juxtaposition of "Aboriginality-as-resistance" and "Aboriginality-as-persistence". The significance of this work is clear. As with the revisionist historical accounts it questions the view of Aborigines as passive "victims".

Along with this shift in research thinking comes a greater concern with Aboriginal power and politics. Following in the tradition of Rowley, Hartwig and Beckett who, if from rather different perspectives, were addressing the issue of inequity in relations between Aborigines and Europeans, researchers have been concerned to assess the effectiveness of self-determination as a policy, the viability of an independent Aboriginal movement, and the extent to which their "leaders" have been incorporated into "White society" (Howard 1982). In a parallel stream of research, feminists have been concerned to study changes in the social position and power of Aboriginal women in the post-colonial context.

Much of the concern with structures of inequality stems from an increasing disillusionment among the anthropological community with the limited changes brought about by self-determination; a policy for which many of their number have been prominent advocates. Self-determination has itself become an academic battleground between two theoretical camps; one utilizing conflict, the other consensus models. But what is singularly lacking in the debate is convincing data on the reality of "Aboriginality" and the level of incorporation.

The key problem here is methodological. How is one to measure "reality", and particularly that of "community leaders" when the emphasis on accurate and faithful description precludes treating this reality as a phenomenon to be explained? Arguably it necessitates a radical re-evaluation of the rôle of research and the relationship between research and theory. Certainly, the existence of this debate reflects important changes in both the anthropologists' rôle and their relation to the Aborigines they study. No longer can they easily retain their self-image as dispassionate observers of a "traditional" group in whose welfare they take a concerned (some would say paternalistic) interest. Instead, they find themselves actively involved through their "expert" status in representing "their" people both informally and formally, in advice to government administrations and in legal cases where information on Aboriginal culture is relevant (as, for example, in cases involving ownership and entitlement to land rights). Although the rôle of adviser to government is not new (Wise 1985) anthropologists now find themselves in situations where Aboriginal groups have a much more active rôle in presenting their views and aspirations. This has in turn provoked a reflection not just on their rôle but on the adequacy of their theorizations and on the data on which these are based.

Perhaps the most important by-product of the empowerment process is the active interest in, and vetting of, the research and the researcher by the Aborigines themselves. As in the UK, USA and elsewhere, a general increase in "democratization" has led to debates about ethics, the political ramifications of research findings, gender issues, the employment of local people, ownership of data, forms of dissemination/publication, and the relative "benefits" gained from the research (Schebeck 1986, Sullivan 1986: 18).

76

Many (non-anthropological) researchers over the last twenty years (e.g. Stevens 1972) have highlighted the extensive material disadvantage of the Aboriginal population. Despite the lack of standard census data until 1966, the available data demonstrates marked inequalities in areas such as unemployment, imprisonment, health, and educational achievement. In conjunction with the historical material it is being used to analyze the institutional treatment of Aborigines by Europeans and the extent of institutionalized racism. Such analysis counters anthropological work which, within a cultural deficit theory framework, evidences unemployment, alcoholism and a "spoiled identity" (Cowlishaw 1988: 72).

Another area of theorizing, which has provoked debates parallel to those in the UK and USA, concerns "mainstream" feminism. An acrimonious (and very public) debate between a prominent anthropologist and, in the first instance, a group of mainly tertiary-educated Aboriginal women (Huggins et al. 1991) illustrates the point well. The latter's anger centred on anthropological accounts of "intraracial" rape, and in particular the potential dangers of publishing such material (Bell & Nelson 1989, Bell 1990, 1991a,b). Clearly this might strengthen negative perceptions about Aboriginal society, but similar information can, as Bell has shown (1991a,b), be found in other recent reports and sources, some of them produced by Aboriginal women.

However, the key issue lies in the priority given to patriarchy, rather than to the state, as the focal point for racially-based oppression. The anthropologist's assumption that intraracial rape was her (and every woman's) business simply underscored for the Aboriginal women the equal involvement of White women (with men) in colonial exploitation. The fact that co-authorship was attributed (by Bell) to an Aboriginal woman simply invoked the feeling that she was being "used" by Bell to give "authority" to her account.

This debate illustrates very clearly the interaction between methodology (in the broadest sense), empirical data and the generation of effective theorizing. It could be argued, for example, that the anthropological tradition has led not only to a blinkering of debates, by focusing on internal relations between Aboriginal groups (rather than external relations with Europeans), but also to a theoretical myopia, in de-emphasizing both the rôle of the state and the resistance of Aboriginals to colonial (and post-colonial) oppression. Researchers such as Beckett (1988), Cowlishaw (1988), Keeffe (1988) and Morris (1989) have shown the potential gains from exploring alternative, neo-Marxian approaches. But, largely because they are widely

perceived as treating Aboriginal groups "as if they are no more than anomalous subclasses appended to a capitalist structure" (Sullivan 1986: 17), "traditional" Marxian accounts have been rare. By way of conclusion, it has to be said that the area of Aboriginal studies is dominated by policy- and action-oriented research and as such remains comparatively under-theorized.

Research on non-Aboriginal groups

The corpus of research on non-Aboriginal groups, which essentially began with the post-Second World War influx of immigrants, differs radically. For one thing, a variety of disciplines were involved from the outset, ensuring that no one discipline, such as anthropology, dominated the literature. As a result, there is a far greater diversity of data collection methods, theoretical frameworks and research problematics. Secondly, research usually tackles the question of relations between different ethnic/racial groups. A third, and important, difference from Aboriginal research is that, possibly due to the broad "ethnic" mix of researchers, tensions between "us" (academe) and "them" (the researched) are less in evidence; so much so that the relationship remains largely unproblematized.

The initial aim of research was to chart the development and nature of post-war immigration. Extensive use has been made, for these and more explicitly theoretical purposes, of official statistics including census returns, records of births, marriages, naturalization and immigration and, more recently, labour market data (see Hugo 1990). However, the utility of these statistics depends on the material collected which, in turn, reflects the ideological framework influencing government policy (Hirschman 1986); a point well illustrated by the Australian Census which excluded Aborigines prior to the repeal of the relevant Constitutional provision in 1967. Birthplace and religious affiliation data were always collected, though published categories depended on the size of the respective groups and the boundaries and legal status of particular nations. The failure until 1976 to include a question on parent's birthplace and, until 1986, to seek information on ethnic ancestry reflects the initial commitment to assimilation and the more recent impact of multiculturalism, which allocates services and resources on ethnic criteria.

Hostility to Asian immigration on the part of the Federation of the Australian colonies ensured that data on "race" was collected from the very first national census in 1911. In contrast, prior to 1971 the only section of the Aboriginal population to be enumerated were those living in settled areas. Then (in 1971) the political agenda dictated a reformulation of "racial" options to "European", "Aboriginal", "Torres Strait Islander" or "Other" (Aboriginals and Torres Strait Islanders being linked in government policy). The abandonment of the more general "race" question by 1981 was justified partly by reference to its "racist" overtones, and partly due to the revision of Australia's immigration policy, which had ceased distinctions on "racial" criteria. Also with rising levels of immigration from Southeast Asia and the increasing heterogeneity of the "European" population it had become a very poor indicator of "ethnicity".

The inclusion of additional measures such as nationality and (in 1976, 1986 and 1991) language proved of limited use to researchers and policy makers. While the census data provides the *potential* to examine shifts in ethnic identity, it is often only published, or analyzed, in terms of the broad policy categories of "NESB" or "ESB". The "NESB" data provided in many non-census publications is derived from an individual's birthplace, with the indirect effect of transferring to the whole NESB group the experiences, whether in health, the labour market or other areas, of the foreign-born population.

Additional problems stem from inter-censal shifts in the inclusion and formulation of questions, but research with a contemporary focus is better served because of the increasing scope of data now collected and, since the 1981 census, the availability of sample data. The Census and other official data sources are able to provide important data on economic and educational attainment and disadvantage and form the basis for research within both Stratificationist (Evans & Kelly 1986, Withers & Pope 1985) and neo-Marxian paradigms (Collins 1984, Lever Tracey 1981a,b).

Almost three decades of work by Jean Martin provides a basis for charting the shifts in research agenda and theoretical frameworks. This is both because of the sensitive and innovative nature of her research and the critiques of it that have appeared since her death. Trained as an anthropologist, her first research project was an ethnographic study of a group of East European refugees in Australia (Martin 1957). The guiding theme of her work, and that of others during the 1950s and 1960s, was the process of adjustment experienced by new arrivals. As in the UK and elsewhere in the West, "assimilation" was both state policy and the dominant theoretical model of social change. Not surprisingly, therefore, Australian studies, whether based on social psychological tests, questionnaires, interviews or community studies, often sought to establish the extent of assimilation; conceptualized either as an individual or group phenomenon. Even where researchers chose simply to explore "change" rather than "assimilation" they were confronted with methodological problems, since both depended on specifying a particular socio-cultural model: the "traditional" pre-migration society in the former and the "receiving" or "host" society in the latter.

Recent scholarship has been highly critical of the assimilation phase of research, branding it as conservative and ethnocentric (Wilton & Bosworth 1984). Yet, an important result of the research was to highlight the inappropriateness of government policy and its disjuncture with empirical reality; thereby contributing to the reconstruction of knowledge and the abandonment of assimilationist policy (Martin 1978).

Although "assimilation" as a research paradigm largely disappeared, the social welfare implications of continued immigration spawned many, usually small-scale, policy-oriented studies by community groups and government bodies (Holton 1990: 174–200). These failed to contribute significantly to the theorization of ethnic relations, but they stimulated some important academic debates. While much early research indulged in "blaming the victim" by suggesting that migrants were at least partly, if unintentionally (through limited English, particular cultural practices etc.), responsible for many of their "problems" (Martin 1978: 36), researchers began to emphasize both the diversity of the "migrant experience" and the error involved in depicting migrants as passive and powerless individuals. Nevertheless there was a tendency, particularly among ethnic community workers, to continue to stress "disadvantage" and powerlessness lest a more "optimistic" prognosis might provide a rationale for governments to cut funding to a variety of social welfare programmes.

The strength of feeling engendered by research presenting "optimistic" findings came to the fore at the 1992 Women and Migration Conference organized by the Bureau of Immigration Research. This called both for a greater sensitivity to the potential use and misuse of research data, and a reevaluation of the rôle of the researcher vis-a-vis the researched. Arguably it is the lack of conflict in the latter area, which accounts for the fact that non-Aboriginal research has not witnessed the sort of epistemological revolution we saw earlier in the case of studies of Aboriginal groups.

While commentators had long questioned the effects of extensive migration on Australian society and culture, researchers in the 1980s sought to focus much more on the economic impact of immigration and, now, more

recently on the environment (Fincher 1991), all areas of significant importance for policy in the 1990s. Another focus of research was the examination of ongoing, institutionalized patterns of ethnic relations; stressing
in particular the characteristics of the ethnic group, its continuity and form.

The often highly descriptive nature of such accounts is well illustrated
by the entries in *The Australian People:An Encyclopedia of the Nation, Its
People and Their Origins* (Jupp 1988) which was published as an Australian
Bicentennial project. Research here has tended to treat the "ethnic community" as a bounded and easily identifiable entity. Whereas the salience
of "ethnicity" varies, "community" is seen as static and non-problematic;
the key issue being whether these "communities" are enduring collectivities
bound by ethnic solidarity, or are merely reactive in the sense of responding
to the external forces of racism and discrimination (Price 1963, Martin
1972a).

While minority ethnic groups tend to live in the major urban areas, research shows that residential concentrations are not generally as high as
among (say) Black populations in the USA, or even the UK. Despite this,
much Australian research has targeted these concentrations and ignored
individuals who live outside them (Burnley 1985). There is, therefore, a
danger not only of wrongly characterizing collective ethnic identity, but
also of distorting, for example, age/class distributions and obscuring social mobility.

Again paralleling research in many Western societies, studies of young
people have problematized individual ethnic identity and, in particular, how
the young are affected by being "between two cultures". In contrast to early
studies, which tended to emphasize extreme conflict and personal problems, more recent research has provided a more positive perspective on
"coping" in different social milieux (Bottomley 1979, Johnston 1972,
Tsoldis 1986). Shifts in theoretical approach are clearly implicated here.
Symbolic interactionist models are common in these recent studies, and
"resistance theory" has begun to influence ethnographic work in schools
(Walker 1987).

In marked contrast to Aboriginal research, the political construction of
ethnicity among (ethnic) minorities has been largely ignored, except by
those concerned with the rôle of the State (Castles et al.: 1988). However,
ethnic leadership and political participation, insofar as they are studied, do
raise interesting questions; in the former case about intra-community class
divisions (Kakakios & van den Velden 1984) and, in the latter, about the
impact of multicultural policy on incorporation in the existing party political

system (Jupp 1984, Holton 1990: 204–6).

Mirroring the race-class debates in the UK and USA, a major feature of research on non-Aboriginal groups is the widespread and often bitter debate stemming from the differential prioritization of "class" and "ethnicity". Various theoretical polarities are in evidence – Stratificationist vs Marxist, neo-classical functionalist vs institutional political economist, culturalist vs structuralist – and lending particular passion to conflicting conceptualizations of culture and ethnicity is the conflation of the theoretical debate with the political debate about multiculturalism.

Academics who attack multiculturalism for its emphasis on cultural maintenance rather than equity and social justice, have emphasized how those studying culture and ethnicity have become actively involved both in the formulation of the policy through membership of advisory committees and as advocates of cultural maintenance programmes, especially in education: but the sharp personal distinctions between researchers have blurred over the last decade as multicultural policy has broadened to encompass issues of social equity and justice. Concurrently, the economic determinism of earlier Marxian accounts has been replaced by more complex neo-Marxian analyses that address culture, power and the independent, autonomous interplay of gender and ethnicity as well as class (Bottomley & de Lepervanche 1984).

In the 1970s social inequality was a dominant theme in both policy-oriented and theoretical work. Jean Martin (1975, 1976), for example, analyzed the economic situation and "disadvantage" of migrants with the aid of national survey data (1975, 1976). However, she did so within a non-Marxian framework that drew attention to the variations between ethnic groups and the effects of period of residence. Similarly, her longitudinal study of the educational outcomes of high school students demonstrated that (educational) success varied both by ethnic and class background (Martin & Meade 1979). The significance of this work lay in its implicit critique of overly simplistic Marxian analyses which argued that differential experiences were reducible to class-based explanations.

The work of Castles and Kosack (1973) on "guestworkers" in Europe had provided the major theoretical inspiration for Marxist analyses. Early accounts of labour market segmentation used highly aggregated NESB/ESB data from the census (Collins 1978, Lever-Tracey 1981a,b). More recent analyses have begun to examine theoretically important variations in the labour market positions of different non-Aboriginal populations, taking account of internal class divisions and involvement in industrial conflict

(Lever-Tracey 1984, Lever-Tracey & Quinlan 1988). Weberian scholars were also using census data to assess social mobility, but here the (im)mobility of individual groups was often explained in terms not of institutional barriers and discrimination but of differential levels of individual resources and skills; thus illustrating the truism that theoretical/political paradigm, rather than data source, is often the major determinant of research "findings" (Jacubowicz & Castles 1986, 1988 Evans & Jones 1987, 1988).

In the same way that research on inequality and disadvantage tends to ignore variations within large aggregate groups such as "migrants" or "NESBs", there is often a failure to examine the experiences of women. When they are "visible" it is usually within the "social problem" agenda discussed earlier. Although the first major collection of Marxian-inspired writings on ethnic minorities indicated in its title *Ethnicity Class and Gender in Australia* (Bottomley & de Lepervanche 1984) the need to consider gender issues, they remain undertheorized. A recent article has argued that this reflects the way in which radical positions both of the Left and Right have been constrained by existing (male) theoretical agendas at the same time as the whole "migrant" issue has been marginalized in "mainstream" political and social thought (Jeannie Martin 1991: 111). She then illustrates (ibid.: 120) how the work of Jean Martin (1978), which she sees as presenting a Weberian interest-group theory, is bedevilled by the location of women within the family. Ethnicist or culturalist approaches are seen as similarly flawed. Without offering a way out of the impasse of theoretical invisibility, Jeannie Martin does propose a number of methodological guides designed to ensure that "what is female is situated fluidly, ambiguously and variously in the space between each side, and accepts that a feminist account proceeds from here." (ibid: 131).

In contrast to the paucity of research on "minority women", "the State" has generated an extensive literature from a number of well developed theoretical perspectives. Neo-Marxian writers, in providing a critique of immigration policy and practice, have analyzed the rôle of the State in structuring ethnic relations (Jakubowicz 1984). Others, such as Martin (1978) and Foster & Stockley (1984), reflecting the influence of Weberian and "sociology of knowledge" perspectives, have provided revealing accounts of the factors underlying shifts in State policy.

It is arguably this focus on the State as the major determinant of ethnic relations that has led to a lack of concern with individualized prejudice and discrimination. Even an inquiry by the Human Rights Commission into race-motivated violence involving both Aboriginal and non-Aboriginal victims, and the prioritization (by AIMA) of "racism" as a research area following anti-Asian discourse in the immigration debates of the 1980s, failed to influence the agenda markedly. Despite the fact that the terms "racism" and "racist" are common in both colloquial and political discourse, studies of racism and prejudice are rare. Although perhaps betraying a myopic ethnocentrism not afflicting colleagues in (say) the UK and USA, the relative absence of violence in Australia and the generally high levels of tolerance, combined with the absence of long-established minorities are also important in understanding why "racism", with its often implicit explanation in terms of psychological or ethnic stereotypes, has not been a major focus of research. Australian research has instead emphasized class, gender or the level of human capital as key elements in structural disadvantage. However, a recent survey of discrimination in the workplace (Foster et al.: 1991: 111) has drawn attention to the need to consider "institutional racism". It has essentially been left to historians to redress the balance somewhat. Studies of the relationship between the labour movement, the racism of anti-Asian and -Pacific migration campaigns, and 19th-century Australian nationalism, addressed the question of whether working-class racism was propagated by capital (Burgmann 1978: 33; 1984, 1985) or was embedded in the capital-labour nexus (Curthoys & Markus 1978: xv, Markus 1985).

In general, both historical and statistical materials have been regarded essentially as supplementary research data. But, the emergence of oral history has proved a valuable recourse for those who have repeatedly criticized surveys and other sociological methods for failing to take account of "the individual" (Wilton & Bosworth 1984). Unfortunately however, the implicit theoretical and epistemological assumptions lack articulation. Nevertheless, an emphasis on the "reality" as experienced by hitherto "invisible" groups contains the basis of new insights (and has been recognized as such by ethnic agencies and groups, which have become increasingly active in sponsoring such research). Whether novel theorizations, taking account of ethnic diversity, will emerge from this work remains unclear.

The need for brevity has inevitably led to an over-simplification of theoretical positions and may at the same time have reified the boundaries between competing positions. Indeed, it has to be said that at times rhetoric alone divides the different theoretical "camps".

Conclusion

Research on ethnic and race relations can take a variety of forms, ranging from the study of particular "ethnic" or "racial" groups to the examination of the perspectives, policies and practices of the dominant group, to studies of relations between dominant and minority groups. All three are present in Australia, although there is a major bifurcation of methodology and theorization in research involving Aboriginal and non-Aboriginal groups.

Despite this, similarities in the two research agendas can be detected in the rejection of static descriptions, a greater concern with social change, and (though it applies more to research involving non-Aborigines) a shift in focus away from specific ethnic or racial groups and towards "majority society". This reflects such diverse influences as policy changes (e.g. self-determination), the realities of research funding, and a reassessment of the locus of "disadvantage". Hence the research problematic is clearly seen to depend not only on theory formulation at the "interpersonal" level but on developments in "social" and "institutional" contexts.

It is clear that theoretical paradigms can impose parameters constraining research; witness the continued emphasis in Aboriginal research on "traditional" culture and institutions. But this research agenda also stems from legal, political and policy considerations related to such issues as land rights and self-determination. The latter concerns may partly explain the theoretical bifurcation, and the lack of innovative theoretical work on Aboriginality.

The research bifurcation has had a crucial impact on the scope of the research agenda. But one key element remains unexplored. Apart from one account which allocated Aborigines to a distinct segment of the larger economy (Collins 1978), researchers, even those espousing a "majority–minority" approach, have avoided analyses of relations between Aboriginal and non-Aboriginal groups. The conventional answer is that this is simply too difficult on both theoretical and political grounds. As Bottomley and de Lepervanche state "Our exclusion of Aborigines was by choice, partly because of the difficulty of fitting Aborigines, as a category, into the kind of analysis we have used, but also, because of the political implications of lumping them together with migrants" (1984: x–xi).

The avoidance of the task may not be surprising given that research and theorizing about "racial and ethnic groups" has been ignored by mainstream sociology. Their absence from mainstream theorizing is certainly reminiscent of the ideology of "denial" underlying the policy of assimilation, and remains perhaps the most enduring "blindspot" in the Australian research agenda.

Notes

1. The now common use of Anglo-Celtic rather than Anglo-Saxon to refer to the dominant ethnic groups in Australian society indicates the extent to which the population of Scottish and, especially, of Irish, origin has ceased to be viewed as a distinct minority as was the case until the Second World War.
2. The major (Asian) countries of birth are Vietnam (119,000), Lebanon (68,000), the Philippines (62,000), India (55,000), Malaysia (54,000), and Hong Kong and China (both 46,000). Those of Chinese origin are the major Asian ethnic group (Bureau of Immigration Research 1991:20–1).
3. Countries considered English-speaking by the Australian Bureau of Census are the United Kingdom, Ireland, New Zealand, USA, Canada and South Africa.

References

Austin, D. 1984. *Australian sociologies*. Sydney: Allen & Unwin.
Australia 1985. *Aboriginal education: Report of the House of Representatives Select Committee on Aboriginal Education*. Canberra: Australian Government Publishing Service
Beckett, J. 1988 Aboriginality, citizenship and the nation state. *Social Analysis* 24: 3–18.
Bell, D. 1990. Reply. *Anthropological Forum* 6 (2), 158–65.
Bell, D. 1991a. Letters to the Editor. *Women's Studies International Forum* 14 (5), 507–13.
Bell, D. 1991b. Intraracial rape revisited: on forging a feminist future beyond factions and frightening politics. *Women's Studies International Forum* 14 (5), 385–412.
Bell, D. & T. N. Nelson 1989. Speaking about rape is everyone's business. *Women's Studies International Forum* 12 (4), 403–16.
Bottomley, G. 1979. *After the odyssey: a study of Greek Australians*. St Lucia: University of Queensland Press.
Bottomley G. & M. de Lepervanche (eds) 1984. *Ethnicity, class and gender in Australia*. Sydney: George Allen & Unwin.
Burnley, I. H. 1985. A comparative analysis of first and second generation immigrants: residential and occupational mobility in Metropolitan Sydney. *Austral-*

ian Geographic Studies **23**, 269–90.

Burnley, I. H., S. Encel & G. McCall (eds) 1985. *Immigration and ethnicity in the 1980s*. Melbourne: Longman Cheshire.

Burgmann, V. 1978. Capital and labour: responses to immigration in the nineteenth century. In *Who are our enemies? Racism and the working class in Australia*, A. Curthoys & A. Markus (eds), Sydney: Hale & Iremonger.

Burgmann, V. 1984. Racism, socialism and the labour movement, 1887–1917. *Labour History* **47**, 39–54.

Burgmann, V. 1985. Who our enemies are: Andrew Markus and the baloney view of Australian racism. *Labour History* **49**, 97–101.

Castles, S. & G. Kosack 1973. *Immigrant workers and class structure in Western Europe*. London: Oxford University Press.

Castles, S. et al. 1988. *Mistaken identity: multiculturalism and the demise of nationalism in Australia*. Sydney: Pluto Press.

Collins, J. 1978. Fragmentation of the working class. In *Essays in the political economy of Australian capitalism*, vol. 3, E. L. Wheelwright & K. Buckley (eds). Sydney: Australia and New Zealand Publishing Co.

Collins J. 1984. Immigration and class: the Australian experience. In *Ethnicity, class and gender in Australia*, G. Bottomley & M. de Lepervanche (eds). Sydney: Allen & Unwin.

Cowlishaw, G. 1988a. Australian aboriginal studies: the anthropologists' accounts. In *The cultural construction of race*, M. de Lepervanche & G. Bottomley (eds), 60–79. Sydney: Sydney Association for Studies in Society and Culture.

Cowlishaw, G. 1988b. *Black, white or brindle: race in rural Australia*. Melbourne & New York: Cambridge University Press.

Curthoys A. & A. Markus (eds) 1978. *Who are our enemies?* Sydney: Hale & Iremonger.

de Lepervanche, M. 1980. From race to ethnicity. *Australian and New Zealand Journal of Sociology* **16** (March), 24–37.

Eckermann, A-K. 1988. Cultural vacuum or cultural vitality? *Australian Aboriginal Studies* **1**, 31–9.

Evans, M. D. R. & F. L. Jones 1987. Objective research on immigrants in Australia: why Jakubowicz and Castles are wrong. *Journal of Intercultural Studies* **8** (2), 69–77.

Evans, M. D. R. & F. L. Jones 1988. Wrestling with Proteus: a second response to Jakubowicz and Castles. *Journal of Intercultural Studies* **9** (1), 85–7.

Evans, M. D. R. & J. Kelley 1986. Immigrants work: equality and discrimination in the Australian labour market. *Australia and New Zealand Journal of Sociology* **22** (July), 187–207.

Fincher, R. 1991. *Immigration, urban infrastructure and the environment*. Canberra: Australian Government Publishing Service.

Foster, L., A. Marshall & L. Williams 1991. *Discrimination against immigrant workers in Australia*: A Report Prepared by the Bureau of Immigration Research for the International Labour Office. Canberra: Australian Government Publishing Service.

Foster, L & D. Stockley 1984. *Multiculturalism: the changing Australian paradigm*. Clevedon: Multilingual Matters Ltd.

Hartwig, M. 1978. Capitalism and Aborigines: the theory of internal colonialism and its rivals. In *Essays in the political economy of Australian capitalism*. E. L. Wheelwright & K. Buckley (eds), 119–41. Sydney: Australia and New Zealand Book Co.

Hirschman, C. 1986. The making of race in colonial Malaya. *Sociological Forum* 1, 330–61.

Holton, R. 1990. Social aspects of immigration. In *Australian immigration: a survey of the issues*. Canberra: Australian Government Publishing Service.

Howard, M. C. 1982. Australian Aboriginal politics and the perpetuation of inequality. *Oceania* liii, 82–101.

Huggins, J. et al. 1991. Letters to the Editor. *Women's Studies International Forum* 14 (5), 506–7.

Hugo, G. 1990. Demographic and spatial aspects of immigration. In *Australian immigration: a survey of the issues*, M. Wooden et al., 24–109. Canberra: Australian Government Publishing Service.

Inglis, C. 1986. Policy issues in the education of minorities in Australia. *Education and Urban Society* 18 (4), 423–36.

Jakubowicz, A. 1984. Ethnicity, multiculturalism and neo-conservatism. In *Ethnicity, class and gender in Australia*. G. Bottomley & M. de Lepervanche (eds), Sydney: George Allen & Unwin

Jacubowicz, A. 1986. *Social Science, ethnicity and immigration: an overview of research in academic institutions in Australia*. Paper presented at the Australian Institute of Multicultural Affairs Conference, Melbourne.

Jacubowicz, A. & S. Castles 1986. The inherent subjectivity of the apparently objective in research on ethnicity and class. *Journal of Intercultural Studies* 7 (3), 5–25.

Jacubowicz, A. 1988. Why objectivity need not lead to understanding: a rejoinder to Mariah Evans, Frank Jones, Jonathan Kelley et al. *Journal of Intercultural Studies* 9 (1), 80–4.

Jennett, C. 1987. Race and inequality in the West: incorporation or independence? The struggle for aboriginal equality. In *Three worlds of inequality: race, class and gender*, C. Jennett & R. Stewart (eds), 57–93. Melbourne: Macmillan.

Johnston, R. 1972. *Future Australians: immigrant children in Perth, Western Australia*. Canberra: Australian National University Press.

Jordan, D. 1984. The social construction of identity: the Aboriginal problem. *Australian Journal of Education* 28, 274–90.

Jupp, J. (ed.) 1984. *Ethnic politics in Australia*. Sydney: Allen & Unwin.

Jupp. J. (ed.) 1988. *The Australian people: an encyclopedia of the nation, its people and their origins.* Sydney: Angus & Robertson.

Kakakios, M. & J. van der Velden 1984. Migrant communities and class politics. In *Ethnicity, class and gender in Australia,* G. Bottomley & M. de Lepervanche (eds), 144–64. Sydney: George Allen & Unwin.

Keeffe, K. 1988. Aboriginality: resistance and persistence. *Australian Aboriginal Studies* **1**, 67–81.

Langton, M. 1988. Being black: Aboriginal cultures in "settled" Australia. Canberra: Australian Institute of Aboriginal Studies.

Larbalestier, J. 1991. Through their own eyes: an interpretation of Aboriginal women's writing. In *Intersexions: gender/class/culture/ethnicity,* G. Bottomley, M. de Lepervanche & J. Martin (eds), 75–91. Sydney: Allen & Unwin.

Lever Tracey, C. 1981a. *Post war immigrants in Australia and Western Europe: in reserve or centre forward?* Paper presented to the Ethnicity and Class Conference, University of Wollongong.

Lever Tracey, C. 1981b. Labour market segmentation and diverging migrant incomes. *Australian and New Zealand Journal of Sociology* **17** (2).

Lever Tracey, C. 1984. A new Australian working class leadership: the case of Ford Broadmeadows. In *Ethnicity, class and gender in Australia,* G. Bottomley & M. de Lepervanche (eds). Sydney: Allen & Unwin.

Lever Tracey, C. & M. Quinlan 1988. *A divided working class.* London: Routledge & Kegan Paul.

Markus, A. 1985. Explaining the treatment of non-European immigrants in nineteenth century Australia: a comment. *Labour History* **48**, 86–91.

Martin, Jean 1957. *Refugee settlers.* Canberra: ANU Press.

Martin, Jean 1972a. *Community and identity.* Canberra: ANU Press.

Martin, Jean 1972b. *Migrants: equality and ideology.* Meredith Memorial Lecture, Bundoora Vic.: La Trobe University.

Martin, Jean 1975. The study of the economic condition of migrants. In *Commission of inquiry into poverty welfare of immigants.* Canberra: Australian Government Publishing Service.

Martin, Jean 1976. *A decade of migrant settlement.* Canberra: Australian Government Publishing Service.

Martin, Jean 1978. *The migrant presence.* Sydney: George Allen & Unwin.

Martin, Jean & P. Meade 1979. *The educational experiences of Sydney High School students* (Report No. 1). Canberra: Australian Government Publishing Service.

Martin, Jeannie 1984. Non-English-speaking women:production and social reproduction. In *Ethnicity, class and gender in Australia,* G. Bottomley & M. de Lepervanche (eds). Sydney: Allen & Unwin.

Morris, B. 1989. *Domesticating resistance: the Dhan-Gadi Aborigines and the Australian State.* Oxford: Berg.

Myers, F. R. 1986. The politics of representation: anthropological discourse and

Australian aborigines. *American Ethnologist* xiii, 138.

Price, C. A. 1963. *Southern Europeans in Australia.* Melbourne: Oxford University Press.

Price, C. A. 1985. The ethnic composition of the Australian population. In *Immigration and Ethnicity in the 1980s,* I. H. Burnley, S. Encel & G. McCall (eds). Melbourne: Longman Cheshire.

Reynolds, H. 1989. *Dispossession: Black Australians and White Invaders.* Sydney: Allen & Unwin.

Rowley, C. D. 1970. *The destruction of Aboriginal society.* Canberra: ANU Press

Rowley, C. D. 1971a. *Outcasts in White Australia.* Canberra: ANU Press.

Rowley, C. D. 1971b. *The remote Aborigines.* Canberra: ANU Press

Schebeck, B. 1986. After successful fieldwork: what to do with all of the "material"? *Australian Aboriginal Studies* 1, 52–8.

Stevens, F. S. (ed.) 1972. *Racism: the Australian experience,* vol. 2. Sydney: Australia and New Zealand Book Co.

Sullivan, P. 1986. The generation of cultural trauma: what are anthropologists for? *Australian Aboriginal Studies* 1, 13–23.

Tsoldis, G. 1986. *Educating Voula*: A Report on Non-English-Speaking Background Girls and Education. MACMME, Victorian Ministry of Education.

Walker, J. 1987. *Louts and legends: male youth culture in an inner city school.* Sydney: Allen & Unwin.

Wilton, J. & R. Bosworth 1984. *Old worlds and new Australia: the post-war migrant experience.* Ringwood, Vic.: Penguin.

Wise, T. 1985. *The self-made anthropologist: a life of A. P. Elkin.* Sydney: George Allen & Unwin.

Withers, G. & D. Pope 1985. Immigration and unemployment. *Economic Record* 61, 554–63.

Chapter 5

South Africa:
from "race" to non-racialism?

Rupert Taylor

The dominant analytical model for explaining South African social "reality" is to see it as a racially divided society where the categories of "black" and "white" constitute the society's central dynamic. "Race" is understood to be a basic independent determinant of social identity and 'conflict is seen as the inevitable outcome of given racial . . . differences' (Boonzaier 1989: 175–6). This approach, articulating with key tenets of cultural pluralism and a liberal politics that linked apartheid to the force of racial prejudice, held firm ascendancy up until the 1970s (van den Berghe 1965, Wright 1977). Then, the rise of Marxism and class analysis came to pose a radical challenge by positing economic relationships as constituting the basic social structure. Consequently, to this school of thought, "race" is not an independent factor but the manifestation of those underlying material conditions and class forces that made apartheid functional to the needs of capitalism (Johnstone 1982).

However, the Marxist approach has been unable to specify theoretically just how class intersects with non-economic factors, and has been open to charges of economic reductionism. As a result, the emphasis on "race" has not been significantly displaced in academic and everyday understandings. Since the 1980s, there have been calls for a move towards a synthesis of the "race" and class paradigms (Posel 1983, Welsh 1987), but to date this line of thinking has failed to develop a meaningful critical sociology of South African society. The question of the relative salience of "race" and class in South Africa (Webster 1991) remains undertheorized. It would seem therefore that it is time to recast the terms of this debate and develop a new line of enquiry. The way forward suggested here is to take non-racialism seriously.

Defining non-racialism

To date, in South Africa, there has been limited understanding of, and much confusion over, what is meant by non-racialism. It is a difficult word. While all major political organizations, bar those to the right of the National Party, proclaim commitment to a non-racial society, there has been little, if any, serious analysis of non-racialism itself. It is one of the most often used, yet least-defined concepts in South African politics. As Don Foster has written, "When you ask academics what they actually mean about non-racialism . . . I suspect that we are left rather nonplussed" (1991: 23).

"Non-racial"/"non-racialism" does not feature in standard dictionaries. In the twenty volume Oxford English Dictionary (1989), only the word "non-racial" appears tucked away under the "Non-" words. Moreover, you will not find the word in *The International Encyclopedia of the Social Sciences*, *The Social Science Encyclopedia*, *A Dictionary of South African English* or *The Dictionary of Contemporary Politics of Southern Africa*. It is not clear when the term was first used in South Africa, but few of the key books on South Africa written prior to the Second World War used the word. Even today it is rare to find "non-racialism" as an index entry. There is no adequate, let alone critical, history of the idea. The only book length study on non-racialism, Julie Frederikse's *The unbreakable thread* (1990) fails to provide any "clarity as to what she understands 'non-racialism' to mean" (Seekings 1991: 190).

Part of the problem is that non-racialism has various meanings; it can mean "different things to different people within the same narrow organizational and ideological tradition, and on occasion, different things to the same person" (Carter 1991: 358). Thus, to advance understanding, the distinct definitions attached to the term must be discussed.

Historically, non-racialism was very narrowly related, in the context of apartheid's segregationist logic of parallelism of the 1940s/1950s, to upholding notions of having "separate but equal" political organizations and institutions for racial groupings. This position can be seen in key debates in the African National Congress (ANC) around the formal establishment of the Congress Alliance in 1955, with equal representation for each racially-based Congress partner, regardless of size and strength.[1] The emphasis was on advancing "racial co-operation" not inclusive membership of the ANC: the ANC, under the sway of African nationalism, was not prepared to let "whites" join their movement. It was in these terms that Congress leaders described the Congress Alliance as non-racial (Everatt 1990).

Given mounting criticism and dawning recognition of just how closely such an understanding articulated with apartheid ideology, non-racialism soon became reformulated to have wider meaning. From the late 1950s onwards, non-racialism began to be widely used to reject racial segregation and advance integration through challenging official racial categorization and encouraging organizational openness. Here, while the existence of distinct "races" was not doubted, "race" was not to be used to allocate distinct rights and set compulsory boundaries between people; as in such apartheid legislation as the Population Registration Act (1950), Group Areas Act (1950) and Reservation of Separate Amenities Act (1953).

From this perspective, the attack on racism comes down to challenging individual racist attitudes and furthering procedural, institutional, organizational and policy issues with regard to non-discrimination on the grounds of "race"; to eliminate racist barriers and, more recently, provide affirmative action programmes. This type of non-racialism is of a reactive nature, synonymous with non-discrimination, and is indistinguishable from the dominant use of "multi-racialism".[2] Accordingly, the language of non-racialism can be made to coexist comfortably with that of "race"; as with the use of such terms as "racial understanding" and "racial equality" and it is thus, for example, that Donald Horowitz talks of "a multiracial state with nonracial institutions" (1991: 96). To most people, this is the present-day understanding of non-racialism. At an organizational level the ANC became fully non-racial in 1985; the National Party in 1990.

However, within the ANC there is some attempt to go beyond this and confront the meaning of "race" itself as a form of identity; to question racial categories as a basis not just for representation but for identification. Here, "race" is no longer taken to be a primary factor in self-identification or in the identification of others. To move from treating non-racialism as a reactive to pro-active principle emphasis is placed on the irrelevance of "race" and the building of a democratic society in which racial divisions are swept away by forging a common South African identity (van Diepen 1988). This position, however, stops short of engaging in a radical deconstruction of "race" and as such is still trapped in multi-racialism. Paradoxically, the language of non-racialism still coexists with that of "race"; "to speak of the 'irrelevance' of 'race' still assumes the reality of 'race'" (No Sizwe 1979: 136). The disregard for "race" does not actually go as far as the rejection of the concept of "race" as a constituent trait of human identity. Typical examples are The Freedom Charter's claim "That

South Africa belongs to all who live in it, *black and white*" (Suttner & Cronin 1986: 262, emphasis added) and Oliver Tambo's oft cited explanation that; "[By non-racial] We mean a society in which each one feels he or she belongs together with everybody else, where the *fact* of race and colour is of no consequence" (Cape Times [Cape Town] 4 November 1985, emphasis added).

Clearly then, non-racialism is a critical concept. It is an ideal by which reality is tested and found wanting: but, that said, there are different readings of the ideal depending on the particular salience given to "race". To distinguish more rigorously, and unravel evolving meanings of, non-racialism it must be recognized how they are inextricably bound up with the problem of "race". Non-racialism must be set against different understandings of the idea of "race" and how these have changed over time; especially given that the scientific standing and basis of "race" has been increasingly disputed.

The popular meaning of non-racialism has been shaped by the prevailing academic understanding of "race" developed in the context of the 1930s–60s where an important distinction is made between "race" and "racialism"/"racism".[3] This is most neatly argued in Ruth Benedict's influential book, *Race and racism* (1942) where "race" is seen to exist as a biological reality that can be studied scientifically but racism is something to be vehemently opposed as this is to hold a 'belief in the superiority of a particular race leading to prejudice and antagonism towards people of other races' which has been discredited scientifically (*Oxford English Dictionary* 1989, entry for "racialism"). Here racism is a hostile word, whereas "race" is not. It is not hard to see that in this framework, non-racialism must be concerned to oppose the opinions and actions of proponents of racial superiority or discrimination, but beyond this need not question the idea of "race" per se.

From the 1970s onwards, however, a different approach to "race" began to make its presence felt. As a 1982 survey of the dominant viewpoint in American texts of physical anthropology has shown, almost two-thirds of books written in the period 1932–69 argued that "races" exist compared to just under a third for 1970–79, whereas the number stating that "races" do not exist rose from under one-sixth to over one-third (Littlefield et al. 1982: 642). The shift from the acceptance of the scientific "fact" of "race" to its rejection has been advanced through such works as Ashley Montagu's *Man's most dangerous myth*, where, contrary to the biological "fact" of "race", it is maintained that there are no pure and distinct "racial" enti-

94

ties, and there is no genetic or other deterministic base to "race". This dictates an outright rejection of "race" and the reality to which it supposedly refers. As Morton Fried has noted: "nobody is really white . . . there is no white race . . . there never *was* a white race" (1975: 39).

The implications of this for the meaning of non-racialism are important. It pushes the idea to a far broader terrain, where one must not just challenge racialism but the very existence of "race" itself. As Neville Alexander has been one of few to argue, "when we speak of non-racialism we mean that our position is determined by the scientific fact that 'race' is a non-entity" (1987: 36). Indeed, as the term "race" has no real referent it should be dropped from our vocabulary, ruling that "race" must be analyzed by non-racial social theories. By this definition, non-racialism rejects any talk of multi-racialism, it challenges the need to see and analyze South Africa in terms of "black" and "white", and it directs concern to the elimination of "race" as a significant feature of human identity. It dictates the breaking-down, not the accommodation, of racial differences.

All this, however, has not as yet been fully taken up in the discourse of non-racialism; we have not witnessed a dramatic reappraisal in everyday understandings. Some ANC intellectuals have travelled some way towards this position with their emphasis on the "irrelevance of race" but this is only a partial movement: as recently as 1991, Nelson Mandela stated, "Coloured communities would like to see coloured representatives. That is not racism, that is how *nature* works" (*The Sunday Star* [Johannesburg] 29 November 1991, emphasis added). What has happened is that, "Popular conceptions of race change slowly and in a jumble as ideas from the past become linked with newer formulations producing an intellectual sediment of the conceptual old and the new" (Wetherell & Potter 1992: 20). Thus, while it is possible by drawing the discussion of changing conceptions of non-racialism and "race" together to present the following positions (Table 5.1), these alternative and contradictory conceptions of non-racialism must be seen as evolving, overlapping and rarely crystallized in everyday thinking.

Table 5.1 Competing understandings of non-racialism.

		Race	Racialism/racism
Non-racialism	past	accept (segregation)	reject
Non racialism	present	accept (integration)	reject
Non-racialism	future	reject	reject

Far too often these distinctions are not explicitly recognized and one often finds statements that slip and slide, reflecting ambivalent postures and contradictory meanings.

The move to the new vocabulary of non-racialism, to refuse to explain South Africa in terms of "black" and "white", has yet to be fully made; it is of the future. Given the dominance of the position that "race" appears to exist there is but an ephemeral grasp of the move. There are times when, especially in ANC discourse, use of the word "non-racialism" seems to "float" further, as in Nelson Mandela's statement that "We have no Whites; we have no Blacks. We only have South Africans" (frontispiece to Frederikse 1990). However, the accepted wisdom is to argue that non-racialism has little content, because, after all, "most people believe that 'races' exist" (Maré 1992: 48).

Denying the obvious?

As yet, the argument for denying "race" has not been taken seriously. A broad non-racialism is taken – in both academic and commonsense under-standings – to be "absurd", "utopian" and "idealist"; for, the seemingly obvious primary "reality" is that "races" do exist, that people do see South African society in terms of "black" and "white". The dominant approach is to reject apartheid definitions but to take "black" and "white" as central subjects of social commentary, to argue that "race" must be seen as a valid form of analysis and to maintain that South Africa will be a multi-racial society long after the "end of apartheid". This forms the dominant consensus in the existing social scientific literature. Such work invariably operates in a closed network, with authors drawing on the canonical authority of "master" narratives of South African history and politics and using each others work in the same citationary way.[4]

The highly influential academic writings of Heribert Adam, Hermann Giliomee, Donald Horowitz, Arend Lijphart, Lawrence Schlemmer, Frederik van Zyl Slabbert and David Welsh all take this position and attempt to exclude, or at least subvert, the non-racial position.[5] Horowitz, in *A Democratic South Africa?*, asserts: "The nonracial society is the plural society's analogue to the utopian aspiration for a classless society" (1991: 28). Likewise, Adam argues that to expect the call for non-racialism to "remove an unpleasant racist reality" is "an act of faith", for "What people perceive as real is real" (Adam 1991: 513). More than this, because non-racialism is seen to deny the "true" nature of South African society, it is a dangerous illusion and should be suppressed in academic scholarship (Horowitz 1991: 26).

A frequent argument against non-racialism is that the ANC does not live up to its professed non-racial position; that non-racialism, compromised by the influence of an exclusivist African nationalism, has not been deeply entrenched, has had few moments of presence and been romanticized (Giliomee & Schlemmer 1989, Bernstein 1991); that, in fact, it was not until 1969 that "non-Africans" were admitted into the ANC's External Mission; 1985 when the movement approved non-racial membership at all levels; and that even at present the Indian Congress Movements, in Natal and the Transvaal, are organized on separatist lines (Desai et al. 1991). All this, however, is to confuse the "real" with the ideal and falsely conflate an understanding of non-racialism with the ANC; important sources of non-racialism are to be found in the history of other political movements such as the Communist Party and Liberal Party.[6]

Outwardly, the most convincing case against non-racialism rests on an appeal to the empirical evidence, often supported by the use of comparative findings. For, a wealth of empirical evidence can be cited to portray the "facts" of racial identity and division and the corresponding lack of support for non-racialism. On the basis of an extensive review of the survey literature, Horowitz concludes that, "it is obvious that, if attitudes are any guide, a nonracial society is not around the corner" (1991: 43). Similarly, Welsh's assessment is that; "on the basis of the comparative evidence there seems little chance in the foreseeable future . . . that 'non-racialism' as an attitudinal pre-disposition will penetrate the warp-and-woof of society" (1992: 4).

Those who want to maintain that South Africa is a racially divided society do, however, face serious problems. Even at the empirical level it must be accepted that "black" and "white" cannot be unproblematically made central subjects of social commentary; survey evidence can be cited to show that such categories simply do not fit, that some people reject racial labelling and that sociological factors such as sex, age, and class hold more saliency (Mayer 1975, Dreyer 1989). Many of the liberation movements have not seen themselves exclusively in terms of "being black" or representing "black interests" (Motlhabi 1988) and a number of English-speaking South Africans and Afrikaners refuse to consider "whiteness" the hallmark of their identity (Louw-Potgieter 1988).

The most important problem, however, is the failure to demonstrate the theoretical specificity of "race" and confront issues of "difference". Just how does one explain the production of "race"? How is "race" a viable autonomous notion? What are the differences demarcated by "race"?

Simply stated, the problem is this; how can the language of "race" be used outside the terminology and understandings dictated by the ideology and practice of apartheid? As Vincent Crapanzano has asked: "How does one objectively describe a social reality that is indigenously described, and legislated, in terms that approximate those of the observer?" (1985: 27). Given that "race" is seen as a significant sociological factor and that racial differences are taken to exist and to have a determining saliency, there is a need to specify the meaning of "race" outside the officially recognized group classifications of apartheid. But with the "fact" of "race" contradicted by scientific research findings in modern biology and genetics, what kind of conceptual terminology of "race" is adequate for such a task?

This is not answered. It is not shown exactly how "race" constitutes the most useful, fundamental and distinct definition of human life. Definitions of "race" are either not offered or one is presented with extensive definition but insubstantial analysis where "race" is invariably fused with distinct conceptions such as "ethnicity" and culture. "Race", as a form of identity, is either taken as "given", or in more sophisticated accounts mixed with a carefully controlled measure of social constructionism where "race" is nonetheless "real"; "race [is] a construct but nonetheless highly significant" (Horowitz 1991: 47; also see Adam 1991). This move means that "race" can still be treated as having independent sociological validity but does not actually help to prove its specificity; for, tellingly, there is no attempt to tap, through qualitative research methods, the in-depth social consciousness of people, to tease out precisely how racial consciousness is made and remade (Taylor 1992).

The important point is that as the issue of "race" is not attacked in a resolute way, explanation collapses into simply accepting that everything seems to be about "race" because everything is actually taken to be about "race".[7] Reduced to building understanding on the descriptive foundation of "race", the mainstream position leads to a theoretical dead-end; it ends up merely reaffirming and legitimating "race" on the grounds that it is "real" because people see it as such. This is a non-explanation and represents a pseudo-sociological approach.

All this is hardly surprising; for, in truth, "black" and "white" cannot be made to stand as valid analytical categories for understanding South Africa. As, scientifically speaking, "races" do not exist, racial groupings cannot be examined separately; social or cultural "differences" cannot be related to "race"; and there can be no different and independent "black" and "white" realities.

Part of the problem here is that there is a failure to draw out the material context of the debate. What is called "race" is not adequately theorized as part of the wider social matrix in which there are stark socio-economic inequalities (see, for example, Wilson & Ramphele 1989). There is little attempt to ask who benefits from racial divisions, to focus on how and why the South African state has worked to "manufacture" racial identity through the structural and ideological re-ordering of society. Consequently, there is a failure to understand how recourse to empirical evidence legitimates the status quo which has been established, in part, by apartheid's perverted use of racial categories. Caught in a strongly objectivist frame of reference the mainstream position precludes historical and political understanding of how, over time, the colonial/apartheid order has constructed racial identities and fails to realize that to see things in terms of "race" is to be engaged not in value-free description but in inscription, where a particular interpretation of reality and set of reductive categories is being imposed in line with dominant definitions. In these terms, the fact of "race" as revealed by empirical evidence does not speak for itself; the mainstream position cannot begin to answer the question of what generates racial categorization and the reasons for racial thinking in the first place. The mainstream approach stops at the threshold of serious analysis of these issues.

Clarity on these issues has, however, been clouded by the inability of Marxist accounts to take the question of "race" seriously enough. Marxist analyses of South African society, emphasizing the primacy of class analysis, have been marked by a high level of economic reductionism and have not adequately explained the meaning of "race". It is too simplistic to argue that "race" does not really exist except as an effect of economic exploitation and political oppression. Lacking theoretical depth, the recourse to notions of "false consciousness" does not represent an effective counter-argument to those who seek to affirm the obvious "fact" of "race". To deny the reality of "race" in these terms is not sufficient. A solid defence of non-racialism needs to move away from orthodox Marxist readings of ideology as pure illusion or as "false consciousness" and explain just how and why, in terms of non-racial social theories, "race" has been constructed and has "practical adequacy" at an everyday level (Miles 1989).

Part of the problem here is that it is largely the case that serious theoretical work on this problem, by the South African Left, "ended" in the early 1980s. Frederick Johnstone, writing over a decade ago, stated: "How to bring the non-economic factors back into the picture better, how to avoid overly materialist–structural–instrumentalist–reductionist explanation, how for example to integrate social psychological perspectives with class analysis – these and other related questions pose new challenges" (1982: 24), but this is a challenge to which few have risen.

In this sense, attacks on the Left for having ignored the issue of "race" are on track (Horowitz 1991, Adam 1991, Maré 1992). But the crucial point is that this does not mean that "race" should be addressed in the manner advocated by the mainstream; for this does not take us very far. Instead it points to the need for greater theoretical sophistication in thinking about and advancing non-racialism. The problem is not that non-racialism is inappropriate, but that it has not been fully thought through in academic and everyday understanding.

Advancing non-racialism

To take the debate forward the issue of non-racialism must be sharpened and taken more seriously. To advance such understanding requires exposing the yet deeper reason for the "dead-end" thinking on "race". And this dictates a recognition that: "Thinking is questioning and putting ourselves in question as much as the cherished opinions and inherited doctrines we have long taken for granted" (Heidegger 1968; also see Arendt 1958). For, there has been a refusal to interrogate how interpreting South Africa in terms of "race" is complicit with the formation of one's own identity.

Generally unmindful of its own ideological or political biases, there has been a marked failure to recognize how mainstream understanding is rooted in (and constrained by) unspecified and unquestioned background assumptions emanating from Europe.[8] Apprehension of non-racialism has been blocked by a missing debate surrounding the fact that "race" is a product of Western thought; a dualistic system of thought based on European notions of the constitution of society. As Robert Miles argues, "race" is "a European discourse projected onto various Others" (1989: 72). In this respect, the mainstream view on the "reality" of "race" has not been adequately theorized. There has been a failure to confront the fact that the peoples of Western Europe "sought to enthrone and enshrine themselves and their culture by subverting and neutralizing Others" and explore how

racial identities have been socially constructed through dominant Eurocentric codes and binarisms (Hayes 1989: 80; also see Amin 1989, Giroux
1992).

To effect a displacement of this situation, the gaze must be turned back
on those who advance the primacy of "race". There must be an attempt
to unravel how European notions of "race" have been constructed as nor-
mative; a recognition of how "race" at the level of social relations and ideology has been used to contain and represent South Africa in the context
of specific social and material conditions to serve vested power interests.
In the South African context this dictates having to confront earlier colonial frameworks of ordering and interpreting the country which, through
normalizing certain social practices and understandings, made it open to
outside exploitation. Of particular import in this regard is the construction
of European identity in terms of a "white" Self as advanced by concern
to protect and advance "White Civilization" and build "A White Man's
Land" (Neame 1953, Pheko 1992).

All those who adhere to the belief that South Africa is a racially divided
society must begin to examine their own complicity in the construction of
"race"/racism, to see how their own identity-formation is implicated in that
of the Other. In particular, the way the "problem" of South Africa has
commonly been viewed must be subverted; for, to see it as a "black problem" is to reveal more about the "white" Self than the Other. "Race" is
not something which essentially has something to do with "blacks", to be
combated through an actual knowledge of "blacks". It cannot be so neatly
separated. The issue of "race" is not something that is restricted to the
Other, it is also tied to the Self; "blackness" and "whiteness" are not
produced independently of each other; they "can only be understood as a
pair . . . no-one says anything about 'blacks' without at the same time
saying something about 'whites'" (Thiele 1991: 184). The cartoon below
plays on this deep meaning of how "white" identity – significantly shown
as an authority figure – is connected to the Other through the symbol of a
shadow.

To explode this "black"/"white" duality requires a radical shift to a level
of consciousness that dissolves racial boundaries, sees the death of the
"black" and "white" worlds, and leads to a sense of wholeness which encourages diversity.[9] Such inner transformation can be achieved through reflexive social analysis in which society is taken apart to reveal that "race"
is a social construction that – analytically speaking – does not exist, that
life is not to be seen in terms of stark dualisms but constitutes a totality of

Source: *Contact* (South Africa's Non-Racial Fortnightly), 3(6), 19 March 1960, p. 6.

interconnected processes. This is to arrive at a state of mind which grasps the fluid, open and complex nature of identity; it no longer being seen in terms of binary oppositions, as something that is fixed or "given" (consider, for example, Taylor 1989). This is to reach a sociological understanding of racial identity and marks a conceptual turn to non-racialism.

A broad non-racialism is the starting point for developing a critical sociology of South Africa; it provides an analytic frame for breaking down and rejecting the dominant manner of thinking whereby "reality is conceived purely in terms of a total polarity of absolutes" (Ndebele 1989: 40). Stressing the need to rethink the issue of identity outside the disabling essentialisms of the past, non-racialism points to a realm of indeterminacy where the future is open to the development of a radical democratic politics; a politics that stresses "difference within unity . . . around a shared conception of social justice, rights, and entitlement" and is concerned to create new spaces and modes of sociality outside the European pattern of the sovereign nation-state (Giroux 1992: 81). The way forward requires that attention must focus on strategies to make people aware of the deeper meaning of non-racialism and its implications for identity politics. This necessitates; exploring forms of participatory action-research; assessing the function of art, literature and the mass media; and considering the rôle which Christian symbols and theology can play in dismantling fixed notions of identity.[10] Charles Villa-Vicencio has noted that: "Most South Africans are aware that something different must be born if the country is not to be torn apart by competing ideologies" (1992: 6): a thoroughgoing non-racialism is that "something different". Only by embracing this rethought meaning of non-racialism will South Africa truly move out of the apartheid era. The ruling National Party, however, has other ideas.

102

For, instead of "reckoning" or "coming to terms with the past" in the sense of aiming for genuine self-reflection and understanding through retrospection (Adorno 1986, Habermas 1989), leading National Party politicians are concerned to "draw a line over the past", to wipe the apartheid era from memory. In the words of State President F. W. de Klerk: "If we dwell on real or imagined sins of the past, we shall never be able to find one another in the present, nor shall we be able to work together in building the future".[11]

Not just De Klerk, but other Cabinet Ministers, make constant references to the need to "close the book on the past". Instead of apologizing for the past, of acknowledging that past acts were morally wrong, apartheid has been repudiated on the grounds that it was a grand experiment that failed (Asmal 1992). This is clearly seen in De Klerk's so-called "Apology for Apartheid" speech of October 1992 in which the State President said sorry for clinging too long to the apartheid idea of separate nation states, but continued, "There are powers that are trying to manipulate our country's history by trying to portray it as dark, suppressive and unfair . . . Yes, we have made mistakes. Yes, we have often sinned and we don't deny this. But that we were evil, malignant and mean – to that we say 'no'!" (*The Citizen* [Johannesburg] 10 October 1992). Archbishop Desmond Tutu later responded: "You are either sorry or you're not. You don't say, 'I'm sorry, but . . .' " (*Weekend Argus* [Cape Town] 26 December 1992).

The consequence of the National Party's position is clear; "white" identity is absolved from critical questioning and retains its "centred" position. In fact, the "white" Self remains, if not in name by metonymy, the central reference point in present constitutional designs and power ploys (Taylor 1990, Manzo 1992, MacDonald 1992). Not surprisingly, the National Party's use and commitment to a "non-racial" South Africa is restricted to a limited meaning of the term. The past, however, is never dead and without a concern to take non-racialism seriously, the "New South Africa" is open to neo-colonial designs and will be built on a false incorporation.

Notes

1. The Congress Alliance was made up of the Executive Committees of the ANC, South African Indian Congress, South African Coloured People's Organization and the South African Congress of Democrats.

2. Multi-racialism came into widespread use from the late 1950s. *The Oxford English Dictionary* (1989) defines "multi-racialism" as; "the conception of a state in which members of different races, peoples, or ethnic groups live on amicable and equal terms".

3. On the distinctions between "race", "racialism" and "racism", see Williams (1989: 248–50, entry on "racial").

4. In many ways this mirrors Said's (1991) analysis of Orientalism.

5. See, most notably: van Zyl Slabbert & Welsh (1979), Lijphart (1985), Giliomee & Schlemmer (1989), Adam (1991), and Horowitz (1991).

6. Foster (1991: 23) and Everatt (1990). Also see strands of non-racialism present in the history of the Pan-Africanist Congress, Unity Movement and Black Consciousness Movement. Consider: Pogrund (1990), Lewis (1986), Pityana et al. (1991).

7. This echoes Johnstone's (1976) critique of cultural pluralism.

8. On putting European consciousness into question, consider Said (1991) and Sharabi (1990).

9. For an initial and shortlived attempt to address these issues, see Kleinschmidt (1972). Also see Saayman (1990).

10. In this regard consider, for example, Fals-Borda (1990), Echevarria (1985), Petersen (1991).

11. Speech by the State President Mr F. W. de Klerk at the function of the Goodwill Foundation, 9 March 1991. Also see Speech by the Leader of the National Party, Mr F. W. de Klerk, at the Congress of the National Party of Natal, Durban, Friday, 25 September 1992 – "Here at the crossroads of our history, we need to turn our backs on the past".

References

Adam, H. 1991. Implications of eastern Europe for South Africa: comparing transitions to democracy. In *A democratic vision for South Africa: political realism and Christian responsibility*, K. Nürnberger (ed.), 510–28. Pietermaritzburg: Encounter Publications.

Adorno, T. 1986. What does coming to terms with the past mean? In *Bitburg in moral and political perspective*, G. H. Hartman (ed.), 114–29. Bloomington, Indiana: Indiana University Press.

Alexander, N. 1987. The national situation. In *Sow the wind: contemporary speeches*, N. Alexander, 23–40. Johannesburg: Skotaville.

Amin, S. 1989. *Eurocentrism*. New York: Monthly Review Press.

Arendt, H. 1958. *The human condition*. Chicago: University of Chicago Press.

Asmal, K. 1992. Victims, survivors and citizens – human rights, reparations and reconciliation. *South African Journal on Human Rights* 8, 491–511.

Benedict, R. 1983. *Race and racism*. London: Routledge & Kegan Paul (first published 1942).

Bernstein, H. 1991. The breakable thread. *Southern African Review of Books* **4** (2), 24–5.

Boonzaier, E. 1989. Afterword. In *South African keywords: the uses and abuses of political concepts*, E. Boonzaier & J. Sharp (eds), 174–80. Cape Town: David Philip.

Carter, C. 1991. Review of Frederikse (1990). *Journal of Southern African Studies* **17** (2), 354–9.

Crapanzano, V. 1985. *Waiting: the Whites of South Africa*. London: Granada.

Desai, A., A. Habib, V. Padayachee 1991. Fighting fire with fire: ethnicity, the NIC and the struggle for non-racialism. Work in Progress (Johannesburg) 75, 28–30.

The Dictionary of Contemporary Politics of Southern Africa. 1988. G. Williams & B. Hackland. London: Routledge.

A Dictionary of South African English. 1991. J. Branford & W. Branford. Cape Town: Oxford University Press.

Dreyer, L. 1989. *The modern African elite of South Africa*. London: Macmillan.

Echevarria, R. G. 1985. *The voice of the master: writing and authority in modern Latin American literature*. Austin, Texas: University of Texas Press.

Everatt, D. 1990. *The politics of nonracialism: White opposition to apartheid, 1945–1960*. D. Phil. thesis, Oxford University.

Fals-Borda, O. 1990. The application of participatory-action research in Latin America. In *Globalization, knowledge and society*, M. Albrow & E. King (eds), 79–97. London: Sage.

Foster, D. 1991. *On racism: virulent mythologies and fragile threads*. Inaugural Lecture, 21 August, University of Cape Town, New Series 161.

Frederikse, J. 1990. *The unbreakable thread: non-racialism in South Africa*. Johannesburg: Ravan.

Fried, M. 1975. A four letter word that hurts. In *The human way: readings in anthropology*, H. Bernard (ed.), 38–45. New York: Macmillan.

Giliomee, H. & L. Schlemmer 1989. *From apartheid to nation-building*. Cape Town: Oxford University Press.

Giroux, H. 1992. *Border crossings: cultural workers and the politics of education*. New York & London: Routledge.

Habermas, J. 1989. *The new conservatism: cultural criticism and the historian's debate*. Oxford: Polity.

Hayes, F. W. III. 1989. Politics and education in America's multicultural society: an African-American study. Response to Allan Bloom. *Journal of Ethnic Studies* **17** (2), 71–88.

Heidegger, M. 1968. *What is called thinking?* New York: Harper & Row.

Horowitz, D. 1991. *A democratic South Africa? Constitutional engineering in a divided society*. Cape Town: Oxford University Press.

International Encyclopedia of the Social Sciences. 1972. D. L. Sills (ed.). New

York: Macmillan and Free Press.

Johnstone, F. 1976. *Race, class and gold*. London: Routledge & Kegan Paul.

Johnstone, F. 1982. "Most painful to our hearts" South Africa through the eyes of the New School. *Canadian Journal of African Studies* 16 (1), 5–26.

Kleinschmidt, H. (ed.) 1972. *White liberation: a collection of essays*. Johannesburg: Spro-Cas.

Lewis, G. 1986. *Between the wire and the wall: a history of South African "coloured" politics*. Cape Town: David Philip.

Lijphart, A. 1985. *Power-sharing in South Africa*. Policy Papers in International Affairs 24. Institute of International Studies, University of California, Berkeley.

Littlefield, A., L. Lieberman, L. T. Reynolds 1982. Redefining race: the potential demise of a concept in physical anthropology. *Current Anthropology* 23 (6), 641–55.

Louw-Potgieter, J. 1988. *Afrikaner dissidents: a social psychological study of identity and dissent*. Clevedon, Philadelphia: Multilingual Matters.

MacDonald, M. 1992. The siren's song: the political logic of power-sharing in South Africa. *Journal of Southern African Studies* 18 (4), 709–25.

Manzo, K. 1992. Global power and South African politics: a Foucauldian analysis. *Alternatives* 17, 23–66.

Maré, G. 1992. *Brothers born of warrior blood: politics and ethnicity in South Africa*. Johannesburg: Ravan.

Mayer, P. 1975. Class, status and ethnicity as perceived by Johannesburg Africans. In *Change in Contemporary South Africa*, L. Thompson & J. Butler (eds), 138–67. Berkeley: University of California Press.

Miles, R. 1989. *Racism*. London: Routledge.

Montagu, A. 1974. *Man's most dangerous myth: the fallacy of race*. New York: Oxford University Press (first published 1942).

Motlhabi, M. 1988. *Challenge to apartheid*. Grand Rapids, Michigan: Eerdmans.

Ndebele, N. 1989. Redefining relevance. *Pretexts* 1 (1), 40–51.

Neame, L. E. 1953. *White man's Africa*. Cape Town: General Publishing.

No Sizwe. 1979. *One Azania, one nation: the national question in South Africa*. London: Zed.

Oxford English Dictionary. 1989. 2nd edn. Oxford: Clarendon Press.

Petersen, R. 1991. Towards a South African theology of non-racialism. *Journal of Theology for Southern Africa* 77, 18–26.

Pheko, S. E. M. 1992. *South Africa: betrayal of a colonized people*. Johannesburg: Skotaville.

Pityana, N. B., M. Ramphele, M. Mpumlwana, L. Wilson (eds) 1991. *Bounds of possibility: the legacy of Steve Biko & Black consciousness*. Cape Town: David Philip.

Pogrund, B. 1990. *Sobukwe and apartheid*. Johannesburg: Jonathan Ball.

Posel, D. 1983. Rethinking the "race-class debate" on South African historiography. *Social Dynamics* 9 (1), 50–66.

Saayman, G. (ed.) 1990. *Modern South Africa in search of a soul*. Boston: Sigo Press.

Said, E. W. 1991. *Orientalism*. London: Penguin.

Seekings, J. 1991. Review of Frederikse (1990). *Social Dynamics* **17** (2), 190-1.

Sharabi, H. 1990. *Theory, practice and the Arab world: critical responses*. New York & London: Routledge.

The Social Science Encyclopedia. 1985. A. Kuper & J. Kuper (eds). London: Routledge & Kegan Paul.

Taylor, P. 1989. *The narrative of liberation: perspectives on Afro-Caribbean literature, popular culture, and politics*. Ithaca: Cornell University Press.

Taylor, R. 1990. South Africa: consociation or democracy? *Telos* **85**, 17-32.

Taylor, R. 1992. Review of Horowitz (1991). *Review of African Political Economy* **55**, 113-8.

Thiele, S. 1991. Taking a sociological approach to Europeanness (Whiteness) and Aboriginality (Blackness). *The Australian Journal of Anthropology* **2** (2), 179-201.

van den Berghe, P. 1965. *South Africa: a study in conflict*. Berkeley: University of California Press.

van Diepen, M. (ed.) 1988. *The national question in South Africa*. London: Zed.

van Zyl Slabbert, F. & D. Welsh 1979. *South Africa's options: strategies for sharing power*. Cape Town: David Philip.

Villa-Vicencio, C. 1992. *A theology of reconstruction: nation-building and human rights*. Cape Town: David Philip.

Webster, E. 1991. The historical search for a critical sociology in South Africa. In *Knowledge and Power in South Africa*, J. D. Jansen (ed.), 69-78. Johannesburg: Skotaville.

Welsh, D. 1987. Democratic liberalism and theories of racial stratification. In *Democratic liberalism in South Africa: its history and prospect*, J. Butler, R. Elphick, D. Welsh (eds), 185-202. Cape Town: David Philip.

Welsh, D. 1992. A "simple majority" democracy won't work. *Reality* **24** (3), 3-5.

Wetherell, M. & J. Potter 1992. *Mapping the language of racism: discourse and the legitimation of exploitation*. New York: Harvester Wheatsheaf.

Williams, R. 1989. *Keywords: a vocabulary of culture and society*. London: Fontana.

Wilson, F. & M. Ramphele 1989. *Uprooting Poverty: The South African challenge*. Cape Town: David Philip.

Wright, H. M. 1977. *The burden of the present: liberal-radical controversy over Southern African history*. Cape Town: David Philip.

Chapter 6

"Race" in Britain:
theory, methods and substance

Peter Ratcliffe

Introduction

This chapter will argue that, although many researchers of "race" issues in Britain pay lip service to the need to integrate theory, methods and substantive findings in a coherent fashion, few in fact do so. As with sociological work in other areas, it is all too often the case that reports of empirical work take the form of an "obligatory" (and sometimes perfunctory) theory chapter(s) followed by "the findings"; giving the impression that "theorizing" and "collecting and interpreting data" are two distinct and separable enterprises. Wrongly, in my view, sociologists often institutionalize these divisions in the delegation of duties within a research team. Thus, for example, survey methodologists are not seen as having anything to contribute to the "real task" of theorizing and similarly the task of analysis is one to be solely entrusted to the "number-crunchers". In this way the needs of the data analyst can be ignored in early fieldwork. Consequently, theoretical questions may remain unanswerable because of decisions taken quite independently of the initial (theorizing) phase. I would go as far as to argue that most major projects fail in some respects to come to terms effectively with the imperative of a holistic approach.

"Empirical" research will be taken to mean, essentially, instances of conscious "enquiry-driven" data collection whether this be quantitative or qualitative in focus, survey-based or ethnographic in style. Mainly for reasons of space, historical and library research will be de-emphasized as will, for example, that based on letters, diaries and life histories. This being said, the analysis and use of certain documentary materials such as census (and other official statistical) data cannot be ignored both because of their centrality to much of the literature and because of the issues they raise in ethical/political, as well as theoretical, terms. Indeed, in the latter context, they generate some of the same sorts of queries as explicitly "sociological" enquiries, by raising points which require theoretical explication.

The chapter is organized in three parts. First, it attempts to outline some of the major theoretical issues and approaches which dominate the British literature. Then, given that one cannot do sociological research, especially in a sensitive area such as "race", without confronting major ethical and political dilemmas, the second section addresses these concerns. Becker's (1970) question "Whose side are we on?" is clearly one element of this. But the problems go much deeper in that, even if we are unambiguously committed to one "side" (some would argue a major problem in itself, being an explicit rejection of value-free research), we have to be aware that the other side, or sides, may exploit our work for their own ends. They are raised here largely because they also provoke an interesting series of questions rarely recognized by sociologists, concerning the theoretical insights which these political and ethical dilemmas expose. I would wish to argue in any case that it is totally unacceptable to divorce the activity of research, whether predominantly theoretical or empirical, from its socio-political context.

The third section looks at research styles and, in particular, at the way theoretical issues have been tackled (or evaded?) in recent empirical work. In arguing that fundamental theoretical, methodological (and ethical/political) problems are not confined to one particular research approach but are endemic to all, it takes a critical look at the various paradigms and ask what (if anything) they have contributed to our theoretical knowledge. The chapter then concludes with a brief overview of the major themes and suggests some strategies for further work.

Theoretical issues

Before launching into theoretical debates it is as well to pause for a moment to consider what is meant by "theory". With the exception of the discussion of overarching paradigms linked, for example, to the work of Weber and Marx, for the purpose of the present chapter it will refer to collections of ideas or propositions about the world which, though possibly not strictly testable in a scientific sense, are nonetheless amenable to empirical investigation. I am essentially dealing, therefore, with the world of what Merton, and others, termed "middle-range" theories. In Britain the central focus of research has been on structural inequality, and in particular the way in which "racism" in its various guises impinges on the "black" population; especially those of (South) Asian and African-Caribbean origin.

Having said this it is as well to start with some critical observations about the research area as a whole. Far too many writers use terms such as "race", "class" and "ethnicity" without any clear appreciation of their underlying meaning (or, in the case of "race", lack of meaning), or the absence of consensus surrounding their use and interpretation. Thus "race" is equated with a delineation of the population into (say) "white"/"black" or "Asian"/"African–Caribbean"/"white". "Class" is reduced to surrogate indicators such as "working class"/"middle class" or more commonly perhaps Socio-Economic Group (SEG). "Ethnicity", despite its conceptual complexity, tends to be seen as virtually coterminous with "religion" and/ or national identity (see, for example, Bulmer 1986). And "gender" is often ignored altogether.

There is also considerable dispute (or perhaps more accurately, confusion) among researchers about the use of the terms "immigrant" and "migrant". Neither adequately describes the collectivities of British residents of non-indigenous origin. Given that approaching 50 per cent of the latter are now British or UK-born, the term "immigrant" is both inappropriate and insulting to those concerned.[1]

The use of "migrant" and "migrant labour", for example by Phizacklea & Miles (1980), Miles (1982) and Phizacklea (1983) is also problematic as a description of those who are British citizens, have settled here and who harbour no "myth of return" (Anwar 1979) to their countries of origin. What the term "migrant labour" does achieve, however, is a certain theoretical sharpness, in the sense that it provides a broader processual focus. It serves as a reminder that one is talking both about a system of migration, conceptualized by some in terms of an "international division of labour" (cf. Froebel et al. 1980) and also a situation where even "black settlers" are seen by some on the political Right as "gastarbeiter" who have outstayed their welcome. In other words, it reflects a form of oppressive, and repressive, ideology which is viewed by many social theorists as central to an understanding of the dynamics of contemporary racism.

It should perhaps be stressed at this point, however, that I am not simply talking about the need for greater conceptual clarification as part of an "objectifying" process aimed at generating more precise indicators. The situation is far more complex. Not only are there major differences in the ways researchers have conceptualized basic social indicators, there are also a variety of paradigms underlying the construction of the middle-range theorizations which concern us here. And, not surprisingly, these issues are at times intimately related. To see this one need look no further than the first concept discussed in this section, namely "race".

Given the already massive literature on the topic there is no need to add significantly to it here (see, for example, Montagu 1964, Banton 1977, 1987, 1988, van den Berghe 1978, Miles 1982, 1989 and Karn et al. forthcoming). Suffice it to say that these authors are agreed that there is no scientific justification for the term's use based as it is on a fallacious biological distinction linked to genotype and phenotype (Montagu op. cit). Some researchers such as Miles (1982) have preferred to see the term as a "mirage"; a socially determined ideological construct. Thus, invidious distinctions are made between groups of individuals, and are ascriptive in nature. In addition, the term is seen to have a reflexive property which contributes to its reification.

The major debate in Britain, however, concerns radically different theoretical and epistemological paradigms. This is seen most clearly in the conflicting approach of scholars such as Rex and Miles; a conflict grounded at one level in the fundamental division between Weberian and Marxian forms of analysis. But this very clear delineation of academic battle lines should not be allowed to conceal major internal divisions within these "camps" or to obscure the work of those who are aligned to neither. There is no space here to pursue a detailed appraisal of the various streams of thought. On the other hand, this has already been done in a recent volume (Rex & Mason 1986) and our main purpose is to look at the ways in which theorizations impact on the process of empirical research. What follows then is a brief and necessarily somewhat over-simplified outline of theoretical approaches.

Marxian analyses were the subject of an extended essay in the Rex and Mason reader by John Solomos. He argues that contemporary Marxists have largely shaken off the shackles of determinism and functionalism. Whereas earlier accounts, stemming from the work of scholars such as O. C. Cox (1948), were guilty of economism and class reductionism, research since the late 1970s has tended fairly consistently to allocate at least a partially autonomous rôle to "race", "ethnicity" and (more recently still) "gender". Thus accounts such as that of Castles and Kosack (1973) gave way, for example, to the work of Miles (1982, 1987, 1989) and Phizacklea

& Miles (1980), on the one hand, and Stuart Hall (1978, 1980) and Birmingham's CCCS (1982) on the other. In the work of Miles and Phizacklea "race" (and gender) are incorporated theoretically using the notion of class fractions. While rejecting race as a "false" construct, racism, or more precisely racialization, is seen as the means by which social actors are located in structurally distinct strata. In the latter case, the authors argue from a critical cultural studies perspective that we need to focus on the production and reproduction of racism and the ideology of "race" at different historical junctures, therefore explicitly rejecting the ahistorical and deterministic analyses of earlier Marxian writers.

Sympathetic critics of the Marxian literature have included two important strands of argument. Robinson (1983) and Rivera Cusicanqui (1988) have attacked what they see as the Eurocentric brand of Marxism which typifies much of this work. Ben Tovim et al. (1986) argue, implicitly at least, that the problem lies in the lack of any real commitment to social change through theory-driven action. In distancing themselves from traditional "case study methodology" they argue that,

> [both] as a source of valid knowledge of the processes and conditions of successful/unsuccessful race relations interventions and as a responsible and purposeful use of research resources, our approach is quite as legitimate and useful as those more conventional methods. We would also insist that this is far closer to the spirit of Marxism, the "unity of theory and practice" or "praxis", than much of the Marxist sociology of race . . . that has in recent years institutionalized Marxism within mainstream social science. (ibid: 151)

But this would not in itself satisfy Rivera Cusicanqui, given that she is also worried about the *nature* of action, and particularly the imposition of class-centric (and in this case also Eurocentric) values by Marxist academics.

It is probably fair to argue that empirical work has not, with the exception of Ben Tovim et al., featured strongly in the work of the above authors. Research of this kind has been dominated by organizations such as the Centre for Research in Ethnic Relations (CRER), the Policy Studies Institute (PSI), the Commission for Racial Equality (CRE) and a host of government departments and local authorities. All but the first of these are directly involved in policy-oriented research and as such are not driven principally by theoretical concerns.

Undoubtedly the two major figures in Britain over the last quarter of a century have been John Rex and Michael Banton. Rex, who describes himself as a "radical Weberian", was responsible for the two major studies of race relations in Birmingham (Rex & Moore 1967, Rex & Tomlinson 1979). Here the central theme was that actors compete in markets and social (or "class") conflicts arise from the competing interests of groups formed in this process (cf. "housing classes", to be discussed below).

Despite heading the forerunner of CRER while it was based in Bristol, Banton has done little empirical work over the past 30 years. Instead he has concentrated on theorizing "race" and on developing "rational choice theory" (Banton 1983), which has been argued by Rex among others to lead to a de-emphasis, or even rejection, of the theoretical centrality of racism as a systematic process.

Except for isolated examples, such as Peter Weinreich, few researchers in Britain have worked within a social psychological framework. Few also explicitly at least, have evoked a plural society model, though some multiculturalists have flirted with the terminology and others such as Banton have been *accused* of being cultural pluralists (Bourne 1980). Sociobiology, while gaining a following in the USA, appears to have had little impact on the British academic literature, though the same cannot be said for the political sphere, in that some of its ideas have been incorporated within the "new racism" of the Right.

Rather belatedly "gender" has found its way onto the academic agenda. It is now a commonplace for theorizations to cite the "trinity" of race, class and gender (Parmar 1982, Phizacklea 1983, 1991; *Feminist Review* 1984). Whether a successful theoretical synthesis has yet been achieved is a mute point but writers such as Carby (1982) have provided a very provocative re-evaluation of existing sociological and historical (or in her terms, "herstorical") accounts of "race" and "ethnicity" by showing the way in which analyses are often fairly crudely ethnocentric as well as male-centred. Ware (1992) shows the extent to which "white" women have historically been part of the "problem" faced by "black" women.

This debate apart, the central controversy still revolves around the relative salience of race and class. Although there is no parallel debate to that provoked in the USA by William Julius Wilson's *The declining significance of race* (1978), a debate kept alive by his more recent book published in 1987 (see Allen in this volume), there is nevertheless academic controversy as to whether the issue of race can be effectively subsumed within a modified stratification theory. Some "black" academics, notably Gilroy (1987) would argue not, as would (from very different perspectives) theorists like Rex and Banton. The crux of the argument within Marxian circles, according to Solomos (1989), is the extent to which "race" and "class" are accorded autonomous status.

Perhaps the key question though relates to the acceptability or otherwise of the "race relations" paradigm. Rex is attacked (Miles 1982: ch. 2) for allegedly reifying the concept of "race" by problematizing "race relations situations" and thereby seeing these as the central research "object". For Miles the focus should be on the production and reproduction of the ideology of "race". Hence the objects of study become racism and the process of "racialization", and not "race relations". However, much of the debate stems from problems of semantics in that Miles not only takes an overly literal view of Rex's "race relations" approach but also misses Rex's central concern with racism as an object of study and as a result slides rather perversely into a culturally reductionist explanation of "racial disadvantage" (ibid: 36). Arguably, the notion of "racialization" begs more questions than it answers in that its substantive content is rarely, if ever, specified.

Another possible route is to take Montagu's (1964) lead and talk not about "race" but about "ethnic groups" and by implication, a "sociology of ethnic relations". This fusion, or rather, proposed fusion, of "race" and "ethnicity" has its own problems, however. For one thing, the abandonment of the former term by sociologists will clearly not be followed by its exclusion from contemporary political debates. More importantly, though, the change may well be dangerously mystificatory by switching the focus of major debates from the ideology of "race" and racism to ethnic differentiation. Thus, the conflict dynamic contained in the work of Rex and others might become obscured, as might fundamental structural questions (Jenkins, 1986). Accordingly, the author in his earlier work (e.g. Ratcliffe 1981), retained the term "race" for theoretical debates involving these social structural concerns, while describing particular collectivities as "ethnic groups".

It is nevertheless clear that this is little more than a heuristic solution to a necessarily intractable problem. The "groups" so described are not "groups" in any meaningful sense (hence the use of the more neutral term collectivities). It would, for example, be misleading to assume communalities of interest between category members. (That would be to beg the empirical question.) "Ethnic group" has to be seen for what it is, simply a less pejorative label representing categories of people defined on the basis (in this case) of geographical origin.

A theoretically convincing measure of "ethnicity" would be a different matter entirely, implying a consciousness of group membership. For Bulmer (1986: 54) it is

> a more inclusive concept than that of race. An "ethnic group" is a collectivity within a larger society having real or putative common ancestry, memories of a shared past, and cultural focus on one or more symbolic elements which define the group's identity, such as kinship, religion, language, shared territory, nationality or physical appearance.

It is perhaps not surprising that the paper does not go on to address the question of its measurement in this form. Clearly it would involve a research project in itself. Ignoring the thorny problem of "situational ethnicity" the most realistic measure may well be a composite variable combining geographical origin, birthplace and religion, as far as "objective" indicators are concerned. Consciousness of group membership could then be assessed by questions on "self-image" which may stress a number of differing dimensions such as colour/class/religion/nationality and country of origin. Thus, respondents in the British context may describe themselves as, for example, "Indian Sikh", "Muslim", "Pakistani", "black middle class" or "black British" (cf. Henry 1982). Each of these potentially tells us a great deal, in a theoretical sense, about an individual's perception of him/herself, especially if the initial "self definition" question is followed by an effective "probe" to contextualize the response.

The end result of this, of course, is a complex web of "objective" and "subjective" measures, the latter being internally generated, externally conditioned (as a result of ascriptive rôle allocation) or a mixture of both. The theoretical lessons to be drawn from an exploration of these basic concepts are essentially tied up with the issues of specificational clarity and sensitivity to the vagaries of self-definition in a highly "political" climate.

This issue is considered further later (p. 130). We now turn to the ethical and political problems which are intimately linked to, and also compound, those which are essentially theoretical/methodological.

Politics, ethics and theory

Most sociologists would agree that their research inevitably entails certain ethical responsibilities and has political ramifications of one form or another. It is, of course, no longer even the accepted wisdom among (natural) scientists that they enjoy such freedoms (Watson 1970). Undoubtedly it is in areas such as "race/ethnicity" that the problems are particularly marked, and need to be openly confronted. What is particularly interesting in the context of the present chapter, though, is the extent to which the nature of research undertaken is influenced by these considerations, and the interaction between "theory development" and "ethics".

The first question to be asked is "why study the subject at all?" Although researchers may not acknowledge them, the underlying reasons could be many and varied; voyeurism, paternalism, political commitment to the cause of oppressed peoples, or simply that the problem is "out there", i.e. is on the (academic) agenda. One thing is clear, though. Both the style and focus of the research, as well as its success, will depend on these considerations.

It is not only junior researchers who are shocked by being confronted with the need to justify themselves to their research "subjects". Certainly these early forays "into the field" can be an extremely painful experience for the relatively uninitiated. In a revealing essay Cashmore recalls one particular incident when a "black" youth reacted sharply to his questioning: "What you need to know about Rasta? Him no want to know you, so why you interested in him?" (Cashmore & Troyna 1982: 12)

He frankly admits to having been shocked by this and also to having failed to learn any lessons from it at the time.

This experience should tell us a great deal more than simply that certain fields of enquiry are more difficult than others, and should be seen as more significant than a respondent's quite understandable wish not to be "studied". It very much reflects Britain's "racial" dynamics. There is the objection, on the one hand, to being faced with a "white" researcher; but there is also the more general concern about being a member of a group that is seen within a broadly racialized discourse as a "minority", or worse an "ethnic minority" or worse still an "ethnic minority" with cultural tenets, lifestyles and beliefs that present a threat to the established social order. Solomos (1989), for example, rightly recognizes the significance of the Thatcher governments' adherence in the 1980s to the notion of an "alien wedge" swamping Britain, thereby entailing a threat to the integrity of traditional values and culture. The "black" youth in our example, is, one suspects, reacting to a manifestation of this prevailing ideology which concretizes and compounds an already disadvantaged material position in British society (Solomos 1988).

Research can be seen, and often is seen, as yet another means by which the white majority exercises its power and legitimates its position. It could even be argued, for example, that the very act of studying "black communities" wrongly locates the problem, albeit unintentionally (within a positive scenario). Such research may lead to an analysis which, even if only implicitly, "blames the victim". If this is indeed the end result, one can hardly express surprise if the "victims" are not so keen to be the subjects of research.

It is far too easy to say that all will be well if the researcher is "black" (cf. Campbell 1980). Ignoring for the moment the very difficult issue of "ethnic matching" we need to assess the position of "black" sociologists studying "their own communities". In simple methodological terms, one would have thought a priori that problems of "negotiating access" would be lessened. This is not necessarily the case, however, owing to an increased political awareness of potential "white blacks" and more generally the "race industry" (the notional conflation of a myriad of institutionalized policy research activity). Such feelings are heightened and legitimated by books such as *Endless pressure* (Pryce 1979). The sense of betrayal among the "West Indian" community in Bristol was unmistakable. And it also meant that subsequent researchers had major problems gaining the confidence and co-operation of local people (Jackson 1983). Pryce had broken the two fundamental "rules" of research ethics (Stacey 1970) by disregarding (albeit unintentionally) the interests of both his subjects and the wider academic community.

All of this would appear to suggest that sociologists in general are regarded with suspicion by their research subjects. This is not the case, of course. One suspects that the majority of Britain's population, both "black" and "white", regards the work of sociologists either with total indifference or is largely ignorant of its nature, content and significance.

Nevertheless, the concerns raised here should provoke us to ask a number of fundamental questions: Should sociologists study the "race/ ethnicity" issue at all? Assuming the answer is "yes" (however heavily qualified), what is an acceptable agenda for such empirical research ("acceptability" being viewed in academic/theoretical as well as moral, ethical and political terms)? What minimum level of data do sociologists need on the social milieu they are attempting to analyze? What are the essential factors that determine and delimit the scope of the agenda? (Indeed should there be a limit to what research may or may not be done?) Finally, are there ways in which the results of such research (at every stage from planning, execution through to publication) can be safeguarded while maintaining the integrity of the various participants (i.e. researchers and researched) and the communities from which they are drawn?

Clearly the issues these questions raise are far too numerous and complex to be treated effectively in the present chapter. Some in any case fall outside the scope of the present book in the sense that they do not have fundamental implications for theory development[2]. Others require urgent answers, however.

There will be sociologists for example, who would argue that not only could no (delimiting) agenda be constructed but (even if it could) it would be undesirable. The latter view is seductive in that it leaves the researcher free to define his/her own interests without reference to those of colleagues or the researched. It is my view, however, that this is ultimately unacceptable. The fact remains that one is invariably talking about the study of the (relatively) powerless by those who have power. Secondly, the methodology and even theoretical paradigms followed may be seen as "male and Eurocentric" in emphasis and content (cf. Robinson 1983), with the result that the "findings" of such studies are open to exploitation by other "Europeans" (largely male) who also have power – notably governments, the police and "media barons".

The suggestion is that the agenda should at least entail an exclusionary process. Certain topics immediately come to mind as "sensitive"; the alleged link between "race" and intelligence, the study of "riots", the development of anti-racist groups, and so on. All of these research domains lend themselves to possible exploitation by those who wish to attack and further weaken the position of Britain's "black" population.

The author is well aware that his views will not be popular in some circles. Pierre van den Berghe and others who champion the cause of sociobiology, for example, would hotly dispute any attempt to limit the research agenda. Their arguments are seductive. Surely we cannot deny the existence of an "interesting academic problem" merely because of the fear of what the results might show and/or what might be done with them? My answer would be that even if a culture-free methodology enabled investigation (say) of the "race"-intelligence nexus any conceivable "gains" to society from such work would be far outweighed by the "losses". After all, the substantive proposition behind the research hypothesis relates to the prospect of making invidious distinctions between "races". Furthermore, as noted by Ratcliffe (1988), fundamental problems within the realm of the philosophy of social science undermine the scientific integrity and utility of the exercise.

Concerns about research on issues such as "riots" and anti-racist groups largely centre around the use to which such research might be put by "interested" outsiders, i.e. certain significant groups of non-sociologists such as the police and the political Right. Some would deride the profession, of course, for not taking an unambiguous political stand; witness Bourne's (1980) labelling of sociologists as "cheerleaders and ombudsmen". The position taken in this chapter is the encouragement of a continual awareness of the dangers of misappropriation and exploitation of our work and at the same time the defence of research which is of theoretical importance but which may not be of immediate political or other use to the "black" population.

Before moving on to a discussion of research methods and their particular problems, we need some idea of what constitutes an "acceptable" terminology and an "essential" database. We now face a familiar problem. As noted in the previous section, "race" (and "ethnicity" for that matter) tend to be reduced to surrogate measures predicated on "colour" or "geographical origin". It is not solely, or even principally, a technical question of definition, of course, as is suggested by writers such as Bulmer (1986). Nomenclature is itself the subject of political debate and, as such, is of significance to the process of theorizing sociologically (Madood 1988). The replacement of "Negro" by "black" and of "West Indian" by "African-Caribbean" did not arise by chance or a simple change in fashion (academic or otherwise). The changes occurred as a result of political struggles and/or of increasing popular consciousness of the legacy of historical experience. Far from being an arid academic debate, the arguments continue in the political sphere and in the "non-indigenous" communities themselves. Hence, "black sections" have been an issue within (say) the British Labour Party and trade unions ("black" incorporating African-Caribbean, Asian, African, and so on).

Throughout the present chapter the term "black" is used in the same sense. Importantly, it does not necessarily imply the existence of a universal collective consciousness, but the common experience or awareness of negative rôle ascription and treatment (cf. Ratcliffe 1981). A failure to fully appreciate this led Banton, in a review of *Racism and reaction* (ibid.), to call for the restoration (presumably at all times) of a finer division based on colour/ethnicity. Insofar as this would deflect attention from the major dimension of lived experience, it could lead to analyses that are dangerously mystificatory. No-one, least of all the present author, is arguing for a rejection of "geographical" or "religio-cultural" labels where theoretically appropriate. Nor, incidentally, would I wish to argue that "racism" has displayed an immutable face irrespective of historical juncture, or that it takes (or took) the same form in relation to all minority groups.

Irrespective of the way in which academic arguments are resolved, though, we have to listen carefully to the rejection of "our" labels by the subjects of our enquiries. Even then there are no simple solutions, given that there is by definition no straightforward consensus about which terms are acceptable. Once again the political dimension looms large. Among some "radicals" the term "black" is widely acceptable (for both "South Asians" and "African-Caribbeans"). It is not, however, generally acceptable among the "South Asian" population (and perhaps "middle class Asians" in particular). This point is illustrated by one major public meeting (attended by the author) where much of the debating time was taken up with disputes over the appropriateness of terms such as these. Here, the audience (largely of Indian origin) objected very strongly to the use of the word "black" to describe them, thinking of it as a term of abuse (but nevertheless seeing it as applicable to the African-Caribbean population). Sociologists need to take full cognizance of such debates in that they have significant implications for theory construction.[3]

We are left finally with the question of basic data requirements. This depends very much on the nature of the "agenda" for research. However, there does seem to be general agreement in the literature that the fundamental questions are about patterns of social inequalities and their underlying determinants. The essential requirement, then, is national data on such areas as housing, employment, education, legal rights and social welfare. The rate of change, or lack of it, also needs to be monitored.

Unfortunately, this is not as straightforward as it appears. In addition to appropriate measures of "race/ethnic origin" in the national census "ethnic monitoring" is needed on a vast scale. Both have proved extremely problematic politically (as well as methodologically).

Birthplace data was no longer a useful indicator of ethnicity even as early as the 1970s. The OPCS therefore put a great deal of time, effort and money into devising and piloting different forms of "ethnic question" (see, for example, Sillitoe 1978). As this research showed there were major problems in devising a question which was logically watertight and would at the same time lead to consistently reliable responses. Far more serious, however, were other problems. It was evident that the aim of the question was to identify "black" residents. This angered many potential respondents and led to high levels of resistance and non-cooperation in areas with large African-Caribbean populations in particular. Fear of a shift in the national political climate further to the Right meant that people were undoubtedly loathe to identify their name, address and "ethnic origin".

The idea of asking such a question in the 1981 Census was finally dropped, ostensibly for cost reasons. It was not until the late-1980s that lobbying from a variety of social scientists and bodies such as the CRE finally won the day. Following further testing, it was agreed that the 1991 Census should include an appropriate ethnic question much, one suspects, to the chagrin of many senior politicians notably Margaret Thatcher who, having bemoaned the presence of minorities, made it clear when Prime Minister that she wished to play down inequalities based on "race" (as well as class). "Ethnic monitoring" has had a similarly chequered history. The one consistent supporter of the idea has been the CRE; their view being that careful monitoring is the only way whereby employers (and service providers) can demonstrate that they are upholding their obligations under the 1976 Race Relations Act. But "ethnic monitoring" is still the exception rather than the rule, and where it has been adopted it often takes a rather patchy or tokenistic form.

As Karn (1983: 17) argues (quoting Francy 1979), the debate on record-keeping has produced rather "strange bed-fellows":

> In favour of record-keeping are the Commission for Racial Equality (who use it as a means of enforcing the law), the Select Committee on Race Relations and Immigration, many social researchers (notably the Social Research Association), and alongside them the National Front and the Eugenics Society. Opposed to record-keeping are some but not all black groups, some sociologists, particularly on the radical Left, some civil liberties lawyers and some white liberals, but among them opponents of positive discrimination and the majority of local authorities, Labour and Conservative.

The fact that a highly contentious political issue produces such a complex picture of alliances means that one should be extremely wary of hasty conclusions. From the point of view of data requirements what appears to be called for is a delicate balancing of the interests of researchers and the researched, taking into account the heterogeneity of both groups. On the face of it problems ought to be lessened by the perceived self-image of most researchers as defending the material interests of the researched. Unfortunately, however, the reality is somewhat different.

As to the census question on "ethnic origin", much has been made of its indispensability for social scientists and the strength of data protection legislation. On the latter point there are many within minority communities who are wary given recent legislation on immigration, nationality,

121

refugees and asylum seekers. On the other hand, one should ask just how serious are the potential consequences of data misuse. Local authorities, the police and certainly the extreme Right in the shape of the National Front, British National Party, and so on, already know where "black" families live; as is witnessed by the disturbing escalation in the numbers of "racial" attacks over the last few years. In reality, the main problem appears to be the *idea* of measurement rather than the additional threat it poses. In other words, it is seen by "blacks" as yet another occasion when they are subjected to "official" scrutiny.

Empirical research: problems and possibilities

This section takes a necessarily somewhat brief look at the major methodological approaches open to researchers, and assesses achievements to date. Central to this is the question of links between "theory" and "method" in existing research, and how they may be strengthened in future work. Because of the sheer volume of survey-based studies (as against ethnographic research) my emphasis is on this style of research; it does not reflect an evaluative judgement.

We begin by questioning the usefulness of surveys in the exploration of theoretical ideas, using selected examples to illuminate theory-data linkages. No attempt will be made, or could be made given the constraints of a single chapter, to review the literature as a whole.

Survey research

Britain boasts a substantial tradition of survey work in the area of "race and ethnic relations". At the national level there was the pioneering study by Rose et al. (1969) and the more explicitly policy-oriented PEP/PSI work of Daniel (1968), Smith (1977) and Brown (1984). Complementing these are major government sponsored enquiries (in addition to the census) which include "race/ethnicity" within their remit; in particular the National Dwelling and Housing Survey (NDHS), General Household Survey (GHS) and the Labour Force Survey (LFS).

Most studies, understandably due to cost constraints, are more parochial geographically. Some add a comparative dimension by using more than one city for fieldwork purposes, for example the "Urban Institutions Survey" headed by Malcolm Cross at the Social Science Research Council's Research Unit on Ethnic Relations (RUER) in the early 1980s. But the vast majority have a single research site.

A number of major projects have been based in Birmingham, beginning with the Sparkbrook research of Rex & Moore (1967) and leading more recently to a study of Handsworth (Rex & Tomlinson 1979, Ratcliffe 1981). Nottingham was the subject of Lawrence's (1974) work and more recently Bedford was chosen by Sarre, Phillips and Skellington (1989) for their housing study. Of course, there have been numerous other town and city based studies; some the work of academic researchers, some based in independent research institutes and the rest emanating principally from local authority departments.

Substantive concerns have spanned such issues as education, employment, housing and residential patterns. We need to ask, though, what these studies have contributed to our theoretical understanding of "race and ethnic relations". "Rather little" would probably be the fairest answer. This is not to say the work is of little merit; merely that "theoretical" concerns have not featured high on the agenda. The PEP/PSI studies are not sociological studies in the true sense of the term. They are quite firmly within the realm of policy research, focusing (quite properly) on the inequitable treatment of minorities in a whole range of institutional areas. It would certainly be grossly unfair to attack them for failing to do what they never set out to do; namely, to answer theoretical questions about the position of minorities in British society. They are undoubtedly of immense value in that they provide a wealth of data that can usefully inform a more theoretically grounded analysis.

Where theoretical concerns are cited, there are usually few attempts to integrate these with empirical, substantive issues. Thus, in the field of "race and employment" research there have been lengthy debates about "dual, or split, labour market theory" and "labour market segmentation" but very little theoretically grounded empirical analysis. The "facts" of "racial disadvantage" in employment are fairly well known. Data abounds, for example, as to occupational distributions and differential unemployment levels by age and gender. Processual analyses then typically link this statistical database to discussions of discrimination in the labour market, both direct and indirect, individual and institutionalized. Terms such as "underclass", "sub-proletariat" and "racialized class fraction" have then been used to conceptualize the position of Black workers when "findings" are slotted back into the general theoretical schema.

What is arguably needed is for cogent theorizing to be much more central to the phase of work prior to the collection of data. This would spell out in detail what counts as a test of one's theory, and might in the present context point to the centrality of (say) "job search strategies", "work evaluation" and the interaction between perceptions of occupational status and allocation mechanisms.

Returning to the literature on housing, and illustrating the argument with the theoretical debate surrounding the concept of "housing classes", we might suggest the need for a clearer idea of its conceptual and empirical referents. In other words, if such classes exist, what does that imply for the actor's perception of her/his social world? The initial formulation in Rex & Moore (1967: 274) essentially specifies "tenure" as the mode of delineation between groups and as the material locus of actual or potential conflict between those so defined. The revised categorization in Rex & Tomlinson (1979: 132) takes account of the "desirability" of the area in which the property is situated, and employs an expanded and more precise definition of "tenure", but is fundamentally unchanged in character.

The advantage of such a measure is its simplicity. A few relatively straightforward questionnaire items lead in most cases to a reliable and valid classification. The problem lies in its theoretical linkages. Forgetting for present purposes problems involved in the conflation of "access" and "achieved position" in the housing market,[4] more work needs to be done to discover the subjective meanings and action frames of reference allegedly specific to those within the putative "classes". The scale in general represents a rational and defensible status ranking.[5] It could, on the other hand, be seen as Eurocentric and possibly "class-centric" (using class now in a more conventional sense). Remarkably little is known about the values residents attach to their housing "careers" or about the ways in which they relate (if at all) to others who share their objective (housing market) position.

More thought also needs to be given to the assessment of the nature and likelihood of "actual or potential class conflict". Considerable methodological difficulties arise at this point, not least of which is the vexed question of prioritizing the "race" and "class" dimensions. Put at its crudest – "Do commonalities grounded in (housing) class position override cleavages based on 'race'?" And, what rôle (if any) does "ethnicity" play here? As noted above we even lack basic data on the meaning and importance placed by different groups on tenure.

These considerations serve to remind us of one of the most fundamental problems; namely the limits of empirical research. Survey work has its intrinsic limitations; but beyond this is the obvious point that many theorizations are not directly testable via empirical investigation. Also, there is clearly a limit to the utility of subjective constructs, however much they provide us with insights into the non-observable world.

Some problems of surveys in "race" and ethnic relations research

The problems of survey work in this area are far too numerous to discuss in depth in a brief chapter such as this. They fall broadly into four categories however; substance, measurement, sampling and data analysis (all of which are interrelated in some sense). All in their different ways generate major difficulties for theory construction and testing.

Dealing with substance and measurement problems first, we assume that interview-based research is the only feasible strategy (beyond the census-type enquiry). Here the dominant problem is interviewer-respondent interaction and the impact this has on the types of question which can be asked and the likely validity and reliability of the measurement process. "Ethnic matching" is seen by some as a central issue here (Rex & Tomlinson 1979, Ratcliffe 1981, Johnson & Cross 1984, Brown 1984). The question is whether validity and reliability are improved by a matching of interviewer and respondent. Intuitively it is the obvious solution to the problem of non-rapport. Unfortunately, as is the case in most of the instances discussed in this chapter, the issues are far more complex than they appear at first sight.

Matching is normally based on broad categories of "colour and/or geographical origin". The problem is that in the case of South Asian communities "caste" and "religion" are also key social markers. There is also the more general interaction bias linked to "gender" and "class". Clearly respondents potentially take many different cues from the interview situation, all of which are threats to reliability and validity. There is in addition the broader issue of suspicion on the respondent's part that despite "matching" at fieldwork level the agenda in firmly in the hands of the "white" majority. One finding in Rex & Tomlinson's work (1979: 325) may be encouraging though, in that "matching", at least of a relatively simple kind, appears to make little difference to the nature or "depth" of response.

However much these problems can be solved, there remain a number of issues which are destined to evade the survey researcher. "Caste" is perhaps the clearest example. Direct questioning of the kind attempted in the Handsworth research is clearly problematic. (Unfortunately, the present author found to his cost that "coming clean" and admitting this simply laid him open to gratuitous attack by one reviewer!) There is little doubt that this and a host of issues related to cultural patterns and social obligations are better tackled by ethnographic research.

Perhaps the most fundamental problem with survey research is that its focus is very much on the individual and in particular the individual's attitudes, actions and material position. As such, the orientation is very much that of the Western advanced industrial society; hence the criticism of Eurocentricity noted earlier. Some have even gone as far as to suggest that the approach is "gender" specific as well as "culture" specific (Oakley 1981).

Turning to sampling problems, perhaps the major stumbling block is the familiar one of targeting relatively scarce populations. Conventional solutions involving, for example, multi-phase techniques would prove prohibitively expensive, particularly in areas with low concentrations of minority residents. One solution adopted by the Handsworth research team (largely under pressure, it must be said, from the market research company that undertook the fieldwork) was to abandon any attempt at a random sampling design. Quota sampling, with proportionate selection from census enumeration districts, was used for the main sample of 900.

The 1974 PEP study reported in Smith (1977) used random selection but excluded areas of low minority concentrations. However, for the follow-up study in 1982 a new approach was deemed necessary (Brown 1984: 4) given that "the (earlier) survey was (only) representative of about 76 per cent of Britain's population of Asian and West Indian origin". Using focused enumeration (Brown & Ritchie 1981), which it must be said raises certain ethical problems, they were able to sample in low concentration areas; thereby boosting the theoretical, as well as empirical, soundness of their project. That they had hitherto achieved by definition only three-quarters coverage in population terms is not simply a pedantic technical point. It leads potentially to dangerously misleading inferences about Britain's Black population. In testing labour market theories (to take a case mentioned earlier) it might, for example, produce strong empirical support for near perfect segmentation. The inclusion of low concentration areas, and the inevitable increase in the number of middle class "blacks", may therefore provide an important corrective.

Another, rather more technical, problem stems from the use of "white control groups". It could be argued that, although it is clearly sound practice to generate a sample of "whites" in (say) Handsworth when the focus of inference is the area itself, the "white" and "black" samples are effectively different entities. This is because the former are less representative than the latter of their communities in Britain as a whole. Put simply,

Handsworth (say) is a "typical" area of "black" settlement but not of "white". Accordingly, an "inner/outer area" dichotomy has been used in some more recent studies (e.g. Brown 1984, Johnson & Cross 1984). There is no universally "correct" answer here: much depends on the theoretical focus of the particular study in hand.

The sampling unit should similarly be chosen to fit the theoretical goals of the research. The focus may be on the "individual", the "household" or the "head of household". All are problematic in different ways due to the issue of cultural specificity (and are even problematic in culturally homogeneous populations – Stacey 1969).

Clearly all of these problems have implications for the sociological end-product and analytical requirements should in turn impose constraints on conceptualizations and sampling strategies. But perhaps the most difficult problem relates to the process of categorization and more generally the linkages between words, statements and meanings. These issues are well documented (cf. Cicourel 1964) but are no less intractable for that, and particularly so in ethnically diverse populations.

This is perhaps an appropriate point at which to switch to ethnographic (or field) studies in that this research genre purports to be considerably more effective than survey research in tackling these difficult problems of "meaning".

Ethnographic research

Although survey research has tended to dominate the literature in Britain, numerous ethnographic studies have been published over the last few decades. These have varied enormously in scope, focus and methodology, from small scale studies of specific minority groups within urban settings or institutional contexts (e.g. school or workplace) to studies that essentially focus on the institutions themselves. A number do both, of course; but retaining this distinction in the interests of brevity, the former category would include the works of writers such as Watson (1977), Khan (1979), Pryce (1979), Benson (1982) and more recently Bhachu (1985). The latter category would include the work (discussed earlier) by Ben Tovim et al. (1986), much of the work in the area of educational policy by Barry Troyna, Wendy Ball and Richard Hatcher (Troyna & Ball 1985, Troyna & Hatcher 1992) and in the area of housing and urban renewal by the present author (Ratcliffe 1992).

There is no space here to review these studies but we need to ask what the major benefits of ethnographies are. As to the former typology we can argue that probably the major advantage is the possibility of gaining a clearer insight into such issues as cultural patterns, religious practises, and caste divisions. Secondly, and following on from this, is the opportunity to check and cross-check through repeated observations. The direct involvement of the researcher also avoids the problem of detachment from the researched that the survey analyst necessarily suffers (not to mention the detachment embodied in the interview process itself).

Looking at the other side of the coin, many problems of "field studies" stem from this closeness to the subject matter. Access to one sector of the community may preclude access to another for political or other reasons. "Closeness" may therefore be selective and/or illusory. Perhaps more important, however, is the danger of immersion in the minutiae of cultural and kin patterns to the exclusion of major structural concerns (Jenkins 1986). Hence, ethnographies have been seen by some as mystificatory and/or inconsequential (cf. van den Berghe 1978: Introduction). Further methodological problems involving sampling strategies, ethics and the researcher's rôle as discussed in standard textbooks such as Burgess (1984, 1989).

In some ways more difficult to categorize methodologically are institution-based "field studies". At one level there are those, such as the work of Ben Tovim et al. (1986) which use research teams comprising employees of the organization to be investigated and academics who are also members of political/quasi-local-governmental committees (in this case Community Relations Councils). More common are studies involving academics looking in from the outside. Examples here would be the present author's work on urban renewal (Ratcliffe 1992) and much of Barry Troyna's work in the field of education. Suffice it to say that there tends to be a more explicit attempt here to relate theory to substantive policy concerns by looking at the structural context of discriminatory practises. And there is also typically the explicit aim of avoiding the mystification, stereotyping and pathologizing tendencies to be found in many ethnographic accounts of minority communities. Multi-level and often multi-method strategies are the key to this.

We would argue that surveys and ethnographies should not be seen as alternatives and certainly not as incompatible strategies. An effective research strategy is one that specifies theoretical problems and uses that approach, or combination of approaches, seen as most effective in that particular instance. Each approach has its own advantages; advantages which should not be lost in the morass of disciplinary chauvinisms.

Concluding remarks

Four points summarize the central arguments:
1. Researchers need to be much clearer in the definition and usage of such pivotal terms as "race", "ethnicity" and "class". They should be aware also of the reflexive quality of their terms, and to employ this reflexivity effectively in theory construction.
2. Theoretical issues need to be conceptualized with much greater precision than hitherto and to be spelt out in such a manner as to permit effective exploration.
3. Research strategies should match the level of theoretical sophistication.
4. Multiple research strategies, or triangulation to use Norman Denzin's (1970) term, should be adopted where appropriate and feasible. This implies much closer co-operation between, for example, social statisticians, sociologists, social anthropologists and psychologists.

Notes

1. This is a clear instance of the general phenomenon discussed in the next section; namely where the fact of rejection of a term used by researchers has theoretical significance beyond the realms of ethics and politics (see p. 129-30).
2. These issues will be addressed in more detail in Ratcliffe, P. *Sociologists, the state and social change* (working title; manuscript in preparation).
3. The obvious question is "Why is there conflict over such terms?" In attempting to answer this we can gain useful insights into subjective interpretations of social structure and of inter- and intra-group conflict. The immediate issue here, for example, raises queries as to the complex interplay of "race" and "class".
4. There are other debates on the problem of linkages with an individual's position in the labour market.
5. It is also consistent with the pervading ideology of the "property owning democracy".

References

Anwar, M. 1979. *The myth of return: Pakistanis in Britain*. London: Heinemann.
Banton, M. 1977. *The idea of race*. London: Tavistock.
Banton, M. 1983. *Racial and ethnic competition*. Cambridge, Cambridge Univer-

sity Press.

Banton, M. 1988. *Racial consciousness*. London: Longman.

Becker, H. S. 1970. Whose side are we on? In *The relevance of sociology*, J. D. Douglas (ed.), 99–111. New York: Appleton-Century-Crofts, Meredith Corporation.

Ben-Tovim, G. J. Gabriel, I. Law & K. Stredder 1986. *The local politics of race*. London: Macmillan.

Benson, S. 1981. *Ambiguous ethnicity: interracial families in London*. Cambridge: Cambridge University Press.

van den Berghe, P. L. 1967, 1978. *Race and racism: a comparative perspective*. New York: Wiley.

Bhachu, P. 1985. *Twice migrants: East African Sikh settlers in Britain*. London: Tavistock.

Bourne, J. 1980. Cheerleaders and ombudsmen: the sociology of race relations in Britain. *Race and Class* XXI (4), 331–51.

Brown, C. 1984. *Black and White Britain: The third PSI survey*. London: Heinemann.

Brown, C. & J. Ritchie 1981. *Focussed enumeration: the development of a method for sampling ethnic minority groups*. London: PSI/SCPR.

Bulmer, M. 1986. Race and ethnicity. In *Key variables in social investigation*, R. G. Burgess (ed.). London: Routledge & Kegan Paul.

Burgess, R. G. 1984. *In the field: an introduction to field research*. London: Allen & Unwin.

Burgess, R. G. (ed.) 1989. *The ethics of educational research*. Falmer: Falmer Press.

Campbell, H. 1980. Rastafari: culture of resistance. *Race and Class* XXII (1), 1–22 (Summer).

Carby, H. 1982. White woman listen! Black feminism and the boundaries of sisterhood. In *The Empire strikes back: race and racism in 70s Britain*. CCCS, 212–35. London: Hutchinson.

Cashmore, E. & B. Troyna (eds) 1982. *Black youth in crisis*. London: Allen & Unwin.

Castles, S. & G. Kosack 1973. *Immigrant workers and the class structure*. London: Oxford University Press/Institute of Race Relations.

Cicourel, A. 1964. *Method and measurement in sociology*. New York: The Free Press.

Daniel, W. W. 1968. *Racial discrimination in England*. Harmondsworth: Penguin.

Denzin, N. 1970. *The research act*. London: Butterworths.

Feminist Review 1984. Many Voices, One Chant: Black Feminist Perspectives, No. 17 (Autumn).

Franey, R. 1979. Long Playing Records. Roof: March.

Froebel, F., J. Heinrichs & O. Kreye 1980. *The new international division of labour*. Cambridge: Cambridge University Press.

Gilroy, P. 1987. *There ain't no black in the Union Jack: the cultural politics of race and nation*. London: Hutchinson.

Hall, S. et al. 1978. *Policing the crisis: mugging, the state and law and order*. London: Macmillan.

Hall, S. et al. 1980. *Culture, Media and Language*. London: Hutchinson.

Henry, I. 1982. *The growth of corporate Black identity in Birmingham*. PhD thesis, University of Warwick.

Jackson, A. 1983. *Ethnogenesis and associational behaviour: the political organization of welfare in ethnic communities in Bristol*. PhD thesis, University of Warwick.

Jenkins, R. 1986. Social anthropological models of inter-ethnic relations. In *Theories of race and ethnic relations*, J. Rex & D. Mason (eds), 170–86. Cambridge: Cambridge University Press.

Karn, V. 1983. *Research on housing and race in Britain: current themes and future priorities*. Paper presented to a conference sponsored by the SSRC Environment and Planning Committee under the title "Housing Research in Britain: The Next Decade", University of Bristol, 12–14 September.

Karn, V., D. Phillips & P. Ratcliffe (forthcoming) Race, Housing and Economic Change, in preparation.

Lawrence, D. 1974. *Black migrants, White natives: a study of race relations in Nottingham*. Cambridge: Cambridge University Press.

Madood, T. 1988. "Black", racial equality and Asian identity. *New Community* **XIV** (3), 397–411.

Miles, R. 1982. *Racism and migrant labour*. London: Routledge & Kegan Paul.

Miles, R. 1987. *Capitalism and unfree labour: anomaly or necessity?* London: Tavistock.

Miles, R. 1989. *Racism*. London: Routledge.

Montagu, A. (ed.) 1964. *The concept of race*. New York: Free Press.

Oakley, A. 1981. Interviewing women: a contradiction in terms. In *Doing feminist research*. H. Roberts (eds), 30–60. London: Routledge & Kegan Paul.

Parmar, P. 1982. Gender, race and class: Asian women in resistance. In *The empire strikes back: race and racism in 70s Britain*. CCCS, 236–75. London: Hutchinson.

Phizacklea, A. (ed.) 1983. *One way ticket: migration and female labour*. London: Routledge & Kegan Paul.

Phizacklea, A. & R. Miles 1980. *Labour and racism*. London: Routledge & Kegan Paul.

Phizacklea, A. 1991. *Unpacking the fashion industry: gender, racism and class in production*. London: Routledge.

Pryce, K. 1979. *Endless pressure*. Harmondsworth: Penguin.

Ratcliffe, P. 1981. *Racism and reaction: a profile of Handsworth*. London: Routledge & Kegan Paul.

Ratcliffe, P. 1985. *Race, class and residence: the case of Afro-Caribbean house-*

holds in Britain. Paper presented to Anglo-Dutch Conference, University of Leiden, the Netherlands, March.

Ratcliffe, P. 1988. Race, class and residence: Afro–Caribbean households in Britain. In *Lost illusions: Caribbean minorities in Britain and the Netherlands*, M. Cross & H. Entzinger (eds), 126–46. London: Routledge.

Ratcliffe, P. 1992. Renewal, regeneration and "race": issues in urban policy. *New Community* 18 (3), 387–400.

Rex, J. & R. Moore 1967. *Race, community and conflict: a study of Sparkbrook*. London: Oxford University Press/Institute of Race Relations.

Rex, J. & S. Tomlinson 1979. *Colonial immigrants in a British city: a class analysis*. London: Routledge & Kegan Paul.

Rivera Cusicanqui, S. 1988. The social sciences and the ethnic question in Latin America: the cases of Columbia and Bolivia. In *Linkages between methodology, research and theory in race and ethnic studies*. M. W. Murphree (ed.), np. Harare: Centre for Applied Social Sciences, University of Zimbabwe.

Robinson, C. 1983. *Black Marxism*. London: Zed.

Rose, E. J. B. et al. 1969. *Colour and citizenship: a report on British race relations*. London: Oxford University Press.

Sarre, P., D. Phillips & R. Skellington 1989. *Ethnic minority housing: explanations and policies*. Research in Ethnic Relations Series. Aldershot: Avebury.

Sillitoe, K. 1978. Ethnic origins: the search for a question. *Population Trends* 13, 25–30.

Smith, D. J. 1977. *Racial disadvantage in Britain: the PEP report*. Harmondsworth: Penguin.

Solomos, J. 1988. *Black youth, racism and the state*. Cambridge: Cambridge University Press.

Solomos, J. 1989. *Race and racism in contemporary Britain*. London: Macmillan.

Stacey, M. (ed.) 1969. *Comparability in social research*. London: Heinemann.

Stacey, M. 1970. Professional code of ethics. *Sociology*, 114–17.

Troyna, B. & W. Ball 1985. *Views from the Chalk Face: School Responses to an LEA's Multicultural Education Policy*. Policy Papers in Ethnic Relations, No. 1. CRER/ESRC: University of Warwick.

Troyna, B. & R. Hatcher 1992. *Racism in children's lives*. London: Routledge.

Wallman, S. (ed.) 1979. *Ethnicity at work*. London: Macmillan.

Ware, V. 1992. *Beyond the Pale*. London: Verso.

Watson, J. D. 1970. *The Double Helix*. Harmondsworth: Penguin.

Watson, J. L. (ed.) 1977. *Between two cultures: migrants and minorities in Britain*. Oxford: Basil Blackwell.

Wilson, W. J. 1978. *The declining significance of race: blacks and changing American institutions*. Chicago: University of Chicago Press.

Wilson, W. J. 1987. *The truly disadvantaged*. Chicago: University of Chicago Press.

Part Three
ETHNICITY, NATION AND ETHNO-NATIONALISM

Chapter 7

Linkages between methodology, research and theory in race and ethnic studies: a case study of Sri Lanka

Radhika Coomaraswamy

Introduction

An inquiry into the state of research on race and ethnicity in the Asian Region must begin with one important question. Why is it that well developed research communities in Sri Lanka and India did not predict, or even devise concepts to understand, the nature and degree of Sri Lanka's ethnic conflict or India's regional violence? Why were they so unprepared that when the conflict finally became intractable, there was no literature to offer a satisfactory explanation of the phenomenon, no empirical evidence on which to begin further exploration and very few conceptual insights into the historical roots of the violent social upheavals that were taking place? The same questions have been raised in other areas of the world where ethnic and racial tensions have erupted into overt conflict.[1]

The reason for this lack of awareness and preparedness must be located to some extent in the priorities for research that have conditioned social science in South Asia. Since Independence, such research has focused on economic aspects of development, on the one hand, and on the creation of a nationalist ideology to unite the newly independent states, on the other. Research into ethnic relations was a marginal field often dismissed as being of interest only to anthropologists and to rather quaint obscurantists.

Recently, H. A. I. Goonetilleke, Sri Lanka's leading bibliographer compiled a comprehensive listing of all articles written in Sri Lanka on the country's ethnic conflict. Before the "ethnic riots" of 1983, there were only 167 books and articles on the ethnic question. In the two years following these events, however, there were no less than 500. These statistics in themselves indicate the unprepared state of the intellectual community (Goonetilleke 1985).

A historical bias

Writings on race and ethnicity in South Asia are biased towards the broadly historical. These historical debates take on ideological importance when they are reproduced as school texts and disseminated through the mass media. They become part of the shared "knowledge" of the community and an essential aspect of the construction of a post-independence nationalist imagination. They are primarily responsible for the content of any form of nationalist consciousness. In fact, for a long period, history and archaeology were the exalted fields within the arts and social sciences. Most of the scholars from India and Sri Lanka who have earned international reputations are historians. Romila Thapar (1978), in her article on interpretations of Ancient Indian History, chronicles in detail the phases of historical writing in India. The historical literature is an extremely important aspect of Asian ethnic studies, even when analysis is ostensibly confined to a purely "fact-finding" exercise. In South Asia, most groups see ethnic conflicts in terms of their historical rights. Grievances whose roots may be located over ten centuries ago become a part of contemporary discourse and debate. It is the research of historians transformed into popular beliefs about history that has created the volatile mix which is South Asian ethnic consciousness.

The first Indian and Sri Lankan historians in the early 20th century, such as R. G. Bhandarkar, followed the models of British historians and the writings of political history. The scholarship gave birth to a rich tradition dedicated to the study of historical documents and a commitment to a thorough methodology. The impact of this British model is still felt, animated by a love of the Oxbridge tradition of historical writing (de Silva 1973). This research still provides the source material for debates about ethnic conflict over the last two centuries or more.

However, the most influential schools of thought came with the nationalist movements in India and Sri Lanka; symbolized in India by historians such as Basham (1971, 1977) and Majumdar and in Sri Lanka by Paranavitana. These historians and archaeologists, writing in the 1940s and 1950s conducted original research into the ancient sources, and helped recreate and reinterpret the history and traditions of South Asia so that the new nation-states would acquire distinctive cultural identities. In its early phases, the writing of nationalist history was seen as a progressive aspect of the anti-colonial struggle. But once independence was achieved these writings led to the institutionalization of certain assumptions about history.

The perceptions of, and insistence on, the historical rights of the majority were often at the expense of minority groups in society. These in turn were transformed into uniform nationalist ideologies through school texts and the mass media (Anderson 1983).

Romila Thapar (1978: 11-14) describes in detail how the biases of these authors made them stress political unity in Indian history at the expense of diverse regional histories, and the Hindu Golden Ages at the expense of the Muslim experience. In Sri Lanka the same process took place. Nationalist authors stressed political unity over the long periods of regional regimes and the glory of Sinhala Buddhist civilization over that of the Tamil Hindu. In India, Muslims were the "other", the "invader". The Tamils occupied the same space in popular consciousness in Sri Lanka. Contemporary perceptions of issues such as "race" and "ethnicity" are deeply conditioned by this literature.

Diversity was suppressed and homogeneity encouraged in the hope of building up a modern nation-state. This strategy was implemented through standardized school texts and standardized mass (and especially electronic) media presentations. It led also to the homogenization of culture at the national level. Writers such as Karl Deutch (1969) have rightly stressed this aspect of nation-building in their writings.

This process of historical development, encouraged by nationalist historians, provoked the predictable reaction from minority groups in these societies, especially those who were territorially segregated. These groups put forward their own histories, which glorified the regional heritage and provided alternative "ethnic" interpretations of history. Nilakantha Shastri's work in India and the writings of Professor Pathmanathan (1978) in Sri Lanka are attempts to place regional ethno-political realities within the mainstream. Politically, however, the dialectics of history and "counter"-history have led to ethnic conflict based on "historical rights". Who came first and where? Who were the "legitimate" dynasties? Who are the authentic sons (sic!) of the soil? This remains the primary agenda for debate in the political arena. The work of historians, therefore, has directly intervened in the political process, and conditioned both the discourse and rhetoric of political debate.

The "left" perspective

The second school of scholarship that has deeply influenced attitudes to-wards race and ethnicity is the research conducted by the intelligentsia of the "left" in these societies. The agenda here was conceived as having two parts: first, to provide a critique of the existing literature and prevailing interpretations of social, economic and political phenomena. In this, they used class analysis as a means of situating "race" and "race relations" within the context of the production process in any given society. Secondly, they sought to write the "forgotten" history of the classes and tribes that was ignored or concealed by mainstream history. This has, in fact, cul-minated in a new type of research called "Sub-Altern" studies (Guha 1985). These attempt to record and analyze the various social movements and formations throughout history which are not represented in the political history of elites or dominant classes.

The "left" perspective on studies of ethnicity in South Asia was origi-nally that of regarding "ethnic research" with a great deal of contempt and scepticism. They saw such research as "obscurantist", and even the word "ethnic" is challenged as a misnomer. Their emphasis is on social classes and specifically on the workers and the peasantry. This perspective led in turn to a view of revolts, hitherto defined as "ethnic", as in reality move-ments led by parochial elites against forces of modernity and at the expense of social liberation for the masses. These intellectuals saw "ethnic" re-search as actually aggravating the problems of society by reifying, and thus legitimizing, the concept of ethnicity. They felt that the less the idea was stressed the better, because it would then be more likely that a person's "antiquated attachments" would gradually fade. This approach was directly tied to the belief that such problems only exist in "capitalist" or "feudal" societies and that socialism would eradicate all the differences. Bipan Chandra (1979: 273), one of the most outspoken members of this school in India writes:

> The reality of Indian politics was that there could be no solution, whether radical or conservative, to the communal problem within the framework of the existing nationalist politics. Only strong left-wing and mass-based politics could have provided this. Such politics did not, however, exist and a short cut could not meet the situation.

The events of the 1970s and 1980s have forced a radical rethink by some leftist historians and writers, and a new type of approach appears to be emerging. Kumari Jayawardena's writings (1986) on ethnicity and class in Sri Lanka are a prime example. In the South Asian context, the term "class" has often been redefined to conform to and reflect contemporary realities. Thus, the term "intermediate class" is becoming widely accepted as an important category; a category which Marx may have seen as a petit-bourgeoisie. There is increasing belief that this "intermediate class", which has had access to social mobility through control of the vernacular press and local industry, is the most dynamic class since independence and has spearheaded nationalist and chauvinistic temperament. Jayawardena's book analyses the relationship between class and ethnicity in these terms.

He also attempts to use the methods of structuralist deconstruction that have appeared in western Europe. For the first time the myths and legends which contribute to the creation of ethnic ideologies are dealt with directly, and confronted. There is a purposive attempt to separate fact from fiction and to provide an alternative discourse to nationalist history. Historians such as Romila Thapar in India and Leslie Goonewardene in Sri Lanka have begun to engage in this type of research activity. In addition, as a response to the societal crisis, the Social Science Association of Sri Lanka (1986) published an important volume stressing the need to free certain concepts and legends from the stranglehold of nationalist interpretation. Moreover, the writings of Western Marxists such as Benedict Anderson (1983) and Ronald Munck (1985) on the phenomenon of nationalism in the 1980s are now widely read and have undoubtedly had an impact on South Asian intellectuals. These theories point to the fact that the resilience of nationalism and ethnicity in contemporary society reflects a failure of "left" theory, and a renewed attempt must be made to understand these phenomena using other categories such as the nature of the state and the construction of political ideology.

There is another aspect of left-thinking that has to be understood in this context, especially considering recent developments in eastern Europe. Much of Marxist thought in South Asian countries was disseminated through the Soviet Publishing House, which translated important Marxist works into popular vernacular languages. This simplified literature, often a caricature of Marx and Lenin, was the major source of inspiration for many youths growing up in the 1960s and 1970s, and the vocabulary and modes of discourse deriving from this literature still abound on political platforms. Unfortunately, since ethnicity was not recognized as a valid concept or category, there was little written in this field. But, in related areas of political and economic thought, Marxist paradigms, simplified and sloganized in terms such as "exploitation", "capitalism" and so on . . . , remain important elements of political discourse and indeed have a currency beyond mainstream Marxism. They are often attached to movements seeking an indigenous socialism, or nativistic, ethnic perceptions of nationalism.

The empirical void

In western Europe, research on ethnicity is undertaken primarily by sociologists and social anthropologists (see Ratcliffe, in this volume). In South Asia this is not the case. There is very little empirical research involving the collection of primary data, and especially data on the relationship between ethnicity and socio-economic status. There are many reasons for this. In the West, race relations usually concern first or second generation migrants, and sociological data are deemed by many as necessary in terms of the social management of conflict.

Clearly, then, most of the migrants came to the West after Durkheim and the development of sociology as a discipline. In South Asia, ethnic relations are extremely political and there is a history which is not tested by resort to paradigm shifts in research agenda and methodology. This sensitivity of "the received tradition" often serves as a deterrent to original research. What we have are analyses of census and survey data, often gathered for specific purposes, such as the study of household patterns, structure, and so on; but there are very few studies which openly address the problem of ethnic conflict and thereby develop the categories and the methodologies to attempt to capture empirical reality; especially in such sensitive areas as employment, land rights and the relationship between ethnicity and class. As a result there is very little data to help us understand the material factors contributing to ethnic conflict. This lack of empirical evidence then feeds into the dialectic and further encourages the reliance on historical arguments. It also amplifies the rôle of myth and legend over statistics.

Another reason for this void is that the most dominant research paradigm in "Third World" societies today constitutes what may be termed the "development studies" school, with its special emphasis on the economic aspects of development. If one were to analyze the progress reports of the Marga Institute, a non-governmental institution funded by international NGOs (and often considered the foremost NGO in the Third World), this becomes immediately evident.

The Marga Institute is located in Sri Lanka and is dedicated to socio-economic research. In the years before the riots of 1983, and even after ten years in existence, it had not produced a single study on the empirical reality of Sri Lanka's ethnic relations. Their surveys concerned housing, social welfare infrastructure, fertility, labour force participation, micro-village profiles, education services, and so on. There was no attempt to capture the empirical reality of life in the Tamil periphery which was on the verge of rebellion; nor was there even an attempt to study changes in the fields of education and employment which may have affected inter-ethnic equity.

After the 1983 riots, and spurred on by a sudden sense of urgency, the Marga Institute finally produced a monograph on the Sri Lankan "Ethnic question" (Marga Institute 1985), but this simply collated existing official socio-economic data on certain areas of contention between the communities such as land rights, education and employment (to show the relative positions of the various ethnic groups). Although undoubtedly a useful document, its reliance on existing census data means that it gives no insight into the real causes of the conflict, or changing patterns of ethnic relations.

Primarily to fill this void an International Centre for Ethnic Studies (ICES) was set up in Colombo in 1982. Its objectives were to conduct comparative research into ethnic relations on themes such as devolution, education and employment. The first two publications of the Centre (Goldman & Wilson 1984, Rothermund & Simon 1986) follow this remit. The data are again drawn from census and Sri Lankan Central Bank reports but the articles do at least attempt to analyze them in terms of their impact on ethnic relations. For example, there is a discussion as to whether education policy, which introduced ethnic quotas or the language requirement of Sinhala only with regard to employment in the expanding state sector, invoked a positive or negative response from the various ethnic groups. (The article by S. W. R. de A. Samarasinghe (1984) on education and employment is particularly noteworthy.) Recently the Centre has begun to publish a series of monographs on the theoretical aspects of nationalism and ethnicity arising from its lecture and workshop series. Importantly, there has also been an attempt recently to disseminate research findings via the mass media, and especially television.

The ICES has an International Board but a Sri Lankan management. Its agenda reflects the growing belief that ethnic problems are often approached as "unique to one country" and takes it as axiomatic that much more valuable information can be elicited through comparative research and intervention. Research in the area of devolution, education and employment does indicate that certain legislative models and procedures are already commonly employed to manage social conflicts involving ethnic factors; but there has thus far been very little research into their actual impact. For example, the setting of quotas and the use of affirmative action and preference policies have been widely in evidence since the 1960s, but their effectiveness has yet to be assessed. This is particularly true in India with regard to the Scheduled castes and the Backward classes, and in Sri Lanka with regard to university admission on the basis of ethnic criteria. The furore in India over the Mandal Commission Report of 1982, and the ensuing riots and self-immolation by students, demonstrates how controversial such issues are. The first ICES publication (Goldman & Wilson 1984) attempts to analyze these strategies in terms of long term prospects for conflict management.

It would be wrong to argue that *no* research on ethnicity was undertaken in Sri Lanka or India before 1983. There were a few political scientists working in this area, primarily influenced by Western theorists such as Karl Deutsch and, in particular, his analysis of the problems of national integration. The best known of these South Asian scholars is Michael Roberts, who from the 1970s has been warning of an impending crisis in Sri Lanka.

Roberts (1979) attempted to synthesize "interest groups" theory with the communications theory developed by Deutch, in the process of stressing the importance of sub-national group identities, especially in newly developing countries. He argued that independence does not automatically lead to integration and that unless enlightened policies are pursued there is always the possibility of what he terms "nation-breaking" rather than nation-building. Although foreign scholars of political science also warned Sri Lankans of an impending crisis, their arguments were often rejected by nationalist scholars who felt that by focusing on ethnic divisions such scholarship actually contributed to the problem. With time, however, they have begun to accept the link between the study of nationalism and a politicized ethnicity. But few national scholars (apart perhaps from Roberts himself) adopted these models with a view to understanding their political relevance.

In India too, work on ethnicity was often related to studies of nationalism. Bipan Chandra, along with Kosambi, saw the problems of ethnic conflict as the failure of nationalism. They felt that it should be understood only in that context. A recent study by Partha Chatterjee (1986) attempts to form a structuralist analysis of India's nationalist leaders. It indicates

that the ethnic and religious leanings of the Indian leaders and the nationalist movement were always destined to lead to a situation of communal
strife. It was seen as inevitable that a powerful nationalist ideology would
be firmly rejected by certain regional and tribal groupings.

Populism and ethnicity

One approach to social science that is popular in South Asia, especially due
to the influence of Buddhism in Sri Lanka and Mahatma Ghandhi in India, is what may be called the "populist school of social research". This
emphasizes indigenous ideas and concepts, and is extremely critical of both
Western and Eastern political thought. It also focuses a lot of energy on
criticizing the values of the national intelligentsia within South Asian societies. In their view social science is only justified if it results in social
action at the grassroots level. Such research should be indigenous and re-
sistant to foreign influences, especially in the area of research funding
(Wiles & Canovan 1981). Many of the leading intellectuals in India and
Sri Lanka can be said to subscribe to this school of thought to some degree (see, Goonatilake 1986).

The contribution of populist thinkers has been extremely important in
documenting the lifestyles of tribal groups and other ethnic minorities who
have been marginalized by "modern" development in South Asia. Often
animated by a glorification of rural values, this research into the life-style
and grievances of the Naga tribesmen, or the Vaddas, or the marginalized
Sinhala peasantry, has given an added dimension to ethnic studies. It is not
aimed at contributing to anthropological inquiry but unequivocally at in-
forming social action geared to the protection and enhancement of the rights
of these groups against vested interests and capitalist domination (Dasgupta
1985).

Ironically, the ideological bias of populists towards marginalized groups
does not naturally lead to them accepting the larger ideals of "sharing
power" with less vulnerable ethnic groupings and the development of a
multi-ethnic identity at the national level. There is a rejection of the "politicized ethnicity" of powerful ethnic groups that would find expression
in legal and administrative arrangements for national power sharing.
Hence, the Sikh cause in India and that of the Tamils in the north and east
of Sri Lanka are not accepted as valid. They reject the claims of powerful ethnic groups, i.e. those which enjoy substantial economic power and

professional status, on the grounds that they are not economically marginalized – though they may be politically discriminated against in the use of language and religion. Economic marginality is thus the only criterion for ethnic grievance.

Serena Tennekoon (1987) analyzes attitudes to ethnicity and race in terms of Sri Lankan populist consciousness, using as a database the feature stories and articles by scholars and academics in the pages of the Sinhala newspapers of Sri Lanka. These revealed that the ideology conveyed, especially in the midst of ethnic strife, was an extremely ethnocentric one, and exclusivist in its views of ethnic identity; being expressed in terms of historical rights and a "chosen people". In fact, many of the arguments rested on biological claims of difference based on Aryan vs Dravidian myths, and claimed that the Tamils and Sinhalese were *racially* different groups. This is compounded by the fact that there is no Sinhala or Tamil word for ethnicity, only for race or Jati.

However, the same discourse, while it accepted racialism and racial stereotypes, also called into play the ideology of populism; that the Sinhala peasantry was the most downtrodden and vulnerable sector, and should be protected. The emphasis, it was argued, should not be on the "achievement-oriented" ethnic minorities. But this type of approach was also based on an ignorance of the social composition of the Tamils which, despite having a significant middle class, also had a large working class in the form of plantation workers on the tea estates. This peculiar approach to ethnicity, "through peasant eyes", has a distinctively South Asian flavour, and its appeal is often attributed to Buddhist values or Gandhian freedoms. Research by indigenous scholars, especially those educated in the vernacular, is deeply influenced by this type of populist approach. As a result, the ideological and historical processes of ethnic identity and ethnic struggle are not studied as ends in themselves. In fact, the studies are heavily influenced by a "victim consciousness" and a sense of moral purpose. When this is allied to the study of marginalized peasant groups it has particular moral force and a fundamental imperative for social action. As in Latin America, the purpose becomes one of documenting and giving expression to the myths, legends and aspirations of a "forgotten" community; but, when the "victim consciousness" is transformed to apply to the majority community, such as in Sri Lanka or Malaysia, then it has the contours of an oppressive monolithic ideology which, having captured state power, does not entertain democratic pluralist values and is indeed suspicious of diversity. Research into ethnic studies is viewed with great suspicion as an attempt to promote disintegration and chaos in these Third World societies.

Human rights and ethnicity

In recent times one of the major areas of research and debate on ethnicity in South Asia has been generated by the Human Rights Movement. There are files which chronicle "ethnic" incidents such as, for example, the riots in New Delhi and the action by state forces in Sri Lanka. Armed with such data the movement has made suggestions as to a possible resolution of ethnic conflict in terms of administrative and human rights models.[2]

Legal research

The human rights reports by people such as Virginia Leary make additional proposals for administrative and legal solutions to the type of crisis presented by ethnic conflict. This has also become an increasingly important area for socio-legal research in South Asia (Leary 1983). Legal research is also currently being undertaken as to whether devolution or federalism might solve the problems faced by regional minorities. Given the present level of political consciousness among such minorities, it has become necessary to reassess existing constitutional structures and to revise them in such a way as to make them more sensitive to the growing aspirations of these groups. The ICES is currently undertaking a study of Centre-State relations, a study of systems including federalism, devolution, and so on, with the aim of reassessing federalism in countries such as India and Malaysia. The specific remit of the study is to see to what extent federal revision can be used as a means of managing ethnic conflict. Given the recent events in the Punjab and Sabah, these studies (to be undertaken by policy institutes in the two countries) will be of great interest to future policy-makers.

Policy studies

As we have seen, the study of ethnicity in South Asia was for a long time either ignored or left to a small number of anthropologists who duly documented diversity within countries and regions. Increasingly, an awareness

144

has developed that government research is needed that is directly geared towards a revision of government policy. There was the need to take a look at the long-term implications of present policy and to help devise formulae for the management of future conflict. The demand for this kind of research came from concerned scholars in the NGO sector – the Centre for Policy Research in India being an example. But interest has also spread to the government itself, research at the Institute for Policy Research in Sri Lanka being evidence of this. Studies have assessed the effectiveness of "preference policies" and "quota systems" as vehicles for improving life chances for minorities (Dias 1981), and the impact of language policies on ethnic power-sharing within countries (ICES 1990). As yet there is little research concerning state policy on employment and education. Studies of, for example, the indirect impact of large development projects on ethnic relations, and the impact of different governments' economic strategies on those relations, are sorely needed. But given that these are extremely sensitive areas, not least because they threaten to subject to critical analysis the assumptions behind government policy, it is perhaps not surprising that there is a void in the literature.

Inevitably any such research, to be effective, will have to be conducted (at least in part) in collaboration with the state. Certain criteria and assumptions should therefore be laid down to ensure the validity of the process. The next decade will perhaps witness a proliferation of policy studies in these areas as governments in South Asia are increasingly concerned to minimize conflict. (The Institute of Policy Studies recently set up by the Sri Lankan government may be a case in point.) Many politicians believe that economic and social policies since independence have actually aggravated ethnic conflict. However, some governments may prefer to keep the lid firmly on Pandora's box in the hope that the problem will disappear with increasing economic development. But the wave of democratic movements sweeping the sub-continent from Pakistan to Bangladesh has called for more open dialogue and research. In such a situation, scholars may finally have the opportunity to dictate the agenda and pursue policy-relevant research irrespective of opposition from those in power whose interests are threatened.

Anthropological reality

What is apparent from the above survey is that, despite the intensity of

145

ethnic conflict in the South Asian region, the amount of research remains minimal. A researcher clearly has to be prepared to meet criticism that may arise from the exposure of political interests and policy errors. Another factor is that the value positions of most social scientists and historians have been such that they have not attempted to come to terms with the changing reality. Instead they have preferred to research historical documents or non-ethnic socio-economic factors. Research and methodology in the South Asian region have also been "ethnically blind" for political reasons (but also because of the outlook and training of social scientists).

It has been left to anthropologists to draw our attention to the complex ethnic reality of our region. Scholars such as Sri Lanka's Gananath Obeyesekere have, through their research, captured the sense of ethnic diversity, congruence and divergence and have conveyed the spirit of a dynamic culture constantly in the process of re-creating and reproducing itself. The reality portrayed by him is the reality of particular experiences where ethnic groups live side-by-side, their relationships complicated by political ideology but their intermingling resulting in a unique set of cultural syntheses (Obeyesekere & Gombrich 1989).

Recently, social scientists using anthropological data have begun to draw on this work to help demystify political myths which "demonize" other ethnic groups. Scholars have attempted to show joint traditions and a joint history so as to minimise political conflict. But the problem with the anthropological approach is that it is only an exploratory foray into a specific "localized reality", filtered through the subjective perceptions of the author. Anthropological research is rarely concerned with the more general history and political dimensions of identity formation. Nor does it help us relate ethnicity to macro-processes or throw light on the relationship between ethnicity and class, nation, gender and religion. For this reason, although anthropological research may be regarded as a useful starting point, it cannot be seen as an end in itself. Further, it will only provide us with a partial, shaded reality.

Research on the politics of ethnic conflict

Given the form of conflicts in South Asia and the nature of argument and counter-argument, much research is done to further a particular claim of one ethnic group and/or to deny the claim of another. Although all research is ultimately political, some profess or acknowledge an overt political purpose at the outset. Satchi Ponnambalam's book (1983) on Sri Lanka's ethnic conflict, which attempts to present the historical case for a separate Tamil state, does indeed uncover certain archival material that furthers his argument. But, much of the detail betrays an overt political intent. At the same time, there is a controversial article by G. H. Peiris (1985) which states at the beginning that it is an attempt to deny the Tamil concept of traditional homelands in Sri Lanka and to assert Sinhala sovereignty throughout the island. Again, despite the overt political purpose, he does present original data that throw fresh light on the debate. But this ideological commitment leads him to conclusions which are principally motivated by political concerns.

Research methods and paradigms

The historical method still dominates research on ethnicity in contemporary South Asia. As we have already seen the approach usually involves delving into archives (and sometimes archaeology) to determine the claims and counter-claims of various ethnic groups. It is still dominant in the sense that of all the articles set out in the bibliography on Sri Lanka's ethnic conflict, it remains the most popular approach. The next most popular approach to have developed as a result of recent events is what may generally be called the "human rights" method, which analyzes ethnic conflict in terms of the obligations of the state, and which documents the abuse of power perpetuated by police and army personnel; actions directed against specific ethnic groups. A vast amount of empirical data is now available to feed into this work.

There is also some political science literature in the Marxian tradition which focuses either on the problem of "nation-building" or on class conflict and its relationship to ethnicity. There are also, as we have seen, some anthropological writings. What is lacking is a political economy perspective which captures the social dynamics of the present. It is therefore in this area that a great deal of research has to be done in the near future. Such research will not only have implications for policy but will also tend to shift the locus of argument away from a historical focus which situates the debate in emotive age-old conflicts over territory rights.

Future directions for research

If one were to plan a programme for future research in South Asia, one could argue that it has to be divided into two distinct types. The first, as stated earlier, should have a strong socio-economic dimension; focusing on the impact upon ethnic groups of such matters as youth unemployment, migration patterns and state development policies. It could look also at the open economy and its effect on ethnicity, ethnic conflict and statization; the labour force participation of the various ethnic groups; changing occupational patterns, and so on. Finally, there should be additional surveys into perceptions of the various groups, especially with regard to each other. This research has to be done soon if these societies are to develop the data and the policies with which to diffuse ethnic conflict *before* it reaches the point of violence.

Secondly, as many writers have pointed out, the source of much of the conflict in South Asia is ideological, at the level of collective identities. In that sense, it poses different analytical problems from those associated with immigrant labour in Europe, tribal loyalties in Africa or even the position of an indigenous "Indian" population in Latin America. The linkages and loyalties to different religions, different dynamic traditions, different social castes, different but historically powerful linguistic groups, makes the ideological dimension a paramount consideration in South Asia. Conflicts resulting from such loyalties and linkages go beyond the boundaries of nation-states and are fuelled by a strong sense of primordial attachment to certain sets of socio-religious symbols. Theoretical research should be conducted, therefore, into the symbolic construction of South Asian ethnic identity, and the power of symbolic systems over the lives of individuals. Such research will do well to draw on the works of Western structuralist writers such as Foucault, Levi-Strauss and Derrida to help understand the nature of symbolic systems and their relationship to power and politics. In addition, the original and creative works of South Asian scholars such as Ashis Nandy (1983), which explore these symbolic systems from a South Asian perspective and which attempt to understand their power from within, provide perhaps an even greater opportunity for understanding the intensity of the dilemmas before us. Before such a theory can fully develop, it is essential that empirical data on perceptions and values are collected in a systematic fashion.

In this way the development of theory would have a firm foundation, built on a sound primary database, and not represent a reflection of impressionistic ideas, a priori reasoning or philosophical speculation.

Conclusion

More than thirty years after independence, we in South Asia have only just begun to go down the road of self-discovery. This search is no longer propelled by the sort of rigidly fixed categories and externally imposed world views that have directed our social reality. Instead, our understanding of ethnicity in South Asia will require analyses as far as possible free from pre-conceived ideas or dogmatic value positions. This represents a difficult agenda given the intensity of conflict in our societies. There is no alternative but to take another look into the mirror at our social reality. It is to be hoped that the shock to the social science community, when faced with a catalogue of its current inadequacies, will generate critical insights and encourage individuals to take on many areas of research which, because of their "sensitivity", have hitherto remained untouched.

Notes

1. The terms "ethnicity" and "ethnic" are used here in relation to group identities based on linguistic, religious or other culturally determined criteria.
2. See publications of the People's Union for Civil Liberties, New Delhi; or The Movement for Inter-Racial Justice, Colombo.

References

Anderson, B. 1983. *Imagined communities*. London: Verso.

Basham, A. I. 1971/7. *The wonder that was India*. London: Fontana.

Chatterjee, P. 1986. *Nationalist thought and the colonial world: a derivative discourse*. London: Zed.

Chandra, B. 1979. *Nationalism and colonialism in modern India*. New Delhi: Orient.

Das, V. 1989. *Communities, riots and survivors*. New Delhi: Oxford University Press.

Dasgupta, S. 1985. Adivasi politics in Midnapur c.1760–1924. In *Sub Altern Studies*, R. Guha (ed.). New Delhi: Oxford University Press.

Deutch, K. 1969. *Nationalism and its alternatives*. New York: Alfred A. Knopf.

Dias, C. 1981. Quest for equality. In *Ethical dilemmas of development*, H. A. I.

Goonatilleke et al. (eds). Lexington: Lexington Books.

Goldman, R. & A. J. Wilson (eds) 1984. *From independence to statehood: managing ethnic conflict in five African and Asian States*. Colombo: ICES.

Goonatilake, S. 1986. *Crippled minds*. London: Zed.

Goonetilleke, H. A. I. 1985. July 1983 and the National question in Sri Lanka: a bibliographical guide. In *Sri Lanka's ethnic conflict: myths, realities and perspectives*. The Committee for Rational Development, New Delhi: Navrang.

Guha, R. (ed.) 1985. *Sub Altern Studies*, vol. 1. New Delhi: Oxford University Press.

ICES 1990. *Programme on bilingualism in Sri Lanka*. Colombo: ICES.

Jayawardena, K. 1986. *Ethnic and class conflict in Sri Lanka*. Colombo: Navamaga.

Karkar, S. 1986. The communal devil. *India Today* (1 November 1986).

Leary, V. A. 1983. *Ethnic conflict and violence in Sri Lanka*. Report of Mission to Sri Lanka in July–August 1981. Geneva: ICJ.

Marga Institute 1985. *Inter-racial equity and national unity in Sri Lanka*. Colombo: Marga.

Munck, R. 1985. *The difficult dialogue: Marxism and nationalism*. London: Zed.

Nandy, A. 1983. *The Self under colonialism*. New Delhi: Oxford University Press.

Obeyesekere, G. & R. Gombrich 1989. *Buddhism transformed*. Princeton: Princeton University Press.

Pathmanathan, S. 1978. *The Kingdom of Jaffna*. Colombo: A. M. Rajendran.

Pieries, G. H. 1985. *An appraisal of the concept of a traditional Tamil homeland in Sri Lanka*. Colombo: ICES Monograph.

Ponnambalam, S. 1983. *Sri Lanka: the national question and the Tamil liberation struggle*. London: Zed.

Roberts, M. (ed.) 1979. *Collective identities: nationalisms and protests*. Colombo: Marga.

Rothermund, D. & J. Simon (eds) 1986. *Education and the integration of ethnic minorities*. London: Frances Pynter.

Samarasinghe, S. W. R. deA. 1984. Ethnic representation in Central Government and Sinhala-Tamil relations in Sri Lanka 1948. In *From independence to statehood: managing ethnic conflict in five African and Asian States*, R. Goldman & A. J. Wilson (eds), Colombo: ICES.

de Silva, K. M. (ed.) 1973. *History of Ceylon*, volumes 1, 2. Colombo: University of Ceylon.

Social Science Association 1986. *Ethnicity and social change*. Colombo: Navamaga.

Tennekoon, S. 1987. The Divaina Debates. In *Facets of ethnicity*. Colombo: SSA/Navamaga.

Thapar, R. 1978. *Ancient Indian social history: some interpretations*. New Delhi: Oxford University Press.

Wiles, P. & M. Canovan 1981. *Populism*. London: Junction Books.

Chapter 8

Ethno-nationalism in India: political, historical and sociological discourse

Ashok Kaul

Introduction

The explosion of ethnic conflict during the 1960s in many developed countries, and the resurgence of ethno-nationalism in the eastern European block
and elsewhere in Third World countries, has raised serious questions about
the survival of plural societies in the context of the nation-state as currently
conceived. Political developments in the late-1980s and early-1990s have
provoked a marked shift in our understanding of the nature of plural societies and their problems of in-group accommodation. Ethnicity is no
longer regarded as a legacy of primordial social relations: it is being taken
seriously as an analytical paradigm. The debate has become more urgent
in a country such as India, where complex ethnic diversities are seen on
the surface. The present chapter attempts to conceptualize the rise of ethno-
nationalism in the geographically peripheral northern states of India. The
developments are viewed within the paradigm of colonial contradictions,
historical events and differential development.

Ethnic, religious and national divisions:
the colonial context

India is a social, economic and political paradox, "a rich–poor nation with
a weak–strong state" (Rudolph 1988: 1). It has a living history of over four
thousand years with enormous diversity yet cultural continuity. During its
long history, India has encountered many civilizations and cultures. The
most significant was also the most recent; the subjugation for almost two

hundred years (1757-1947) by the British. This has structurally transformed India and knitted it into its present nation-state formation. Despite
British rule promoting its political unification, with the merger of more than
five hundred small states, the contradictions of colonial social engineering remain endemic, even after four decades of independence.

History reveals that Britain subjugated India in the interests of colonial
expansion and Empire-building. Behind the consolidation of political power
was the tradition of Western culture, espousing the values of equity, ra-
tionalism and universalism. As one prominent writer argues:

> The cultural tradition of 19th Century west which overwhelmed the In-
> dian scene was in its ethos and structure fundamentally different from
> the traditional cultural patterns of Hinduism and Islam. Its basic tenets
> were in contradiction with most of the essential attributes of the contem-
> porary Indian tradition . . . it encouraged the values of equality, equity
> and universalism and not those of status and hierarchy. (Singh 1983: 86)

Indian society at this historical juncture was economically stagnant, socially degenerated and politically diffuse. It provided conditions conducive
to the implementation of colonial socio-economic policies, which resulted
in changes in the physiognomy of the social structure of Indian society. In
fact, colonial social engineering was "degenerative as well as regenera-
tive" (cf. Dutt 1970, Desai 1981, Matto 1991). On the one hand, the introduction of new education and legal systems, and the expansion of rail-
ways and communication created a new educated middle class and knitted the country together; on the other, the plundering of raw materials,
fragmentation of land, the introduction of a "permanent settlement land
bill" and the destruction of the traditional artisan class resulted in the
creation of new classes both at rural and urban levels.

The linkages provided by the new changes were instrumental in the development of movements within which emerged the contradictions of caste,
class and communal antagonism that were hitherto unknown to Indian
society. During the process of decolonization, the National Movement,
under the banner of Congress, provided a structure in which all classes and
castes of people with different backgrounds and perceptions were bound
together by the common cause of independence; wherein the contradictions
of under-development remained temporarily concealed, only to reappear
after the transfer of power. India achieved freedom but with a partition,
an artificial division of the country on the basis of a "two nation theory".
This involved brutal and bloody violence and necessitated the mass migra-

tion of people from one end of the country to the other. In many ways, partition has proved a stumbling block impeding the reconstruction of a democratic, secular and plural nation.

Bequeathed with the problems of partition and the legacy of colonial rule, India achieved the "ideal" of national independence without the integration of various regional cultures. It differs from the West, where nationalism was built on the fruits of the Industrial Revolution and expansion of the colonies. These countries already had an abundance of the educational and professional skills generally deemed necessary for a progressive, "civilized" nation. In fact, in Italy and Germany the integration of various cultures into the national culture preceded political unity, so Britain and France were the "pacesetters" in a sense. In the case of India it was different. To quote Singh (op. cit.: 114) once more:

> Both nationalism and democracy in India have come into being in a different historical context. First these values have been derived from an alien tradition and have grown on the soil of India under a colonial patronage . . . for historical reasons these institutional innovations have been introjected in the Indian body politic in a compressed form which in the West had evolved gradually and this phenomenon creates new and far greater cultural stresses than it did in the West.

India became a nation based on a fusion of old society and new state: the old society, being highly stratified with systematic patterns of inequalities; the new state having a written constitution based on equality, and incorporating the principles of democracy, secularism and socialism. The conflict of rationalities seemed to be unending.

> It is a long drawn out competition with occasional pauses and frequent clashes, e.g. Mandal, with insidious encroachments, e.g. public interest litigation and overt manoeuvring. In this struggle equality is able to push back inequality from some aspects of the traditional terrain. (Peter 1991: 7)

These conflicts have from time to time exposed the deep divisions on Indian society along the fault lines of caste and community. Coming late to the quest for "developed" status, the country had to skip many stages. It adopted the path of capitalist development through a planned programme; But the initial phase laid emphasis on growth and took distribution for granted. The results were uneven distribution and distorted development, which created pockets of affluence and large areas of poverty. Significantly, with this social differentiation, a new conflict emerged in the ownership and control of productive capacity, in that the process of democratization and uneven development exposed these social cleavages in an ethnic form.

The display of ethnic affinity is "based on certain shared perceptions of distinctive commonness often augmented by diachronic continuity" (Dasgupta 1975: 467). This shared commonness is expressed in terms of various identifiable groupings based on, for example, religion, language and region, and yet the society is "multi-ethnic both in terms of plural social division and multiple personal identification. This multiplicity leads to a perplexing series of cross-closures for bargaining, rivalry and combination that are quite different from the mutually reinforcing ethnicities" (Peter op. cit.: 10). In Punjab and Kashmir, the two northern border states of India, the ethnic sentiments have taken on secessionist overtones. In each state a section of the population has waged a war "against the state", and both have now been under a siege of violence for over a decade, entailing heavy loss of life, deteriorating conditions of law and order and the revival of religion-based politics. Indeed, extremist policies – involving killing, looting and kidnapping, combined with the exodus of minorities from these states – have posed a serious threat to the survival of India as a nation-state.

Ethno-nationalism and social conflict:
two case studies

Punjab

Notwithstanding the long history of rancour and hatred between Sikhs and Muslims during the Aurangzeb regime, pre-partition Punjab had, over three hundred years, developed a common, cohesive composite culture based on accommodative elements of Hinduism, Sikhism and Islam. It was reflected in the common Punjabi language, in rituals, customs, folk tales, epics, music and mysticism. Since the time of Ranjit Singh, the heyday of Sikh rule, Lahore had been a cultural centre and the capital of a unified Punjab. The Punjabis, and especially the Sikhs, had developed a sense of identification with it and the surrounding places of worship. The loss of these places in the process of partition has remained an irreconcilable factor for the Sikh's psyche. Indeed, it can be argued that it is this break in cultural continuity that triggered the emergence of Sikh nationalism.

After partition, the fragmented Punjab became a land of two com-munities; Sikhs and Hindus linked by intermarriage and shared history. The Sikhs form a slight majority of the population at 53 per cent, concentrated mainly in villages and comprising the major part of the peasantry. In contrast, the Hindus live more often than not in towns and cities and are dependent largely on small business and professional work. To overcome the blemishes of partition, the Centre adopted a "softer" policy towards Punjab as compared to other states. As a result of the second five-year plan, Punjab experienced a boom. The advent of the "green revolution" undoubtedly made the state more prosperous than others but it fragmented the peasantry into various classes such as rich peasants, capitalist landlords, and the marginal and poor. The main beneficiary of this revolution was the big peasantry, which became even more powerful through the patronage of the Akali Dal party and its off-shoot Kissan unions. The gains from production of the middle peasantry were short-lived due to the repayment of loans and the cost of raw materials (such as fertilizers, tractors, pesticides). The withdrawal of subsidies within a couple of years following the "revolution", created a surge of indebtedness that marginalized both groups.

However, even the big peasantry became discontented as the surplus, which might have led to investment and the enhancement and generation of capital, found no such channel, because of the absence of planned industrialization. The economy remained stagnant and frozen. What was initially thought of as a boom rapidly became shrouded in disillusionment. "Riddled with discontent and violence, Punjab has been left with diseased soils, pest-infested crops, waterlogged deserts . . . instead of a peace Punjab has inherited conflict and violence" (Dang 1988: 4). Since the Centre controls agricultural policy, fixes its price and manages its distribution, it became the natural target of protest. The Kissan unions mobilized the peasantry and submitted a charter of demands to the ruling party. These included higher prices for their products, better redistribution systems, more subsidies for their raw material costs and more water and power supplies for their fields.

Coincidentally, during the 1960s Congress was the ruling party both at the Centre and at state levels. Sensing the opportunity to wrest power from Congress, the Akali Dal, a local (regional) political party, turned the genuine peasant unrest into a political movement by adding more demands formulated on ethnic lines. The most dominant of these argued for the creation of "Punjabi Soba" on the basis of the Punjabi language. The Centre responded by meeting the demands partially, and the state of Punjab was reorganized on a linguistic basis in 1966. There was a brief respite until 1971, when war led to the second partition of the subcontinent. At this time Bangladesh was created on the basis of, and as a national "home" for, Bengali culture. The humiliation of defeat was never reconciled by the military leader-ship, and after the assassination of Bhuto, its military regime (through "Operation Topac") started a proxy war against India by creating insurgency in Punjab and Kashmir.

Those who were easy prey to propaganda from across the border included unemployed youths. They were organized, trained and indoctrinated in the belief that the Hindu centre was hegemonic and working against the interests of the Sikhs. The political crisis of the 1970s added fuel to the worsening situation. In this context, the formation of Janta Dal (a coalition of local and national parties) represented another turning point in the Indian political scene. The regaining of power by the Congress Party in the mid-term poll in 1980 was a serious setback to these regional parties. To re-emerge from this identity crisis, they began to communalize their politics.

The Akali Dal was no exception. It formed a new movement with a different agenda focusing on religious concessions and a demand for greater autonomy to the state. Mobilization was on communal lines and therefore quite different from the situation in the mid-1960s. A new religious symbolism was created to "demonstrate" that the Sikhs were a different, and distinct, nation. Soon, however, the movement developed beyond the control of Akali Dal and fell into the hands of overtly extremist organizations, who had already gained ground with the tacit support of India's hostile neighbour. These groups marginalized the political parties and waged a war against the state calling for a separate nation of Khalistan.

These military organizations have not only rendered the political parties irrelevant but also destroyed the character of the former political movement by virtue of its fragmentation into different factional parties. The response from the state was the reassertion of power, which in turn led to "Operation Blue Star", the assassination of Mrs Gandhi, and the emergence of Hindu fundamentalism. The end-products are well known; continuing violence, state repression and the denial of democratization.

Kashmir

Kashmir, on the other hand, has socio-cultural patterns which make it a society quite different from Punjab. It became a Muslim-dominated state during the four centuries of Muslim rule beginning in the 14th century. The impact of Islam in Kashmir was two-fold (a) mass conversion through the process of Islamization by kings and missionaries, reducing the stratified pre-Islamic Hindu majority to the single verna of a Brahminic community, and (b) the emergence of syncretic cultural patterns through the interaction of two religions. By the time Islamization had begun in Kashmir, Islam had itself undergone many structural changes through its contact with Persian and Hindu society. Moreover, Kashmir was experiencing a strong transformative movement of mysticism in its indigenous (popular) "Rishi" tradition, of which "Lal Ded" was the founder. She was a poet-saint, a local reformist. Her powerful expressions of "Shaivite" philosophy in simple common language (Lal. Waakh) have been passed down from generation to generation via an oral tradition. They embody a forceful message of understanding and tolerance, "endowing it with qualities of affective metaphor and imagery drawn from familiar surroundings with memorable sayings that have become current coin (age) . . . she is more significantly the maker of modern Kashmiri language as well as literature" (Kaul 1973: 185). It was around this "Rishi tradition" that the Kashmiri culture, which had knitted the two communities together for centuries, evolved.

The conversion to Islam in Kashmir proved only a veneer. In the context of patterns of adaptation, it is important to recognize that Islam in Kashmir underwent a process of transformation not only in its social and interpersonal sphere but also in its identity and cultural aspects. The "greater" traditions of Islam are dominated by the pre-Islamic "minor" traditions. Its religious tenets of monotheism accommodated "peerparti", faith in shrines and polytheism in one form or another. Similarly, it did not remain a homogeneous and monolithic Muslim entity, but gave rise to the very different patterns of social stratification that were observed prior to the advent of Islam. While retaining its pre-Islamic cultural traditions, it provided some blending of these traditions since, "Kashmir Pandits . . . as Brahmins offer a unique example in India of close affinity with Islamic customs and manners. They took to learning of Persian, [and] meat eating, which is generally taboo among Brahmins" (Singh 1983: 80). Thus the culture of the Kashmiri is hybrid in character; pre-Islamic traditions are fused with those of Islam. Because of this there is no overt conflict between the two communities. Indeed, this was the logic of the age-old Hindu-Muslim coexistence and the reason for the secular character of the valley.

With the establishment of British rule in India, Kashmir was annexed to Jammu and became the state of the Dogra dynasty for about seventy years prior to independence. During this period the Muslim elites not only lost their pre-eminent status but also refused to modernize their community on the basis of the new Westernization. On the other hand, the Kashmiri Pandits, traditionally an educated community, benefited most from the process of modernization and the new education. A lag in the development of the Muslim middle classes was to become responsible for the subsequent growth of communal forces in the valley.

During the development of the National Movement an uprising against Dynasty rule was led by the National Conference, a local party under the leadership of Sheik Muhammad Abdullah. With the help of Nationalist leaders, it was able to dethrone the rulers of the Dynasty. The popular leadership of the National Conference wanted to keep Kashmir a free zone between India and Pakistan; against the wishes of a small section of Muslim religious elites (Bakra) who wanted to join Pakistan. But its insecurity and geographical vulnerability was exposed soon after independence, when part was annexed to Pakistan by aggression. This forced the local leadership to join India via the instrument of accession, but with a privileged position under Article 370 of the Constitution (which guarantees its special status within the Indian state). The choice was made on the grounds

(a) that the secular democratic India would allow local popular representatives to assume power,

(b) that, being a Muslim majority state, it would be possible for Muslims to regain lost status and prestige without sacrificing their cultural identity, and

(c) the influence of the Nationalist leaders on local leadership, and the rôle played by the local Brahminic community during the struggle against the Dynasty rule, were recognized and respected.

No doubt it marked a new phase in the progress and prosperity of the state but for many years the Muslim religious parties did not participate in elections. They constantly opposed the accession to India and supported the claims on Kashmir of Pakistan, on the grounds that "Islamic tradition admits no pluralistic or secular state" (Singh 1983: 72). And, "even for the nationalist minded Muslim elites, who were against the partition, it was often difficult to justify existence of Islam within a Hindu Majority state" (ibid.: 72). It created a deep schism between religious and secular values.

After the death of Sheik Mohammad Abdullah, the founder of the National Conference and the most prominent leader of Kashmir, the National Conference started losing its base to communal politics. In the absence of genuine political socialization, a "false consciousness" centred on the political significance of religion was created by the different political parties in order to gain votes at the ballot box. The rôle of the Centre in toppling local governments from time to time and violating Article 370, has also led to the emergence of Kashmiri patriotism.

With the growth of fruit production, handicrafts and tourism, a new affluent class has emerged throughout the valley; a class which has found its way into education, civil administration and the new and growing business sector. They have also benefited from the general process of development; but the other major sections of society have been less fortunate. All of these, from tenants, landless labourers and the working class to middle class professionals, have experienced little by way of radical change. The new rich class has identified itself with Muslim ethnicity and has replaced the traditional secular elites. Those most affected are the non-Muslim minority community, "a traditional educated local Brahminic community, that over the years has acted as the agent of development for the vast Muslim community and socializing and disseminating literacy" (Kaul 1987: 61). As part of the democratization of the general mode and tenor of life, this was a natural outcome, but it could be argued that the community lost its share of the fruits of economic development far beyond "proportionality". Over the centuries, this community has kept the secular character of the valley intact.

The broader historical developments in the late 1970s such as the rise of Islamic fundamentalism in Iran, the denial of democracy in Pakistan and the internal crisis stemming from political instability in India, all have contributed to the emergence of the present ethnic movement in Kashmir. Unlike the mood of the past, the movement is no longer a peaceful demonstration against the perceived excessive interference of the Centre in its internal systems of administration and political representation; it has adopted a more combative stance, challenging the very accession of Kashmir to India. Many would agree that the movement has fallen into the hands of "militant radicals", who run it in a fashion parallel to that of the proponents of Punjab militancy. Patronage is provided by orthodox religious elites, who were previously isolated by the secular forces of the National Conference. By inducing moral panic, an emphasis is placed on the banning of alcohol, the closure of cinemas, and the replacement of popular traditional literature.

These are part and parcel of the process of orthodox Islamization which is being implemented by these radical militant organizations. This conscious religious identification with the Iranian model is geared to tear the valley away from the mainstream plural culture of India. It has brought about the mass exodus of the minority, suspension of the constitutional Assembly, deadlock in the political process and, not surprisingly, the suffering of ordinary people caused both by the State and by the "militants".

Conclusion

To sum up, we entered into a discourse which recognized (a) that India is a country of many religions and widely varying cultures, and (b) that the territorially segregated nature of these religions has resulted in the generation of distinct "ethnic pools". We then saw that over the years since independence there has been a gradual rise in the growth of ethno-nationalism within these pools. The recent major uprisings in Punjab and Kashmir accompanied by politically grounded religious extremism have posed a serious challenge to both the pluralism and territorial integrity of the country. A comparative analysis of these movements reveals that even if the socio-cultural patterns differ, the process of ethno-nationalism manifests a striking similarity. It revolved around the following issues: the deterioration in the Centre-state relationship, break-down in the process of modernization and secular–ization, and (arguably) the need for a Common National Culture.

Since cultural integration did not precede political unification, the imbalances of the "old society" and the rationale behind the "new (nation-)state" created structural inconsistencies. As Singh (op. cit.: 210) argues, these include

> democratization without spread of civil culture (education), bureaucratization without commitment to universalistic norms, rise in media participation (communication) and aspirations without proportionate increase in resources and distributive justice, verbalization of welfare ideology without its diffusion in social structure and its application as social policy, over-urbanization without industrialization.

The end result was that the process did not allow the modernization paradigm to become a "melting pot" for cultural integration. Hope now rests on the formation of a new economic policy with clear unambiguous priorities in the area of conflict; priorities geared to make the development process more equitable, and demonstrably so.

In the post-Nehru era, there has been an abrupt decline in the political culture of the country. Both the National and regional parties have vitiated the norms and procedures of democracy by using the state, capital and even physical force in the quest for power. This has not only communalized politics along religious and caste lines but also produced a shift in the power structure of the country. The new power elites are heterogeneous in composition and are dominated by the casteists and religious revivalists; in marked contrast to the traditional, homogeneous elite which was secular and educated. With the National culture disappearing, ethnic identity has found political articulation through the regional parties, which are often out of line with the ruling party in the Centre. There is arguably a need to make the state "more federal", and in so doing provide channels through which to air political demands and conflicts on the way to finding effective solutions. This will also enable the positive dimensions of ethnicity to develop into a common broadly-based, multi-layered culture. The core elements of this common culture are already in place, but in an isolated "unfertilized" form.

It is probable that central to this will be a discovery of the literary tradition, music and mysticism, and the development of a common law, a common market and modes of worship in keeping with the "world-view" of the peasantry. In order to support this process, the neutrality of the state would need to be ensured as, in the past, this position has too often been violated by the ruling party in order to appease one section or another for political purposes. Above all, although easier to say than to do, a procedure has to be evolved whereby religion is separated from the polity, i.e. is constrained strictly within the "private domain" (Rex 1991).[1] A dispassionate appraisal of the contemporary nation–state suggests that, without a serious attempt to address these issues, the society faces the prospect of escalating levels of factional conflict with the "real" catalyst being socio-economic inequalities concealed by religious, cultural and ethno-nationalist modes of discourse.

Notes

1. Rex's paper evaluates the "two domains" thesis with regard to the accommodation of ethnicity in a multi-cultural plural society.

References

Dang, S. 1988. *Genesis of Terrorism*. New Delhi: Patriot.

Dasgupta, J. 1975. Ethnicity, language demands, and national development in India. In *Ethnicity: Theory and Experience*, N. Glazer & D. P. Moynihan (eds), 466–88. Cambridge, Mass.: Harvard University Press.

Desai, A. R. 1981. *Social background of Indian nationalism*. Bombay: Popular.

Dutt, P. 1970. *India today*. Calcutta: Mansa.

Kaul, A. 1987. Synthesis in Kashmir. *Kala Sarovar* **1** (2).

Kaul, J. 1973. *Lal Ded*. New Delhi: Bharti.

Matto, A. 1991. *Reform movements and social transformation in India*. New Delhi: Reliancs.

Peter, R. 1991. *Ethnicity and Integration: Political Rationalities*. Seminar on Ethnicity and National Integration, Gandhian Institute, Varanasi, India.

Rex, J. 1991. *The Political Sociology of a Multi-cultural Society*. Seminar on Ethnicity and National Integration, Gandhian Institute, Varanasi, India.

Rudolph, 1988. *In pursuit of Lakshmi*. Oxford: Oxford University Press.

Singh, Y. 1983. *Modernization of Indian tradition*. New Delhi: Thompson.

Chapter 9

The dialectics of theory and research on race and ethnicity in Nigeria

L. Adele Jinadu

Introduction

In the context of Nigerian scholarship it is relatively easy to assess the salience of the two central concepts, namely "race" and "ethnicity". The former, intensely problematic as it is (Montagu 1969, Miles 1982, 1989, Rex & Mason 1986) tends to dominate analyses in societies polarized in terms of perceived phenotypical differences, usually skin colour. Hence, in the USA much debate surrounds the issue of the "colour line" (Allen, in this volume, and Farley & Allen 1987). Similarly, in Britain (Ratcliffe, in this volume) sociologists have tended to focus on the differential positions of indigenous "whites" on the one hand and "South Asian" and "African Caribbean" people on the other. Apartheid in South Africa makes it almost inevitable that "race", as loosely defined here, is seen as the key concept.

In Nigeria and much of West Africa, however, the absence of settler-type colonization has meant that these societies are, in this narrow sense, relatively homogeneous. Nor surprisingly, therefore, "ethnicity" rather than "race" is generally seen as the key delineating factor. The questions addressed in this chapter, then, are twofold. How much has empirical research on ethnic relations in Nigeria contributed to theory formation and, per contra, how have theoretical insights enlightened the research process?

The relationship of empirical research to theory

To answer this question, one must explore, necessarily somewhat briefly, the nature of the relationship between empirical research and theorizing, especially the epistemological implications of any presumed relationship between the two sets of activity. It would be a mistake to see this relationship as unproblematic. Much depends, for example, on what we mean by "empirical research" and "theory".

Some would argue that empirical research seeks to produce the evidence or experience on which science as scientia (or knowledge) is founded and constructed. It requires, in other words, the gathering, processing and cumulation of information or data which is then validated by, and shared among, a community of scholars. However, this is a grossly simplistic view. It is actually a far more complicated process that involves questions of methods and methodologies, of what is or is not acceptable data and of how and what inferences may legitimately be drawn from the data.

A theory, on the other hand, is in Abraham Kaplan's (1963: 294) view "the symbolic dimension of experience, as opposed to the apprehension of brute facts". It is "the device for interpreting, criticizing, and unifying established laws, modifying them to fit data unanticipated in their formation and guiding the enterprize of discovering new and more powerful generalizations" (ibid.: 295).

In a generalized way it seems that empirical research is ultimately bound up with theory-formation, providing in other words the material out of which ("middle range") theory is built. One implication of this is that empirical research via the replication of previous research provides the opportunity to test the validity of general laws, and leads to the "building block" view of sociology criticized so effectively by C. Wright Mills (1959). Less controversial is a view that sees the theory/research interface as complex and dialectical.

Kaplan (1963: 57–8) has talked of an "empirical-theoretical continuum", arguing that "no observation is purely empirical – that is, free of any ideational elements – and no theory (in science, at any rate) is purely ideational". This turns partly, among other things, on whether one is aiming for what has been prescribed as grand theory or middle-range theory and whether one proceeds to build such theory through inductive or deductive reasoning.

Much depends on what empirical research is intended to achieve. Discussing the behavioural movement in political science, Leys (1969: 5) for example, referred to its "particular way of pursuing research, quite alien to British traditions, by looking for facts to illuminate a theory rather than the other way round". But he also referred to the "procrustean" approach to empirical research 'in which the researcher brought to the field a set of theoretically derived hypotheses to be investigated in relation to appropriately selected facts . . . " (ibid.: 8).

There are two important points to make here, however. First, empirical research should not be confused with methodology, in the specific sense of technique or the scientific method (Kaplan 1963: 19). Secondly, in the sense of the two kinds of activity used here, it is important to bear in mind Leys' (1969: 8) admonition that "empirical research and general theory-building are essential to each other". The issue, in this latter view, is therefore not whether empirical research influences theory in race and ethnic relations, but whether and how they interact and affect each other. It is to an examination of this interdependence of empirical research and theory in the area of ethnic relations studies in Nigeria that I now turn.

Nigeria as a case study of the linkages between research and theory

Nigeria is a plural society; the term "plural" being used here in a special sense to denote what some have referred to as "deeply divided" or "ethnically split" societies. In such societies political conflict is waged along essentially ethnic lines. Belgium, Sri Lanka, India, the Netherlands and the former Yugoslavia, come to mind as further examples of such plural societies. It must be pointed out, however, that ethnic differences need not generate political conflict. They only give rise to such conflict when set within a particular type of social or plural diversity.

The term ethnicity refers to identity affiliations based on primordial attachments such as common language, religion, culture or caste. Ethnicity (or ethnic relations) as an aspect of political process in Nigeria is therefore about ethnic group relations, although, as some have pointed out, such groups need not be homogeneous (Nnoli 1978: 5). For example, each of the three largest ethnic groups in the country – the Hausa-Fulani, Yoruba and Igbo – is also made up of substantial numbers of sub-ethnic groups (see Odetola 1978: 165–6, where 29 sub-ethnic divisions are identified among the Hausa-Fulani, 12 among the Yoruba and 32 among the Igbo).

A number of questions flow from these basic demographic data. For

Table 9.1 Ethnic composition of Nigeria.

Ethnic units	Estimated population	Estimated percentage
Hausa-Fulani	15,370,000	29.0
Yoruba	10,800,200	20.0
Igbo	9,180,000	17.0
Tiv and Plateau cluster	4,860,000	9.0
Ibibio and Semi-Bantu	3,240,000	6.0
Kanuri	2,484,000	5.0
Edo	1,784,000	3.3
Idoma-Igala-Igbirra	1,404,000	2.6
Ijaw	1,083,000	2.0
Bororo Pastoral Fulani	957,000	1.5
Nupe	682,000	1.2

Source: Based on data from T. O. Odetola, *Military in Nigerian Politics*, New Brunswick Books, 1978, 165–8.

example, how have relations between these various ethnic groups been explained? In what way has a priori theoretical reasoning influenced empirical research on "ethnic politics in Nigeria"? In exploring these questions one must take into account not only the value position that informed the approach of the researcher but also the way in which this influenced the formulation of problems to be investigated.

All of this clearly has an important bearing on the research "findings" and on how the task of theory formation is conceived and executed. Disciplinary backgrounds have also influenced the nature of research, although the theoretical and methodological eclecticism, which the behavioural movement in political science encouraged, has tended to lead, at least among political scientists, to a multidisciplinary approach to the study of ethnic relations in Nigeria and elsewhere in Africa.

The study of ethnic relations in Nigeria has passed through a number of phases, reflecting changes in the country's political status as well as changes in fashions and trends in the social science research agenda. For much of the colonial period the study of ethnic groups and ethnic relations was carried out by missionaries and cultural and social anthropologists whose interest was mainly cartographic. Much of this was not informed by explicitly theoretical considerations, the research being largely ethnographic in form and relying heavily on participant observation as a technique. What primarily emerged from such studies were profiles or biographies of ethnic groups – their histories, cultures, languages, laws, customs, and so on.

Much of this was useful in facilitating colonial rule. For example, in some cases research data had a direct influence on the policies of the colonial administration. Indeed, as I have pointed out elsewhere, the raison d'etre for the creation of the West African Institute of Social Research at the University College, Ibadan, Nigeria in 1950 was social and applied anthropological research geared to facilitating colonial administration and social control, especially at the local level (Jinadu 1986). This development was preceded by the creation of specialized institutions in Britain for the study of "native" peoples in the colonies (Mabogunje 1982).

In this way we can characterize the origins of ethnic studies in Nigeria and in other parts of the British empire in Africa. However, the final decade of colonial rule in West Africa, which roughly spans the decade between 1950 and 1960, witnessed a shift away from cartographic studies of individual ethnic groups that located them in their communities, to studies which broadened the focus to their social and political relations with other ethnic groups (in the context of competitive urban and national politics).

This shift was due partly, as studies by Dugbaza et al. (1974) in the case of Ghana, and by Onoge (1973) in the case of Nigeria have shown, to the failure of social anthropology to transcend its colonial origins and preoccupations. The shift also coincided with the growing interest in African area studies by North American researchers and scholars who brought with them quite different methodological and theoretical concerns from those of their British predecessors.

The ethnic mosaic of the USA, highlighted by the political impact of ethnicity (and race) in urban, state and national politics, was a factor which readily predisposed US researchers to turn to ethnic politics in Africa to test the cross-cultural, cross-national validity of theories of race and ethnic relations based on data drawn from their own country. For them ethnic groups were more than simply anthropological collectivities.

Indeed the growth of area studies in the USA in the immediate post-Second World War period was linked to the need to develop social science theories which took account of, and were applicable to, the non-Western, non-European world. It was against this background that US scholars increasingly turned their attention to research on race and ethnic relations in Africa, the Caribbean, Latin America and Asia. Indeed it could be argued that the strategic need of the (US) state for a better understanding of these regions of the world as it pursued its hegemonic global interests also fed this nascent academic pursuit.

The next phase of the study of ethnic relations in Nigeria and elsewhere in Africa was therefore characterized by a preoccupation with theoretical and methodological questions. An initial concern was to explain the relationship between urbanization and modernization and its impact on ethnic relations. This investigation drew upon the rich stock of sociological theory then available, especially that which equated development or modernization with increasing complexity and functional differentiation. The argument (or hypothesis) deriving from this can be formulated in the following way.

The modernization process leads to urbanization. The urban centres thus created will attract individuals from various ethnic groups, inducing them to leave their villages in search of jobs. In this way, newly developed towns will become "melting pots" with cross-cutting ties increasingly weakening the "pull" of ethnicity or at least making it more ambiguous as a determinant of social relations. Thus, in his study of Africans in an urban community on the Northern Rhodesian Copperbelt, Epstein (1958: xii) refers to "interdependence between all sections of the population, whose interaction make up the social system and keep it working". As a result, Epstein further observed "the African in the town is involved in a variety of sets of social relationships, many of which perforce cut across tribal lines" (ibid.: 232).

The assumption underlying this argument is that the process of detribalization so described is a sine qua non for the political integration of the new nations of Africa. The logic of modernization would increasingly make ethnicity fall into desuetude in Africa. Ethnicity, therefore, is seen as something dysfunctional to, inherently antagonistic to, or even incompatible with, "modernization".

But what the theory reflects, more than anything else, is an inadequate and highly ethnocentric, interpretation of the process of social change in Europe and North America. It wrongly assumes, for example, that ethnicity or tribalism had been swept aside by industrialization and urbanization in these regions of the world and that the "modern" Europe or America was "detribalized". To the extent to which African societies were "follower-societies", the same process or development was seen as being replicated in Africa.

This was one theoretical perspective which informed empirical research on ethnic relations in Africa in the 1960s. But to what extent has the work of researchers informed this theoretical formulation? The assimilationist perspective that underlay the detribalization thesis has been exposed as a form of ideological mystification, providing neither a true picture of the salience and persistence of ethnic differentiation in Europe and North America nor a valid account of the dynamics of social relations in post-colonial Africa. It simply did not reflect empirical reality on the ground. The claim that urbanization weakens ethnic ties runs, we would argue, counter to data which strongly indicate not only the persistence, but also the progressive intensification, of "active" ethnicity even in urban centres.

This theoretical reformulation of the relationship between ethnicity and urbanization was based on the analysis of data collected during research into ethnic relations in urban centres. The work of Abner Cohen (1969) on the Hausa community in Ibadan, Western Nigeria, then the largest city in Nigeria, readily comes to mind in this respect. This particular community, according to Cohen, is a politico-religious one, most of whose members are engaged in the long distance trade in cattle and cola between the North and South of the country. Their domination of this trade is maintained by a high sense of ethnic solidarity and cohesion in that it facilitates the exclusion of their Yoruba hosts.

Based on this ethnographic data, Cohen suggests that rather than leading to detribalization, urbanization is conducive to retribalization, which he claims is:

> a process by which a group from one ethnic category, whose members are involved in a struggle for power and privileges with the members of a group from another ethnic category, within the framework of a formal political system, manipulate some customs, values, myths, symbols and ceremonials from their cultural tradition in order to articulate an informal political organisation which is used as a weapon in that struggle (1969: 2).

The concept of retribalization enables Cohen to situate ethnic relations in a conflict or competitive situation over access to, and control of, scarce resources. It also suggests a conception of ethnicity as a focus for conflict around which (ethnic) groups assert and emphasize their ethnic identities and exclusiveness. This ethnic assertiveness amounts to a moral imperative. But why does urbanization lead to retribalization?

Cohen's answer is that this is because

> ethnicity is essentially a form of interaction between culture groups operating within common social contexts. It is for this reason that the

phenomena of ethnicity are so dramatically evident in the cities in both developing and developed countries. Here the division of labour is usually highly advanced and the struggle for resources, like employment, wages, housing, education and political following is intense.

Data collected by other researchers of ethnic relations in Nigeria have confirmed this reformulation. Melson and Wolpe (1970) and Nnoli (1978), for example, have pointed to the salience and persistence of ethnicity in Nigerian politics, although their concern extended beyond viewing and explaining ethnicity primarily in socio-cultural terms. But does this reformulation necessarily suggest that the data on which the detribalization thesis was based must be rejected and with them the thesis itself?

One answer is given by Epstein (1968: 228–9):

> There is of course an explanation of these divergences of viewpoint which will at once spring to mind. Over a continent marked by wide regional differences . . . it is clearly to be expected that there will be a wide range of variation in the process of urbanisation itself . . . But a further possible explanation is that the divergent views . . . are correct in themselves, but represent only a partial view of that situation; they are an expression partly of ambiguities in the concept of tribalism itself, partly of ambiguities in the emerging social system of the town.

The problem thus touches on the vexed question of the usefulness of case studies as a strategy for theory formulation; and also whether social phenomena, time-bound and culture or situationally specific as they usually are, embody an inherent uniqueness which means that they are not readily amenable to generalization.

This debate marked another phase in the study of race and ethnic relations in Africa. But the recent focus on what has been described as "ethnic revival" or "ethno-nationalism" has shifted the theoretical debate beyond explaining the relationship between urbanization and ethnicity. In retrospect the debate appears to have been an excessively academic one. What was needed was a theoretical approach which, avoiding psychocultural and structural-functional explanations of ethnicity, located it in the context of the material forces that gave rise to it and in reaction to which it is manipulated. Such a theoretical approach would require a methodology and data of a quite different kind. What was lacking was, according to Nnoli (1978: 17), a willingness "to investigate rigorously the impact of the nature of the socio-economic and political structures of society on the emergence and persistence of ethnicity". Moreover, there was a need to move from micro- to macro-sociological analysis, something which social or political anthropology was, perhaps, inherently incapable of doing.

Nnoli's own study proceeds on the assumption that "we cannot fully comprehend the ethnic phenomena in Africa without an adequate understanding of its historical origin and objective economic basis" (Nnoli 1978: 21). This requires a focus on the class basis of ethnicity since "the ethnic formation is a historical entity. It encompasses and penetrates all social formation including class structures, and, in a certain sense, it is a spatial framework for class relations and contradictions" (ibid.: 20).

With this materialist theoretical framework, Nnoli locates the origins of ethnicity in Nigeria in colonial racism and shows how what he describes as the "ethnic ideology" is used to mask the exploitation of local resources by ex-colonials. He also explains how the various ethnic factions of the Nigerian petit-bourgeoisie have used ethnicity to advance and protect their class identity. According to him, "the struggle of the various regional factions of the petty bourgeoisie and comprador bourgeoisie for the division of the national wealth contributed to the emergence of contemporary ethnic identity, feeds on it, and is masked by it" (ibid.: 277-8).

In this way the politicization of ethnicity or rather the ethnicization of politics in Nigeria is related to the process of class formation and class political behaviour. Although his concern was primarily with the study of Nigerian political parties, Richard Sklar (1963) has made the same point with respect to the manipulation of ethnicity by the emergent petit-bourgeoisie to advance their class interests. What this theoretical formulation has brought to the fore is the conjuncture of ethnic and political consciousness, their socio-economic roots and the rationality of the petit-bourgeoisie in mobilizing ethnic consciousness for their politico-economic ends. This needs some further elaboration.

While closely linked to the retribalization thesis, this theoretical formulation, as was indicated earlier, shifts the analysis of the connection between ethnicity and modernization beyond concern with the progress of urban migration and resource competition. This is reflected in the focus on the rôle of the state and class political behaviour in structuring ethnic relations. Put differently, the concern here is not with urban migration and resource competition as such. Rather, it is with the mediatory or catalytic rôle of the state and the emergent class structure in shaping ethnic relations in a polity going through a process of social change.

The theoretical implications of this perspective are clear enough. First,

171

the colonial and post-colonial state is actively involved in the process of class formation and the politicization of ethnicity. Nnoli (1978), for example, has stressed the indelible effect which state policies in colonial and post-colonial Nigeria have had on ethnic relations, in structuring the composition of, and the relationship between, the various ethnic factions of the petit-bourgeoisie, and in shaping differential access to public goods (e.g. education, employment, housing, etc.) by ethnic groups; that is, in regulating what is often referred to as "the spatial diffusion of modernization" (Bates 1983: 15).

For these various reasons control of, or rather access to, state power becomes a life-and-death matter since it is bound up with ethnic group advantage and the ability to use the instrumentalities of the state to advance ethnic and class interests. This is why in Nigeria, for example, party politics, often drawn along ethnic lines, have tended to be a zero-sum affair even when there appeared to have been some elite consensus or accommodation on regulatory mechanisms and rules for managing both intra-class and ethnic cleavages (Jinadu 1985).

Data drawn from other African countries support this interpretation of the intersection of class and ethnic political behaviour and the rôle of state policies in shaping, directing and intensifying ethnic conflict. In their introduction to a collection of papers from a seminar on ethnicity and public policy in Africa, Rothchild and Olorunsola (1983: 3–4) observe that:

> although the specific configurations of class/ethnic power distribution differ widely from country to country, there is a general tendency for the new men of power at the centre to use state instrumentalities to regulate the activities of the society in terms of their distinctive class interests . . . [T]hese state institutions may not prove sufficiently effective to allow them full scope for their organizing activities, but the intent to utilize the state as an instrument of sectional direction nonetheless remains.

A second theoretical implication of the perspective utilized by Nnoli relates to how the state is to be conceptualized in Africa, especially in the context of the interrelated processes of class and ethnic formations. It obviously rejects the liberal notion of the state as a neutral force whose raison d'etre is not only to reconcile various interests but also to aggregate the various demands on it into policies designed to advance a public or national interest. An alternative theoretical formulation arising from the perspective modifies the Marxian notion of the state as an instrument and condi-

172

tion of class domination.

This modification identifies the acquisition of political power as the modality for the acquisition of wealth. Economic power, and with it class relations, rest on the acquisition of political power. This is why the capture of state power is so crucial to the process of class formation in Africa and why ethnicity is manipulated to facilitate or ensure this. This reformulation is well captured by Sklar (1979: 537) when he asserts that in much of sub-Saharan Africa, "class relations, at bottom, are determined by relations of power, not production".

A third theoretical implication of the perspective is the need to focus on the rôle of "ethnic leaders" (who are essentially drawn from petit-bourgeois elements) in mobilizing ethnic consciousness and utilizing it for political ends. Ethnicity in this view is a political resource wielded by these ethnic leaders as they compete among themselves in the political and economic market-place. Ethnic conflict, then, revolves around the hegemonic rivalries of these petit-bourgeois elements.

The rôle of ethnic leaders in utilizing ethnicity to regulate political conflict and to maintain and promote intra-class accommodation has been well-documented in the case of Nigeria. Nnoli has shown that "as a result of their success in ethnic politics, the privileged classes now occupy political and economic positions of power and status in the inherited colonial structures. Therefore, they have an objective interest in maintaining the ethnic pattern of activities and the imperialist structures both of which are inimical to inter-ethnic harmony" (1978: 228).

This intra-class accommodation is also reflected in the adoption of a federal system of government. Writing of the Nigerian political class, Sklar (1967: 527) has observed that they "had a formula for peaceful development . . . It preserved the full regionalization of all political organizations capped by an agreement among regional leaders to respect the political status quo and share the fruits thereof on an equitable basis".

My own work (Jinadu 1985) has sought to show that Nigerian federalism has always reflected attempts by the country's emergent political class to regulate political conflict along ethnic lines by disaggregating constitutional authority between two levels of government – federal and state or regional. I have argued, in effect, that this constitutional disaggregation of political power became increasingly consociational in nature over the years.

This was indeed a strategic device to broaden the ethnic base of the emergent political class in order to resolve contradictions arising from

173

existing patterns of domination and authority. In short, federalism and consociationalism in Nigeria are responses by ethnically-based petit-bourgeois leadership to contradictions in the structure of ethnic relations in the country (ibid.: 72–3).

Implications for theory and research in comparative ethnic relations

I have sought in the previous section to indicate developments and shifts in theoretical formulations on the nature and character of ethnic relations in Nigeria over a thirty-year period. I have indicated the theoretical presuppositions which have influenced empirical research on ethnic politics in Nigeria and how various scholars have sought to explain ethnic relations in the country. It would not have been easy (nor arguably would it have been useful) to completely separate empirical research from theory in order to determine their causative influence on each other.

More appropriate for my purpose has been Kaplan's notion of an "empirical-theoretical continuum". It is, moreover, useful to bear in mind that, consciously or unconsciously, our choice of a research problem – the questions we pose in trying to understand and solve it and the methodologies we adopt in the process – are all fundamentally subject to our orienting cultural gestalt or cognitive maps. This has a theoretically predisposing character to it, no matter how much we might attempt to remain "detached" or value-neutral in our research.

The selective use of data to arrive at or challenge theoretical formulations about certain dimensions and manifestations of ethnicity in Nigeria should have been obvious from the foregoing analysis. While it can be argued, therefore, that the accumulation and analysis of such research-grounded data has added to the stock of theory in ethnic relations, theory has nonetheless, as I have tried to show, perhaps more implicitly than explicitly, affected research and the gathering and interpretation of data in two ways.

First, it has done so by directing researchers to what to look for, providing a framework within which the research problem is to be formulated and organized. For example, the detribalization thesis draws upon a particular theory of the relationship between some aspects of the universal process of social change and ethnicity. For those who utilized that theoretical perspective, their "research" was little more than a ploy to provide

174

further confirmation of a relationship already "observed" in other cultural contexts.

The inadequacies surfaced not so much from problems inherent in the data, but more from the orienting theory guiding the formulation of the research problematic. This is what may be described as the ideological element in the research enterprise. As has been demonstrated by the critique of the modernization school in its study of African politics and society, this ideological "trap" can all too easily result in ethnocentricity or cultural bias.

Secondly, theory has influenced research in the sense that decisions about what data to look at (or for) are themselves not independent of the theoretical framework within which the research effort is cast. "Facts" in the social sciences are, by definition, ultimately a product of "social process" and therefore require a "social" context for their interpretation. To say this is to affirm that one element of this social context is the ideological.

If it appears that the argument being developed here contradicts the "empirical-theoretical continuum" approach which I have already advanced, this is probably because of the conceptualization of that continuum. For, on my understanding of what Kaplan means when he articulates this notion, the relationship is a dialectical one in which the activities cannot be easily separated. To quote again "the human being is himself an instrument of observation and requires, like all other instruments, a theory for its proper use . . . In short, the line between the observational and the theoretical is differently drawn according to the purposes and contexts of our reconstruction of the logic-in-use" (1963: 58–9).

Conclusion

I wish by way of conclusion to indicate some of the comparative dimensions of theoretical work on ethnic relations in Nigeria. For if ethnicity has assumed global dimensions then we need to isolate common elements which make for cross-cultural comparisons. That way, too, the task of theory-formation in this field will be advanced. No less important for purposes of constitutional reform are policy measures for dealing with ethnicity that can emerge from such comparisons.

Starting with the relationship between urbanization and ethnicity, the process of retribalization which Abner Cohen observed in Nigeria has been found to operate in a similar fashion in, for example, the USA. In the concluding chapter of his book (Cohen 1969) he documents in some detail the cross-cultural, comparative utility of his theoretical formulation of the retribalization process in both North America and the Caribbean. Michael Parenti (1967) and a number of other scholars have noted the existence of the same phenomena in the US, highlighting in particular how it is reflected in voting behaviour, and in occupational, housing, recreational and associational patterns.

If we take another dimension of ethnic relations in Nigeria, exemplified in Nnoli's work, its implications for comparative ethnic relations, are once again not difficult to discern. The reference here is to the effect of state policies in shaping ethnic relations and access to public and non-public goods and services by ethnic groups. A useful theoretical formulation for comparative purposes can be found in some of the writings of Hechler (1975, (with Levi) 1979). The argument is that the politicization of ethnicity, reflected in the emergence and ideology of ethno-regional movements, is a reactive process which is due to a shared awareness of relative deprivation. This is indeed one effect of capitalist industrialization. The social, political and economic inequalities between ethnic groups, created consciously by state policies, provide part of the explanation for the rise and appeal of ethno-regional movements in contexts as diverse as Western Europe, North America, Asia and Africa.

Another dimension of research on ethnic relations in Nigeria, which has cross-national comparative implications, is the focus on the rôle of what I call the political class (the nascent petit-bourgeois element) in mobilizing ethnicity for political purposes. The work of Anthony Smith (1981) has tried to place this phenomenon in a comparative perspective. "Ethnic" intellectuals, finding themselves competing for jobs and opportunities in bureaucracies with intellectuals from other (ethnic) groups find it useful, or are even forced, to manipulate their ethnicity.

Thus Smith (1981: 134) argues that 'besides providing a new bureaucratic arena for their career and status aspirations, the historic or ethnic community, suitably transformed into the active "nation", resolves the cultural identity crisis of the intelligentsia, places them at the head of an alliance with other aspirant strata, and breaks down their social isolation from the "people", with potentially revolutionary results'. Van den Berghe (1981: 188) has also argued with respect to consociationalism that it is a form of political engineering which generally depends on this manipulation of ethnicity to advance the class interests of ethnic political leadership.

A further implication of all this relates to the rôle of comparative public policy in dealing with ethnic inequalities and conflicts. After all, one reason for undertaking research and developing theory in ethnic relations is to mitigate some of the deleterious effects of ethnicity. It would be useful to conclude by noting briefly some policy issues which have been raised with respect to the dialectics of ethnic relations in Nigeria.

First, there is the political question of the best form of government for facilitating ethnic harmony; referred to in Nigeria as "unity in diversity". The Nigerian civil war posed this question in concrete terms. The range of options has varied from federalism to confederation to consociation to devolution. In view of the disintegrative potential of ethnicity for the nation-state this is no easy choice to make. The second policy issue is about the fundamental substructural changes that have to be effected to reverse socio-economic inequalities among ethnic groups created by historically-determined state policies. Related to this is the efficacy or appropriateness of what have been described as affirmative action-type policies – proportionality, reverse discrimination and similar compensatory measures – as ad interim measures to mitigate the effect of the inequalities.

References

Bates, R. H. 1983. Modernization, ethnic competition, and the rationality of politics in contemporary Africa. In *State versus ethnic claims: African policy dilemmas*, D. Rothchild & V. A. Olorunsola (eds), 152–71. Boulder, Colorado: Westview Press.

van den Berghe, P. 1981. *The ethnic phenomenon*, New York: Elsevier.

Cohen, A. 1969. *Custom and politics in urban Africa*, London: Routledge & Kegan Paul.

Cohen, A. (ed.) 1979. *Urban Ethnicity*. London: Tavistock.

Dugbaza, G., T. M. Aidoo, S. Adjabeng 1974. The rôle of social anthropology in sociology syllabus of Cape Coast University. *Ghana Journal of Sociology* **8**, No. 2, & **9**, No. 1.

Epstein, A. L. 1958. *Politics in an urban African community*. Manchester: Manchester University Press.

Farley, R. & W. Allen 1987. *The color line and the quality of life: the problem of the twentieth century*. New York: Russell Sage Foundation. (pbk edn, New York: Oxford University Press, 1989).

Hechler, M. 1975. *Internal colonialism: the celtic fringe in British national development, 1536–1966*. London: Routledge & Kegan Paul.

Hechler, M. & M. Levi 1979. The comparative analysis of ethnoregional movement. *Ethnic and Racial Studies* **2**, No. 3.

Jinadu, L. A. 1985. Federalism, the consociational state, and ethnic conflict in Nigeria. *Publius: The Journal of Federalism* **15**, No. 2 (Spring).

Jinadu, L. A. 1986. The institutional development of political science in Nigeria: trends, problems and prospects. *International Political Science Review*.

Kaplan, A. 1963. *The conduct of inquiry: methodology for behavioural science*. New York: Harper & Row.

Leys, C. (ed.) 1969. *Politics and change in developing countries*. Cambridge: Cambridge University Press.

Mabogunje, A. L. 1982. Profile of the social science in Africa. In *Social structure and public policy in the developing world*, L. D. Stifel et al. (eds). Lexington, Mass.: D. C. Heath.

Miles, R. 1982. *Racism and migrant labour*. London: Routledge & Kegan Paul.

Miles, R. 1989. *Racism*. London: Routledge.

Mills, C. Wright 1959. *The sociological imagination*. Harmondsworth: Penguin.

Montagu, A. 1969. *The concept of race*. London: Macmillan.

Nnoli, O. 1978. *Ethnic politics in Nigeria*. Enugu: Fourth Dimension Publishers.

Odetola, T. O. 1978. *Military in Nigerian politics*. New Brunswick: Transaction Books.

Onoge, O. 1973. Counterrevolutionary tradition in African studies: the case of applied anthropology. *Nigerian Journal of Economic and Social Studies* **15**, No. 3.

Parenti, M. 1967. Ethnic politics and the persistence of ethnic identification. *American Political Science Review* **LXI**.

Rex, J. & D. Mason (eds) 1986. *Theories of race and ethnic relations*. Cambridge: Cambridge University Press.

Rothchild, D. & V. A. Olorunsola (eds) 1983. *State versus ethnic claims: African policy dilemmas*. Boulder, Colorado: Westview Press.

Sklar, R. L. 1967. Nigeria politics in perspective. *Government and Opposition* **2**, No. 4.

Smith, A. D. 1981. *The ethnic revival*. Cambridge: Cambridge University Press.

Chapter 10

Community and ethnicity in Israel: interrelationships of theory and practice

Devorah Kalekin-Fishman

Introduction

This essay will trace Israeli conceptualizations of community and ethnicity, and show how they relate to state/nation-building processes. As both have been the subject of general theoretical debate within the social science literature (including Chapter 1 in this volume) the arguments will not be repeated here. Suffice it to say that "community" and "ethnicity" typically symbolize two distinct approaches to social analysis; the former, in various guises, referring to integrative forces; the latter signalling grounds for segregation, and often conflict.

Our concern essentially will be to focus on the political dilemmas that make issues of community and ethnicity problematic, and their interweaving with the linguistic code that governs public discourse. It will then be possible to outline prevailing approaches to theory and research as they appear in the Israeli literature since 1948, the year in which the State was founded.

Political dilemmas of the State

The establishment of separate states for Jews and Arabs in what had been the territory of the British mandate in Palestine was affirmed by UN vote on 29 November 1947. Although the motion was rejected by the Arab leadership, Israel declared its independence when the mandate ended on 15 May 1948. This was the signal for the start of a war between the fledgling state and neighbouring Arab countries. In the course of the conflict, and immediately after it, many Arabs living in the mandated territory were constrained to migrate (Morris 1989). At the same time, large numbers of Jews were pressed to leave neighbouring states and immigrate to Israel.

According to the Declaration of Independence, Israel is a Jewish state, conceived primarily as a solution to the social and political problems of a dispersed, though well defined, collectivity. Since "all Jews are responsible for one another" they constitute a Gemeinschaft (community) by definition. The historical territory to which Israel laid claim was the Promised Land, in which it would be possible to realize for Jews institutionalized communal living.

The Declaration also asserts, however, that Israel is a democratic country in which freedom, tolerance, and brotherhood are the rule, and discrimination on the basis of religion, race, or gender is forbidden (Medzini 1979). Democratic ideals are presumed to be the foundation of a civil society that can accommodate various cultures. And indeed, the political entity that is the State of Israel includes citizens with allegiances to non-Jewish groups; including, notably, the Palestinians. Somewhat paradoxically, Israel embodies a modern universalistic solution to the "traditional tragedy" of the Jews. Nevertheless, in excluding Arabs from true social membership, Israeli society structures minority positions particularistically (Turner 1986).

Ethnicity is at once the source of political dilemmas and part of the social fabric. When the State was founded, the notion that Jews whatever their countries of origin, constituted a solidary entity, was both a moral and a political imperative. There was an urgent need to provide a haven for refugees from the holocaust, and a promise of physical safety for Jews who might undergo persecution in other parts of the world (Eisenstadt 1954). The Law of Return enacted in 1950 specified poignantly that Jews "belonged", and accorded every Jew the right to make a home in the Jewish State (Medzini 1979). Despite this, about two-thirds of the world's Jews live outside Israel (Israel 1988) and the present Israeli population is, in ethnic terms, highly diverse.

By exploring approaches to ethnicity in both popular discourse and the sociological literature, we will be able to assess aspects of civil identity formation in Israel.

Conceptualizing community and ethnicity: the Israeli code

Several different ways of interpreting ethnicity stem from the "social facts" published by the Central Bureau of Statistics (CBS). The Israeli preoccupation with state/nation-building is reflected in CBS usage for specifics of identification, and various boundaries are drawn between Jews and members of other groups. Nationality is recognized as "Jewish" or "Non-Jewish" (Israel 1988); a differentiation of communities which is now acknowledged as legitimating a separate Palestinian nationality.

Religion is another key source of differentiation. The current Israeli population of approximately four-and-a-half million, is described as 82 per cent Jews, 14 per cent Moslems, 2.3 per cent Christians, and 1.7 per cent Druse and others (ibid. 1988). This format, also a long-established custom in Islamic countries (Shipler 1986), is reinforced by the social order. Israeli citizens do not have the option of dissociating themselves from religious groups. Nor, furthermore, is there room for a fine-tuning of religious affiliation. Personal status throughout life – at birth, marriage, divorce, and death – is defined according to the customs of some recognized religion. Each such religious establishment is monolithic. In Judaism, for example, the only approach that is sanctioned (i.e. officially recognized) is Orthodox Jewry. The rights of non-Jewish sects are monitored by political agreement and protected by the State. Differences then, are, specified by religion and can only be eradicated by religious means.

Religious categories are reinforced by political distinctions. All Jewish men and women are conscripted into the armed services at the age of eighteen. Druse men, too, are recruited for military service, while Christians are not. A subtle distinction is drawn between groups of Moslems whose styles of life differ. Because of their unique knowledge of topography and their skills in navigation, Bedouin are often inducted for military service in special units. Among other Moslem groups, on the other hand, there is no conscription, and volunteering is not usually encouraged.

A single religious term binds all the Jews together socially and politically, so differences among Jews are recognized and summarized in terms of geography. In 1987, more than 37 per cent of the Jewish population of Israel were overseas-born (Israel 1988: 3), and this proportion has been rising due to an accelerated rate of in-migration from Ethiopia and the USSR during the 1980s.

The Statistical Yearbook does not present a detailed listing of the 100-plus countries of origin; instead, it refers simply to continents. Apart from those born in Israel, Jews are classified as born in "Asia-Africa" or in "Europe-America". In the relevant tables, the "Israel-born" are further distinguished according to "father born in: Israel [or] Asia-Africa [or] Europe-America" (e.g. ibid.:Table XXII/3, 605). However, the reference to continents is quite loose: "Europe-America" includes most of the countries of the British Commonwealth, and, depending on the frame of reference, "Asia-Africa" may or may not include Turkey, Greece and Bulgaria.

Usage effectively constitutes a typology of communities; the higher status "Western" or "Ashkenasy" Jews, on the one hand, and the lower status "Eastern" or "Sephardi" Jews, on the other. Those who are presumed to have arrived from "modern" societies in "Europe-America" are not usually designated by their community affiliation (Hebrew: eda, plural: edoth); but those who are associated with "traditional" countries of origin in the Middle East, Africa, and those born in Israel but whose ancestry is traceable to Spain, are all assigned to "edoth". There is, thus, a Yemenite "community", a Maghreb "community", and an Iraqi "community" but no Polish or French or South African "eda"; giving rise to its perception as "racial" (at least in a "North-South" sense).

In addition to the classification by religion, non-Jews are often listed according to their mother tongue under the plural heading of "minorities". Official documents therefore present non-Jews as a collection of small groups rather than as members of distinct nationalities. This gives the impression that demographic ratios in the region are reversed within the borders of Israel. It is an ideological device that minimizes the long term significance of minority groups to the Jewish State.

Despite the concern with origins, the term "immigration" is not in common usage. Depending on the country to which one moves, it is a problematic experience for Jews. Jewish in-migrants "ascend" to the country and are "absorbed", while out-migrants "descend". The physical metaphor derives from the Old Testament and is used in the media as well as in government documents. It is the only term available in colloquial discourse and remains unchallenged in social science research.[1] In-migration (ascension) per se reflects glory on the individual migrant. Out-migration is recorded and interpreted as a sinful act: it is an admission of a personal failing and a demonstration of disloyalty to the state and to one's fellows. Non-Jews, however, are not classified according to countries of origin, nor are their movements into or out of the country registered in the Yearbook.

Further demographic classifications locate people in urban or rural enviroments and specify the particular type of rural setting. Villages (k'farim) belong to non-Jews; Jewish villages are categorized according to their economic organization as: kibbutzim, moshavim, and moshavoth, or, collectively as the "working settlements". In this way, rural populations are allocated according to "tribal" affiliations.[2] These are the commonsense distinctions used when reporting voting patterns, the perpetration of criminal offences, and the distribution of employment and social welfare projects (Arian 1981, Greenberg 1979).

These classifications are echoed in "high" and "popular" culture. Literature and literary criticism focus on shifts in conceptualizations of community and ethnicity in a search for clues as to the impact of society on an individual's life. The issue is of central importance because, under the metaphor of "ascent", migration is a constant feature of the social structure. The possibility of a foreign national consciousness having been internalized by "ascending" Jews is vigorously denied. Insofar as possible the tension between participation in the institutionalization of a political entity (the State) and carrying into one's daily life a national culture that was nurtured in an "other" political system is consistently treated as a non-subject (cf. Lithman 1987: 92).

Contemporary social discourse and news media presentations use parallel imagery, with two topics – Arab-Jewish relations and immigration – consistently high on the agenda. The distinctions of ethnicity and community are part of a vocabulary that is "taken for granted". The formalized categories appear in the badgering and swearing of street slang and in popular music, "racialized" imagery attributes "irresponsibility" to Arab minorities, and the fields of entertainment and sport are replete with references to the "types" of populations that constitute performers and audiences (cf. Regev 1990).

It is important to point out that although there are Jews and non-Jews who vary in terms of skin colour, the category of "race" in this phenotypical sense is never used officially. In academic research as well, the possible impact of "colour" on social processes is a non-subject. Popular discourse departs from official terminology, however, to disclose quasi-racist sentiments and attitudes; in it "colour" is shorthand for the conflation of morality, class and ethnicity. Evil people are depicted as having "a black heart". Manual labour, as well as those aspects of an occupation that are routine and taxing, are regularly referred to as "black". Those of European background frequently talk about the members of non-Western communities (Jews as well as Arabs) as "black"; as implied above, these groups are characterized by negative personality traits, such as irresponsibility (mirroring forms of racialized discourse in, for example, the UK and USA).

Theory, methodology and empirical research

Sociological theory has implications which straddle science and practice. Even if only implicitly, theories of social structure necessarily invoke questions of political significance. In a society that prioritizes state/nation-building, both the agenda and discourse of social science will be geared to presenting constructs of "nationhood" and "belonging".

Nomenclature (as discussed above) provides a key to understanding research on Israeli minorities and on migration. The theme of most concerned with Arabs or Palestinians is contestation; leading to conflict-theoretical interpretations of majority-minority relations. As will be shown later, however, there is little systematic attempt to develop theory, as researchers tend to focus on surveys measuring inequalities in the degree to which Jews and Arabs have access to resources (cf. Al-Haj 1991, Nakkara 1985).

Migration, being closely intertwined with national ideology and goals, has led over the last four decades to hundreds of research reports on the ways in which immigrants from different countries have been "absorbed" in "the greater society". Doyen of these "ascension" studies, and prime exemplar of the Israeli structural-functionalist school, is S. N. Eisenstadt. Others, such as Smooha (1978), use pluralist theory to examine cleavages based on religion, ethnicity, and community. Yet others ground their analyses in various forms of "conflict" theory (Rosenfeld 1979, Swirski 1979).

At the time of the mass Jewish immigration in the early fifties (when the population of Israel doubled in three years), Eisenstadt, then a young sociologist who had studied with Parsons at Harvard, was the leading figure in the Department of Sociology and Anthropology in the Hebrew University, Jerusalem. He conducted a research seminar devoted to issues of "ascent and absorption" and publications from it appeared in the then new Hebrew language journal Megamoth [Trends]: Behavioural Sciences Quarterly. This work remains a dominant influence on contemporary studies of community and ethnicity.

As partisans of the revivalist-traditionalist ideology which governed the definition of collective goals and means in the new state, sociologists provided a functionalist interpretation of the collective being forged by this uniquely constituted people. Sociological discussions of immigration, community and ethnicity shared a mode of discourse with the political sphere. From the start however, their work highlighted some of the inherent contradictions in the approach. In the analysis of community and ethnicity there are significant inconsistencies that do not concur with the concatenated structure of the theory or with the functionalist commitment to explanation in terms of systems of relations.

The theoretical framework locates and relocates people in statuses/rôles attached to functions that insure societal continuity and stability. Taking eufunctioning of society as a given, the researchers draw conclusions about ostensible malfunctioning caused by factors "outside" the system of relations. Thus there is a misalliance of form, content, and the approach to explanation. Boundaries between analysis at the level of the system and analysis at the level of the individual personality are not clearly delineated (cf. Kaplan 1964). Israeli functionalists provide hierarchical explanations for social process. Description of society is undertaken with macro-statistics, while explanations are formulated in terms of depersonalized micro-behaviours. The sociologists involved tended to emphasize the deviancy of elements, individuals who "wilfully" detracted from the effectiveness of the system.

A review of the studies carried out during the first years of the State illustrates these inconsistencies. The studies are described as having found that 'the dispersion of immigrants within the absorbing country is positively correlated with (a) the formation in their countries of origin by the immigrants of new primary groups culturally oriented toward the new country; (b) mutual identification and cultural and educational compatibility between immigrants and old inhabitants; (c) strong interdependence in the economic and political spheres; and (d) conditions under which economic development keeps pace with the influx of immigrants, or the immigrants do not constitute a significant numerical problem' (Eisenstadt 1954: 259).

The first three presumably theoretical conditions are in fact a description of the policy and operation of the Zionist movement. In encouraging Jews to make the "ascent" to the new state, or, before 1948, to the state-soon-to-come-into-being, the Zionist movement organized potential immigrants into groups. The understanding was that these would stay together and turn into support groups in the new country. Both before and after their "ascension", the pioneers were familiarized with the accepted ideology. This was a set of beliefs rooted in the cultural heritage of the veteran members of the movement, Jews from Eastern Europe. In the new home, the General Labour Union (the Histadruth) was the arena in which economic and political interdependence was fostered. The Histadruth provided immigrants with jobs, insured a fair wage, and organized communal health care. In addition, the Histadruth was the training ground for most of the key politicians in the new government. As an organization with resources in production, distribution, and policy-making, it could "disperse the labour force as needed".

The theoretical analysis goes beyond empirical findings in taking cognizance of the fact that immigrants may "constitute a numerical problem". That is to say the pace of economic development may turn into an objective difficulty for the state and for the individual immigrant. Only here does the "theory" threaten to cast doubts on the viability of "absorption" in relation to the macro-system.

The insistence that immigrants forget their origins and adopt the social conventions and norms of the country of in-migration led to some paradoxical conclusions. In their research sociologists cite findings which suggest that the less involved the Jews had been in the non-Jewish community in their countries of origin, the more likely they were to develop group solidarity and cohesion. On the basis of their analyses of the veteran residents of the Yishuv, sociologists claimed that immigrants with an enhanced Jewish consciousness before their migration would achieve a high level of self-acceptance in their national identity. This outcome was deemed desirable. But when the real-life new immigrants expressed a desire to preserve their shared traditions, they were considered to be in danger of "failing to adapt" (Eisenstadt 1954). Thus, traits found to be positive in individuals from the absorbing society were devalued in members of "communities".

A consequence of these inconsistencies is a series of contradictory conclusions about what can promote effective adaptation. The errors of bureaucrats, who are likely to act unfeelingly, are interpreted as a technicality that can be solved with good will. When immigrants do not fill proffered rôles, they are held to be suffering from a weak ego or a lack of motivation, either of which signals emotional failure. Truly mature immigrants, it is claimed, will be ready to lower their levels of aspiration in order to fill available niches. Yet, immigrants who are asked to take on low-grade work and do so, are judged to lack social competence. The "ascent" into a "modern" (i.e. clever and progressive) society from a "traditionalist" (i.e. "backward") social context, is apparently only the first step in the long climb to becoming just like those who are established residents. The social context is functional, and therefore good; so the burden of proof is on the immigrant.

Yet Eisenstadt refers to the absorbing society (the Yishuv) as a solidary immigrant community. It "emerged" through the "interplay of the various waves of immigrants – mainly between the two World Wars – . . . *not until the eve of World War II* could it be said to be fully established". In his view, it was fortunate that "in its central and basic stratum – *with the partial exception of the Oriental Jews and of some 'refugee' elements from Central and Eastern Europe* – an almost complete institutional dispersion took place . . . among the various emergent institutional positions and strata" (ibid.: 47 [my added emphasis]). By dating the emergence of social structure a few years ahead of the mass migration of the early 1950s, and simultaneously minimizing the "malintegration" of some groups at that time, the description virtually discredits the newcomers.

The context of the early studies was a wider debate on the nature of the new nation. While philosophers, psychologists, and educationalists argued in Megamoth that Israel was becoming an "ethnic society", functionalist sociologists insisted that Israel was simply undergoing "social change". They were making the political claim, despite evidence of non-absorption in a growing "periphery", that ascending Jews were by definition not of different cultures and must therefore inevitably strive to become part of the Yishuv ("in-group"). Arabs were seen as constituting "complete, closed communities" with a distinct ethnicity. They were therefore *the* "out-group" and only anthropology, with its emphasis on tribal societies, was thought likely to have something enlightening to say about them (Ben-David 1952: 171–2).

Methodology is treated rather cavalierly in many of these early studies. Rudimentary statistics are cited in theoretical papers, but researchers also refer extensively to "impressions". Broad statements about traditionalism and modernity are based on surveys of the literature with no empirical justification for applying these terms to groups in Israel with different cultures.

Studies of stratification carried out during the late-fifties and the sixties constitute a significant advance in methodology. Editors of an anthology (Eisenstadt et al. 1970) devoted to analyses of intergenerational mobility, women's occupational status, aspirations of adolescents, professional status, marriage status, and so on, apologize for the almost exclusively statistical focus of the papers. They admit that there is too little research on 'style of life and group formations of various kinds' (ibid.: 5). A paper that does examine the formation of an association of immigrants from the same country of origin illustrates, however, that the judgmental orientation (towards immigrants' potential for adaptation) has not changed (Bar-Yosef 1970: 490–533).

As in earlier studies of immigration, trends in stratification are regularly explained in terms of cultural competence – shown in predispositions, ego-strength, and status symbols. Ben-David (1970: 380–1), for example, explains adaptive incompetence by reference to "mental imbalance". In the crisis of migration, he maintains, individuals undergo "regression . . . with an inability to plan for the future . . . [They develop] emotional dependence on the representatives of the absorbing society and [give evidence of] . . . immature behaviour generally [sic!]". Remedies are to be found in "primary relationships with individuals of the absorbing environment" although "a bureaucratic framework constitutes a serious obstacle to the creation of such [healing] relationships" (ibid.: 381). Case studies of Jewish communities ("edoth") are presented as evidence that people who "ascend" from traditional societies are likely to experience failure.

Two studies that reject functionalism, and question the exclusive emphasis on adaptation, are worthy of note. Cohen (1970) breaks new ground with his symbolic interactionist study of "social images" in a "development town" (an urban settlement in which most of the residents are new immigrants). And, dating from 1959, Rosenfeld's study of "The Arab Village Proletariat" describes stratification in terms of an uncompromizing historical analysis of class relations.

Community and ethnicity are explored in the first book from the Israeli Sociological Association in its series Studies of Israeli society (Krausz 1980); but although it boasts of a new approach to research in ethnicity, both the preface written by Eisenstadt (ibid: 1–4) and the "Review and Overview" by Weingrod approve of the prevailing approaches. According to Weingrod, "inevitably, the issues of absorption, assimilation, and stratification have centred upon contrasts between the European and Middle Eastern segments of the Israeli population . . . " A provisional summing up of these "classic" issues is to his mind, essentially the contribution of the new volume (ibid: 10).

There are, however, important departures from the rule. Smooha and Peres (ibid.) find that society has to be called to task when the communities ("edoth") of "new immigrants", who had "ascended" in the 1950s still had not made a satisfying social adjustment by the 1970s. On the basis of a pluralist theory, they claim that society can create conditions in which every community will be able to realize its potential. In the one paper that deals with developments among Arabs (*the* ethnic group), Carmi and Rosenfeld link ethnicity with the formation of class relations. As pointed out above, the segregation of Jews and Arabs overrides all intragroup differences and the ghettoization of research on Arabs and Palestinians reflects this social structural reality (cf. the bifurcation of Australian research noted by Inglis in this volume).

Most of the sociological studies of minority groups come from researchers who are not members of the Palestinian, Arab, or Druse communities. Of the 30 studies of Arab society in an important anthology (Haider et al. 1983), only eight were written by Arabs, and four of these were by researchers who live and work abroad: Nakhleh (US) and Zureik (Canada). Indeed, between 1948 and 1976, less than 15 per cent of the country's research output on (Israeli) Arabs came from Arab citizens of Israel. Between 1977 and 1982, this figure rose to 20 per cent, and the 1980s witnessed a significant increase in the number of graduate theses and dissertations; with about a quarter of the research on Arab ethnicity now being undertaken by Palestinians based in Israel or in the occupied territories (Smooha & Saar 1991).

Anthropological research at times challenges the received wisdom, with parallels being drawn (say) with relations between black and white communities in the USA (Lewis 1980). The work of Emanuel Marx, for example, bridges the segregated conceptualizations of community and ethnicity. By studying relatively isolated communities, whether classified as "edoth" or as minorities, he describes the mechanisms of ethno-class formations. In one study, he explores in detail how inequitable access to resources affects both family relationships and the socio-political behaviour of relatively new immigrants in a new (development) town. In another, he traces the threats of modernization to the Bedoui way of life (Marx 1973).

There have been other challenges to theoretical orthodoxy. But one of them, conflict theory, was deemed to be appropriate only to societies "elsewhere", with the consequence that the literature was not translated into Hebrew or Arabic. Then, during the late seventies and the early eighties, an attempt was made by a group of anthropologists and sociologists at the University of Haifa to develop a systematic revisionist critique of theory and research in the area of "ascent and absorption". The group launched a modest journal calling on all those "interested in the social problems of Israel" to join them in attempts to analyze the "oppression, discrimination, alienation and deprivation" that are "inevitable in a class society". The editors of the new journal announced that they would be presenting a critical approach to theory, and called on social scientists to reject "positivistic and supposedly neutral" approaches. This constituted an abrasive challenge to the sociological community.

In the years 1978-1984, the Notebooks for Research and Criticism published studies about social processes that touched on various aspects of community and ethnicity. Basing their work on an examination of historical sources, researchers described anew the problems of Arabs in Israel and the treatment of "desirable" and "undesirable" immigrants. Other papers analyzed market processes, Israeli-Palestinian relations, the condition of Israeli women, and the field of education. Methodologically, the group insisted on the pertinence of macro-factors. They exploited statistical analyses to gain an understanding of process and structure, and related them consistently to historical antecedents and contemporary effects. In some cases there were direct statements about what constituted a "relevant" theory (Bernstein 1981, Kalekin-Fishman 1981, Kamen 1984, B. Swirski 1981, S. Swirski 1979).

Although the journal is no longer published, the challenge it posed was serious enough to be taken up by the functionalist school. Eisenstadt (1986), for example, has addressed the stubborn fact of "malintegration" by attempting to link macro- and micro-social phenomena. As before, however, social cleavages and individual prejudices are coupled and the revision fails to remove responsibility from the malintegrated "edoth". Moreover, his survey of events and policies concerned with "the ethnic problem" in Israel relates only to the Jewish sector; but in the "Recommendations for Research", inequalities and the way in which various cultural groups coped with them are recognized as "processes" in need of further study (ibid.: 36ff.). Eisenstadt now admits quite openly that "the development of the perception and definition of the problems of immigration and of the ethnic groups in Israel . . . the individuals involved and most active in such development – i.e. leaders, intellectuals and the like; and the considerations that guided them in different periods have not yet been adequately researched" (ibid.: 19). The recognition that intellectuals were not always perceptive is especially poignant in light of the affinity between the social science research he has advocated and official policy.

With the intensified ascent of new immigrants in the 1980s (from the territories of the former USSR and Ethiopia) research on "ascent and absorption" has been given a new lease of life. Sociological studies of these groups examine family structure, occupational patterns and political orientations, along with success in Hebrew language acquisition and children's achievements in school. Anthropology-oriented case studies look at customs and habits as well as the "cultural baggage" of the newcomers. Although there is a charitable air to the investigations that is quite different from the impatience reflected in the studies of the 1950s, the kinds of questions asked are still those which test the immigrants' capacity to be absorbed (Horowitz 1989).

As we have seen, in sociological studies of community and ethnicity, it is often difficult to distinguish ideology from theory, and theory from action. The conflation places education at the heart of the project of sociology.

Education in Israel: action and policy

During the late 19th and early 20th centuries, ethnicity was the basis of most schooling, and schools cultivated ethnic distinctions. In the old Jewish communities of Jerusalem and Safed, traditional religious schools were the rule. The Christian and Moslem Establishments provided schools for their respective communities. Immigrants to Palestine from Europe preserved ties with their countries of origin and modeled schools on those of the "mother country".

But in the winter of 1891–92, a small group of teachers formed an association to promote and develop a Jewish State ideology and national solidarity. Instruction in Hebrew was to be a key vehicle for realizing this goal. By the 1920s the various versions of the Hebrew school were winning the day, and when the State was founded in 1948, 90 per cent of Jewish children between the ages of 8 and 14 were in such schools (Nardi 1945).

The Law for Compulsory Free Education was enacted in 1949, and in 1953 the Law for State Education placed responsibility for schools in the hands of Central Government (Medzini 1979). At the time, the Minister of Education explained that a unified system of education would ensure social integration. He pointed out that the communities of new immigrants (Asians-Africans for the most part) were "destitute" and "primitive". Only through centralization would the widely different Jewish communities learn to be one people (Dinur 1957). Separate schools for non-Jewish ethnic minorities were justified, however, by the geographical distribution of Arabic speakers and legitimated by the pedagogical principle that all children were entitled to instruction in their mother tongue. The option of mixed, bilingual education was rejected at the outset (Swirski 1990).

The School Reform Act of 1969, which heralded a major restructuring of the system, seemed to be fool-proof. Students from different socio-economic strata were to be enrolled in well-equipped district schools. The organization would promote social integration. In practice, however, the

Reform reversed the unified approach to education for nationhood as envisioned in 1953. To meet the needs of a diverse population – the "greater society", members of "communities" and the ethnic "minorities" – schools had to generate a variety of curricula.

Ethnicity, community and education:
research and theory

The work of sociologists highlights tensions between the state-generated cultural system as embodied in forms of schooling and curricula, and the concrete relations between groups competing for dominance in the socio-cultural system (cf. Archer 1988). We can see this primarily in the questions asked and the choices of research methods. In the following, I will refer to a few influential studies and evaluate their implications for theory development.

Statistical research demonstrates quite unambiguously that disparities among ethnic groups and communities are at best stable. In fact for some groups of Asians-Africans the gaps have actually widened (Schild 1989). Researchers have shown convincingly that the very policy that is supposed to help disadvantaged students effectively perpetuates disadvantage (Kahn 1977). Ability-streaming has increased achievement differentials, and the structuring of assessment has been shown to perpetuate stereotypical careers for children of different cultures both in school and beyond. Moreover, criteria for career guidance are implemented differentially in assessing students of "European-American" descent (Yogev & Roditi 1984).

Historical studies point to the roots of inequalities in different ways. From an "elite perspective", Ben-David (1989) argues that any increase in the enrolment of students from "traditionalist communities" is likely to pose a threat to the academic standards of universities (and thus concurs with the opponents of positive, or affirmative, action programmes in countries such as India and the USA). In a study of Jewish schools over a period of thirty years, Peled (1984), on the other hand, claims that the educational system has failed the children of non-Ashkenasy families, as evidenced by their being consistently featured among the under-achievers.

Questionnaire-based research has often focused on the extent of "integration". In exploring the social and educational values of children from different (Jewish) communities, Adar & Adler (1966) concluded that the children likely to succeed best at school are those who have been able to

192

internalize what they describe as the values of the "greater society". Other researchers have measured differences in religious and cultural practice, and have assessed levels of hostility to "out-groups" on the part of both teachers and pupils (e.g. Hoffman 1978).

Observational research has examined the explanatory power of "community" in ongoing school interaction, focusing for example on prosocial and antisocial behaviour in kindergartens, and levels of imaginative play. The relatively poor academic achievement in primary school of children from Asian-African communities is "explained" by their failure to devise such play effectively (Hertz-Lazerowitz et al. 1979).

Studies of schools in which Arabic is the language of instruction have looked at differences in the standards of construction and the availability of facilities between schools in Jewish and Arab sectors. Others deal with the degree to which alienation among parents, teachers, and students correlates with rates of educational failure such as dropout, low standards and importantly, the low prestige of the Arab school (Alimi 1981, Said 1984, Shahbari 1980).

In a comprehensive study of education for the Druse on the Golan Heights, Shamai (1990) discovered that the centralized state control of schools had the effect of turning pupils against their teachers. Schools were deemed unimportant by local educators because the "real" world of the ongoing (Syrian-Israeli) conflict over territory revolved around political loyalties.

The overall body of research confirms that there is a clear convergence of community, ethnicity, and structural deprivation. Findings are regularly used to show how education can be improved. In the "values" study mentioned above, for example, Adar & Adler (1966) recommend the solidary value system of the Yishuv as a fitting ideology for all groups within the State. In general, researchers of the Jewish system tend to support the provision of differentiated educational opportunities. But Arab investigators have a different agenda. Their primary aim is to attain access to the types of education prevalent in the Jewish sector and to gain the right to develop a curriculum of their own (Al-Haj 1991, Mar'i 1978).

What is lacking, though, is an explicit macro-social theory. In all policy proposals the conclusions from various pieces of research are collated and used in an ad hoc fashion; the result being a relatively unsystematic collection of findings. The tendency to restrict the agenda to "middle range" theorizations leads to explanations in the form of universal ahistorical laws, and education is thus raised to the level of a positivistic science. Moreover, the emphatically "practical" orientation hinders the development of systematic theory. This situation perpetuates the myth that the aims of education specified in legislation accord with the requirements of a progressive, enlightened society.

As the research findings show, however, Israeli education has undergone, and is undergoing, some changes. The disparities and infelicities that crop up in research with different foci reflect political struggles among ethnic groups in the socio-cultural system (Archer 1988). As a result, the cultural system is in practice steadily moving away from the governing ideology.

Community and ethnicity in Israel: an alternative view

One recent study involved a point-by-point institutional comparison of schools populated by children from "the greater society", from "communities", and from "minorities" (Swirski 1990). Israel, small as it is, "constantly cuts itself down" even further by using artificial systems of classification and thus finding reasons for debasing major components of society, communities and ethnic groups. Because of the "stubbornness" with which class mechanisms operate, people must clarify what education they really need and demand it. The study makes two very important points: first, it stresses the continued relevance of class-based divisions, and secondly it underlines the need for "empowerment".

Although somewhat peripheral to mainstream Israeli sociology, research from widely differing paradigms also contest explicit apologias for the status quo. The model of social structure that emerges in the literature deviates sharply from the ruling nation-state ideology. The uniform educational system envisioned by the founding fathers and mothers of the State, which was geared to transmit the dominant culture, has adjusted to the pressures of a multicultural, multiethnic population. Developments in the educational system can also be understood as the direct outcome (in education) of what the state deems to be its national needs. The state has, for example, to deal with inter- and intra-national economic issues, develop technologies that are suitable to a growing population, cope with political tensions in the region, and deal with the peculiar inter-religious conflicts which arise in an environment saturated with Holy places.

194

Conclusions

It was not substantive bias that led us to devote so much space to the issue of education. Rather it was the fact that education is clearly central to the avowed "nation-building project". But insofar as they deal with issues of nation/state-building, social scientists in Israel do not seem to confront theoretical dilemmas. In fact the lines are quite neatly drawn.

There are those who identify with the official ideology of the state; the impact of this functionalist theorizing being to legitimate the activities of government. "Unsatisfying" (immoral?) actions perpetrated in the name of government are assumed to be the deviations of individuals. Similarly, people who do not conform to the expectations of government-approved acts have themselves to blame for incompetence. Thus analysis in terms of functions and processes serves contradictory theoretical aims, and objectives that are contrary to the interests of individuals. Social scientists who identify with minority populations resort to conflict models: critical theory, theories of class relations or neo-Marxism in various guises.

The results of this theoretical bifurcation are clear. Research in the former genre, often supported by state funds, by simply performing "scientifically", fails to examine the status quo in terms of a comprehensive model of society. Adherents to the latter "camp" identify significant structural weaknesses in the educational system. Some call for a greater degree of community/ethnic empowerment: others for educationalists to be the leaders rather than the led (Yogev 1988). Still others reject the uncritical use of practitioners' terminology and monadic explanations of micro-experiences; arguing that inductive practice demands a reformulation of theory consistent with the data and a shift in the research paradigm (see Kalekin-Fishman, in progress).

As a democratic state, Israel is made up of a multicultural citizenry with civil rights. As a Jewish State, it cultivates its "traditional" religion, value systems, and a consciously shared history. This emphasis is part of the message of the schools, and as such, affects Jews and non-Jews alike. Ultimately, it may well be that the emphasis on differentiated rights in education will lead to a resolution of the dilemmas over national identity. By virtue of the fact that scientific discourse is allied with popular and political discourse, it has the power to demonstrate the nature of reality and take an active part in struggles for change.

Notes

1. In the story of Jacob and his sons, for example, there are repeated references to drought and hunger which cause people to "descend" to Egypt (see Genesis: Chapters XXIV–L).
2. In the framework of the Zionist organization, Jewish villages were founded on an ideological basis. In kibbutzim production and marketing are dealt with collectively. In moshavim, some aspects of production are conducted collectively, but each family also has the right to independent enterprises. The moshavoth were originally set up as residences for those who worked on lands owned by Baron Rothschild or Baron Hirsch. When these connections ended, the villagers became independent farmers. The Arab k'farim "just grew" in agricultural areas (see for example, Cohen 1970).

References

Adar, L. & C. Adler 1966. *Education for values in schools for immigrant children.* Jerusalem: School of Education, The Hebrew University. [Hebrew]

Al-Haj, M. 1991. *Education and social change among the Arabs in Israel.* Tel Aviv: International Centre for Peace in the Middle East.

Alimi, A. 1981. *Social relations of the Israeli Arab adolescents.* MA thesis: University of Haifa. [Hebrew]

Archer, M. 1988. *Culture and agency: the place of culture in social theory.* Cambridge: Cambridge University Press.

Arian, A. (ed.) 1981. *The elections in Israel – 1981.* Tel Aviv: Ramot.

Bar-Yosef, R. 1970. Voluntary associations as vehicles of integration and segregation. In *Integration and development in Israel,* S. N. Eisenstadt et al. (eds). Jerusalem: Israel University Press.

Ben-David, J. 1952. Ethnic differences or social change? *Megamoth* 3 (2): 171–83. [Hebrew]

Ben-David, J. 1970. Socialization in youth movements and social status. In *The social structure of Israel,* S. N. Eisenstadt et al., 457–81. Jerusalem: Academon.

Ben-David, J. 1989. Universities in Israel: dilemmas of growth, diversification, and administration. In *Education in a comparative context. Studies of Israeli society,* vol. IV, E. Krausz (ed.), 148–73. New Brunswick (USA) and Oxford (UK): Transaction.

Bernstein, D. 1981. "Come and grow with us" – women in the workforce and economic growth in Israel. *Machberoth L'mechkar ul'vikoreth* 7 (December), 5–36. [Hebrew]

Cohen, E. 1970. Development towns – the social dynamics of "planted" communities in Israel. In *Integration and development in Israel.* S. N. Eisenstadt et al.

Jerusalem: Israel Universities Press.

Dinur, B. Z. 1957. The law of State Education. In *Values, ways and means: problems of education and culture in Israel*, B. Z. Dinur, 26-40. Tel Aviv: Urim. [Hebrew]

Eisenstadt, S. N. 1954. *The absorption of immigrants: a comparative study based mainly on the Jewish Community in Palestine and the State of Israel*. London: Routledge & Kegan Paul.

Eisenstadt, S. N. 1986. *The development of the ethnic problem in Israeli society*. Jerusalem: Jerusalem Institute for Israel Studies, No. 17.

Eisenstadt, S. N. et al. 1970. *The social structure of Israel*. Jerusalem: Academon.

Greenberg, H. 1979. *Israel: social problems*. Tel Aviv: Dekel.

Haider, A., H. Rosenfeld & R. Kahane 1983. *The Arab society in Israel: a reader*. Jerusalem: Academon.

Hertz-Lazerowitz, R., D. Feitelson, S. Zehavi & W. Hartup. 1979. Patterns of social behaviour and social organisation in free play in the kindergarten. *Megamoth* 25 (2), 239-57. [Hebrew]

Hofmann, J. 1978. Changes in the assessments of national-religious images by Arab youth in Israel. *Megamoth* 24 (2), 277-82. [Hebrew]

Horowitz, T. (ed.) 1989. *The Soviet man in an open society*. Lanham, New York, London: University Press of America.

Israel 1988. Statistical Abstract, No. 39. Jerusalem: Central Bureau of Statistics.

Kahn, S. 1977. Discrimination against communities in teachers' assessment of their pupils. *Megamoth* 23 (3-4): 238-47. [Hebrew]

Kalekin-Fishman, D. 1981. Sounds and control: transmitting the concept of music in the kindergarten. *Machberoth L'mechkar Ul'vikoreth* 6 (June), 5-26. [Hebrew]

Kalekin-Fishman, D. Social worlds and sociological theories (in preparation)

Kamen, C. 1984. After the catastrophe: The Arabs in the State of Israel, 1948-50. *Machberoth L'mechkar Ul'vikoreth* 10 (December), 3-89. [Hebrew]

Kaplan, A. 1964. *The conduct of enquiry*. San Francisco: Chandler.

Krausz, E. (ed.) 1980. *Migration, ethnicity and community*, vol. 1: *Studies of Israeli Society*. New Brunswick and London: Transaction.

Lithman, Y. G. 1987. The immigrants in Sweden – a case of variation. In *Two ways of integrating immigrants: Israel-Sweden, 88-96*. A Report from a Seminar in Jerusalem/Stockholm: Regeringskansliets Offsetcentral.

Lewis, A. 1980. *Power, poverty and education*. Ramat Gan: Turtledove.

Mar'i, S. K. 1978. *Arab education in Israel*. Syracuse, NY: University of Syracuse.

Marx, E. 1973. Coercive violence in official-client relationships. *Israeli Studies in Criminology* 2: 33-68.

Medzini, M. 1979. *Documents of modern Israeli history*. Jerusalem: Ministry of Security. [Hebrew]

Merton, R. 1968. *Social theory and social structure*. New York: The Free Press.

Morris, B. 1989. *The birth of the Palestinian refugee problem, 1947–1948*. Cambridge: Cambridge University Press.

Nakkara, H. D. 1985. Israeli land seizure under various defence and emergency regulations. *Journal of Palestine Studies* **14** (2): 13–34.

Peled, E. 1984. Ideology and political power-producers of educational policy: outline of the policy for the education of disadvantaged children, 1940–1980. *Megamoth* **28** (2–3): 355–69. [Hebrew]

Regev, M. 1990. *Meaning, content and structure in the field of popular music in Israel*. Doctoral dissertation, Tel Aviv University. [Hebrew]

Rosenfeld, H. 1979. The class situation of the Arab national minority in Israel. *Machberoth L'mechkar Ul'vikoreth* **3**: 5–40. [Hebrew]

Said-Ahmad, M. 1984. *Dropping out of Arab primary and intermediate school in Israel*. MA thesis, University of Haifa.

Schild, E. O. 1989. Overview: a policy perspective. In *Education in a comparative context: studies of Israeli society*, vol. IV, E. Krausz (ed.), 10–17. New Brunswick (USA) and Oxford (UK): Transaction.

Shahbari, A. 1980. *The professional self-image of the Arab teacher*. MA thesis, University of Haifa.

Shamai, S. 1990. Critical sociology of education theory in practice: the Druze education in the Golan. *British Journal of Sociology of Education* **11** (4): 449–63.

Shipler, D. K. 1986. *Arabs and Jews: wounded spirits in a Promised Land*. New York: Times Books.

Smooha, S. 1978. *Israel: pluralism and conflict*. Los Angeles: University of California.

Smooha, S. & A. Saar 1991. *Bibliography of publications on Arabs*. Haifa: University of Haifa, Jewish-Arab Centre (mimeo).

Swirski, B. 1981. Battered women in Israel. *Machberoth L'mechkar Ul'vikoreth* **10** (December), 37–62. [Hebrew]

Swirski, S. 1979. Comments on historical sociology of the period of the Yishuv. *Machberoth L'mechkar Ul'vikoreth* **2**: 5–42. [Hebrew]

Swirski, S. 1990. *Education in Israel*. Tel Aviv: Breroth. [Hebrew]

Turner, B. S. 1986. *Citizenship and capitalism: the debate over reformism*. London: Allen & Unwin.

Yogev, A. 1988. Educational policy in Israel related to advancing students from weak groups of the population. In *Planning Education Policy*: Position Papers and Decisions of the Permanent Committee of the Pedagogical Secretariat, Ministry of Education, 175–205. Jerusalem. [Hebrew]

Yogev, A. & H. Roditi 1984. The counsellor as a gatekeeper: guidance of disadvantaged and privileged pupils by school counsellors. *Megamoth* **28** (4). [Hebrew]

Chapter 11

Nation, race and ethnicity in Poland

Antonina Kłoskowska

Methodology and the impact of techniques on research data

In sociological theory and practice there is a constant controversy and discrepancy between the exigencies of formalized research techniques and the complexity of the subject matter under study. This suggests the need for a multiple strategy resorting to methods more subtle but also inherently less amenable to strict empirical control. This dilemma was presented most clearly by Robert Merton (1957) in his consideration of the sociology of knowledge. The same tension between exact findings on trivial problems and less precise knowledge concerning important ones obtains in the domain of nation and ethnicity studies. The use of a multi-method approach or "triangulation" would appear, therefore, indispensable in view of the factual and axiological complexity of the subject matter.

Ethnic and national problems should be considered in several perspectives: historical, sociological (i.e. relating to social structure and its functions), culturological and anthropological-psychological. This necessitates the use of interdisciplinary co-operation and materials, even in what is essentially a sociological study.

The use of historical methods means two things here: not only resorting to past events and longitudinal studies but also using descriptive methods rather than a nomothetic approach aimed at the discovery of universal regularities and the formulation of general laws. The anthropologist's "thick description" (Geertz 1975) can be very useful here in the presentation of inter-ethnic relations. Special attention should be given to the use of personal documents, i.e. autobiographies, personal diaries and the recorded recollections of migrants involved in a transformation of their national milieu, or people living in polyethnic regions (especially in borderland territory). This type of material has been very popular in Polish sociology since the seminal publication *The Polish peasant in Europe and America* by W. I. Thomas and F. Znaniecki (1918).

Content analysis may be included in the category of more formalized methods, especially if applied to mass media, but in the domain of literary fiction much can be done, not through quantitative but through less "formal" analysis. Survey methods, questionnaires and scales on the other hand are widely used in the study of ethnic attitudes, national stereotypes and social distance research (Allport et al. 1953, Klineberg & Lambert 1959).

The present author used such methods on national attitudes and constructs of Polish children (Kloskowska 1961, 1962). The more formalized the instruments of research (e.g. closed questions) the more unambiguous the results obtained. But the very clarity of the results is deceptive. "Race" and "national relations" belong to the realm of "sensitive" issues and accordingly the results of direct studies may be very much influenced by the research situation itself. However this problem can be alleviated by additional, less obtrusive techniques, and particularly by observation, projective methods, and the analysis of "cultural" texts produced and "consumed" by the population under study.

Direct questions on "national characteristics" invite stereotyped answers. The present author has observed that somewhat different descriptions of foreign nations were obtained by asking the subjects "What are they like?" – as in Klineberg's study – rather than asking: "What do you know about them?". In the study of national problems it is especially important to avoid questions which lead the respondent in a biased or non-neutral fashion.

Poland as a "testing-ground" for national and inter-ethnic problems

The First Polish Republic, comprising from the 14th century the Crown territories (i.e. western and central Poland) and the Grand Duchy of Lithuania, was a multi-nation country in which Poles, Byelorussians, Lithuanians, Ruthenians, Jews, Germans, Armenians and Tartars lived side by side. The Polish State, recovering its independence after the period of partition (1795–1918) lost two-thirds of its former eastern territories but the national or ethnic mosaic remained, albeit reduced in number. No less than one-third of the Second Republic's population was made up of "national minorities": about 16 per cent Ukrainians, 10 per cent Jews, 6 per cent Byelo-russians, 2.4 per cent Germans and 0.3 per cent Lithuanians (Tomaszewski 1985).

These ethnic or national peripheries represented a serious political problem. Each of the minorities was the subject of different attitudes and evaluations by those from the dominant cultural group. Ukrainians, Byelorussians and Lithuanians were accepted as autochthonous populations and their respective cultures regarded as mere regional variations of the national culture. As such they were positively evaluated as attractive folkloric additions to the dominant culture.

However, this attitude ran counter to the national aspirations of minority groups. Cossack and Ruthenian (later Ukranian) irredentism has exploded periodically since the 17th century, and the 19th and 20th centuries brought a real nationalist "awakening" of these minorities. In former times their upper classes were absorbed into Polish culture and enjoyed the privileges of Polish "democracy of the nobles". But the new intelligentsia of peasant origin tried to reject Polish political and cultural authority.

In the Second Polish republic (1918–39) this met with condemnation and repression. Most Poles could not and would not comprehend the force of social change and were reluctant to abandon the historical traditions of their powerful state, stretching as it did almost from the Oder to beyond the Dnieper, and from the Baltic to the Black Sea. The national aspirations of the eastern minorities were regarded as an outrage to this historical legacy. Poland, in the 16th century (comprising the Crown territories and the Grand Duchy of Lithuania) was linked by an intimate "personal" union, and as such can be likened to the United Kingdom. When Joseph Pilsudski, national leader and statesman of the Second Republic, protested that he was no Pole but a Lithuanian the opposition of the two identity constructs can be likened to those of "Welsh" and "English" – both "British" (at least from an English perspective).

To understand the state of Polish popular consciousness it is worth noting that the most venerated poem of (national) canonic Polish literature begins with the verse: "Lithuania, o my Fatherland" (Mickiewitcz 1834). In the 19th century there was a "Ukrainian school" of Polish romanticist poetry created by eminent writers but incorporating several folkloric elements drawn from their native region. "Lithuania" and "Ukraine" were regarded in these cases as regions of Poland, and even more: in the poem by Mickiewicz "Lithuania" is a symbol, a synecdoche, representing the entire country, i.e. Poland.

Clearly, however, this view was held solely by the dominant "nation";

no longer by the minorities. One more aspect should be considered: Poles in the eastern regions had for a long time been the masters, the gentlemen, the gentry. Ethnic Byelorussians, Ukrainians, and Lithuanians were peasants, and often servants. "The faithful Cossack", a mounted servant and bodyguard was a very popular character in 19th century Polish literary fiction. But the new national intelligentsia in the eastern regions rejected the subjugation of their respective countrymen to such rôles. The nationalistic attitudes of the Polish majority towards the eastern minorities could be likened to those of "traditionally minded" white Americans from the South to the Negroes; the latter being tolerated (and even liked) so long as they knew, and kept "their place" in the social structure. Another complication in the ethnic and national situation of Poland's pre-war eastern territories was provided by the active communist propaganda inspired by the Soviet Union, who aimed to incorporate Byelorussia and Ukraine into the Soviet state. Both the nationalist and the communist movements were harshly repressed by Polish local government.

Polish nationalistic attitudes towards the eastern minorities contained no explicitly "racial" elements, but there was undoubtedly a negative stereotype of the "blood-thirsty" Ukrainian. It was strengthened after the Second World War as a result of fierce fighting between Ukrainians and Poles in the former eastern territory under German occupation, and because of the active participation of Ukrainian units assisting the SS in the extermination of Jews. The anti-Ukrainian feeling was bolstered by inaccurate wartime reports, also implicating Ukranian units in the suppression of the Warsaw uprising of 1944. (It was in fact Russian-led units comprising various Soviet nationalities – the so-called Russian Liberation Army – who assisted the Nazis at this time.)

After the war Polish retaliation took the form of extremely harsh military repression of the continuing Ukrainian struggle. Then followed the deportation of the remainder of the Ukrainian population still living in territory belonging to the Polish State. (Most of the territory inhabited by Byelorussians and Ukrainians was incorporated into the Soviet Union under the Yalta agreement between the major powers.)

The German as archetypical outsider-stranger

The relations with Germans present a further insight into Polish national, or nationalist, attitudes. Poland's western frontiers, with a Slavonic population and culture, withstood the German impact much longer and more effectively than was the case with the southern Slavs. Despite some mixing of the populations due to German immigration a feeling of unease prevailed in Polish-German relations, as is evident even in the name given to Germans: Niemcy, i.e. the Dumb Ones, people not speaking the natural (our own) language (such was, at least, its popular interpretation).

The contrast between national relations in eastern and western Poland gives rise to a reflection on types of nationalism. A distinction is proposed between acquisitive and defensive nationalism. Polish nationalism in the east was mainly acquisitive, with the notable exception of Russian-Polish relations from the 18th to the 20th century. The term "acquisitive" does not necessarily mean "aggressive". Polish acquisitiveness in the east manifested itself successively in both the peaceful and aggressive variants. The other form, defensive nationalism, can also lead to aggressive measures, but this may be interpreted differently in axiological terms. It could be said that there existed a parallel between, on the one side, German acquisitive nationalism directed against Poland, and on the other, Polish acquisitive nationalism directed against her smaller neighbours. (The existence of such a parallel is not readily recognized by Polish historiography).

In the 19th century, however, with Poland partitioned by Russia, Prussia and Austria, Polish nationalism became defensive on all sides. According to many authors (e.g. Gellner 1983, Tiryakian & Nevitte 1985) the essence of nationalism consists in making claims on behalf of national sovereignty. Polish nationalism in those times claimed the right to its own national language, culture, national institutions, and finally to liberation and unification. It was not a national revival after several hundred years, as in the case of the Czechs, but an unrelenting fight against foreign powers. The national deprivation was resented strongly, and deprivation does not make nations magnanimous and just, any more than it does in the case of individuals.

Thus, in this period great sensitivity was evident in relation to the loyalty of national minorities. Indeed, claims had often remained unfulfilled because national or ethnic minorities had no practical interest in demonstrating loyalty to the national culture of subjugated former masters. On the contrary, it was rather surprising to find that there were numerous cases involving the assimilation to Polish culture of Jews, Austrians and German civil servants or their offsprings despite the political situation. (This would represent an interesting object of sociological research using autobiographical and biographical materials.)

Generally, however, 19th century nationalism in Poland turned most strongly against the major occupying powers, Russia and Prussia. The attitudes towards these nations differ slightly: Germans were generally disliked, Russians often despised as well. Twenty years of independence between the two world wars gave the Poles too little time to rid themselves of their defensive nationalism, and the Nazi occupation brought to a head anti-German feelings.

The character of the occupation, differentiating Poland markedly from the war situation in Western countries, explains (if not justifies) the harsh treatment of the German population in the territories incorporated into the Polish People's Republic after the war, following the Yalta agreement. The expulsion of Germans from these territories was accompanied by the eviction of Poles from the (more extensive) lands of the former Polish State ceded to the Soviet Union.

In general, the war strengthened for a long time the negative attitudes toward Germans, whom it was not easy to distinguish in wartime from the Nazis. This wartime image has been superimposed on the traditional folkloric and literary representation of the arch-enemy, the stranger. This position has been, at least indirectly, strengthened by official socialist propaganda, because of the absolute silence imposed on the rôle played by Stalin's Soviet Union in Poland's (and Poles') fate during the war (Dmitrow 1987, Szarota 1988). However, there was one factor which could prevent the totalization of negative relations towards all "Germanness" in Polish society; German culture. Even at the climax of the war Polish intellectuals were able and willing to distinguish the great symbolic heritage of Germans from war atrocities, and thousands of Polish students from outlawed clandestine secondary schools were studying German literature and philosophy.

An important event in the history of post-war Polish-German relations was the message of Polish bishops to their German counterparts, containing the memorable declaration: "We forgive and ask for forgiveness" (November 1965). This position was nevertheless hard to accept at that time for a section of the Polish population. As recent studies of public opinion show, the attitudes of Polish society reflect the actual political declarations and acts guaranteeing the security of Polish western frontiers. (There are also other shifts in the attitudes and stereotypes which will be presented later, as they have been the subject of sociological research.)

The Jew as an insider-stranger

Despite large scale German immigration into Polish territories going back
to the 13th century, and despite the high level of assimilation, Germans
have been regarded first and foremost as representatives of a foreign, external power. Jewish "immigrants", even after seven hundred years of residence, have been generally regarded as "strangers", albeit "insider" strangers. But this was a category different from Simmel's stranger who comes
and goes. They have lived among the dominant "nation", native but always
peripheral and secluded; often awakening distrust, fear, and sometimes
aggression.

Once again some historical comments are needed to account for this situation. Jewish immigration to Poland in the thirteenth and fourteenth centuries was triggered by the availability of vast lands depopulated by Tartar invasions. It was prompted, too, by the persecution of Jews in western Europe after the plague. In the 14th century this persecution amounted
almost to a holocaust. In Poland and the Ukraine Jews found favourable
conditions for their trade and craft activities; such activities being rejected
by Polish nobility as demeaning their social status and not accessible to the
peasants tied to the soil since the end of the 15th century. In this situation
Polish Jews enjoyed a large measure of local autonomy, but also on an even
larger scale, in the form of Jewish Parliament. Occasional acts of aggression against Jews grew with the so-called "Catholic reaction" of the 17th
century and the establishment of Jesuit schools with their intolerant, turbulent youth, but such acts did not exceed in harshness parallel events elsewhere in western Europe.

Arguably, though, the parallel situation lasted only to the end of the 18th
century. At that time the emancipation of Jews in the West was based on
the principle formulated by a French Enlightenment writer, Stanislas de
Clermont-Tonnerre, who stated that "the Jews should be denied everything
as a nation, but granted everything as individuals" (*Encyclopedia Judaica*
7: 151). Polish political writers proposed a similar regulation of the Jewish population but their plans had been thwarted by the partition of Poland.
The personal emancipation of Jews on Polish territories under Russian and
Austrian rule was not realized until the 1860s, and the expulsion of Jews
from some parts of the Russian Empire combined with their flight from
the (Russian) pogroms in 1905–7 resulted in the growth of the Jewish population within eastern Polish territories.

In France and Prussia at the beginning of the 19th century Jews were forced to relinquish outward symbols of their culture, to send their children to communal schools and to acquire the language of dominant nations. Preserving their religion and family values, they became less conspicuous, less like strangers and much more acceptable as fellow citizens to members of majority communities. This operation, enforced by administrative measures, was painful at the beginning, but subsequently drew the Jewish masses into the industrial and intellectual process which was the essence of the West's progress towards modernity. However, it lost the potentially rich contribution which could have been made by elements of traditional Jewish culture.

In the Russian Empire, and in Austrian Galicia, Jews were abandoned to their traditional way of life. By this time, the former Polish territories had the largest concentration of Jews anywhere in the world. The great centres of Talmudic studies had developed here. It was here also that the Hasidic movement, with its spiritual leaders drawing the faithful from other countries, was born. Here too, the Yiddish language came to maturity and gave us important literary works (from writers such as Sh. Ash, Sh. Aleichem and I. B. Singer). Pre-war Poland was also an important centre for film productions in Yiddish (Tomaszewski 1990, Zebrowski & Borzyminska forthcoming, containing an extensive bibliography in English, Polish and Yiddish).

However, the carriers of this rich, but mainly traditional, culture were separated from the dominant Polish culture. Their social formation was caste-like (Hertz 1961, 1988); entailing life "on the periphery" and breeding mutual distrust and animosity in relations with mainstream social and political groups. It was a phenomenon incomparable (in terms of scale) with the marginal manifestations of traditional Hindu, Chinese or Jewish cultures in some parts of large Western cities. In the period 1918–39, Jews constituted almost 10 per cent of Poland's population and between 40 and 80 per cent in many small towns in the Eastern territories. The estrangement of the core of this traditional group from the surrounding Polish, Ukrainian or Byelorussian milieu was aptly depicted by I. B. Singer (in, for example, *In My Father's Court* 1986) and by other Jewish writers. However, this does not account for all Polish citizens of Jewish origin. In the 1931 Census, 25 per cent of those professing Mosaic religion declared Polish nationality. Yet they were also regarded by many Poles as taking on the character of the traditional population of Jewish city districts and "shtetl" (a Jewish name for a small town with a predominantly Jewish population, or the Jewish quarter of a small town).

From the beginning of the 20th century influential right-wing political parties with pronounced anti-semitic ideology have developed. In the Second Republic their political "bogey" was the triad: Jews, communists and freemasons. During the great recession they blamed Jews for what was essentially a result of the country's general economic underdevelopment. They were opposed to assimilation policies and some of their views were not totally free from the influence of Nazi German ideology.

The paradox of history willed that some of the leaders of this nationalist movement risked their lives to save Jews from Nazi persecution during the occupation. Any assistance given to Jews in occupied Poland was punishable by death (Bartoszewski 1965, Kloskowska 1989). On the other hand, this did not necessarily change their nationalist ideology or their image of Jews as the main source of communist influence in Poland. This was the ideological brand of anti-semitism.

For the ordinary, less-educated person before the war Jews mostly represented the archetypal stranger; in fact the *only* stranger they would meet. In the small towns of eastern Poland Jews often outnumbered the Polish and Ukrainian population. This proximity led to some neighbourly contacts with positive results but separation and mutual distrust prevailed, mainly because of religion, differences in occupation, and disparities in customs and mores.

In the liberal and left-wing circles of inter-war Poland, on the contrary, there were close and friendly relations with intellectuals of Jewish origin: poets, artists, journalists and so on. There was no "Jewish problem" here, but there were admittedly very few Jews involved – at least in the sense of the "Ostjuden". The situation was comparable to that of Western countries with, perhaps, a greater stress on perfect assimilation, stronger attachment to mainstream culture, and the unquestionable loyalty of "converts". (Arguably, it was the price paid for conversion and the mechanics of conversion which raised the most interesting sociological questions.)

In the context of Polish history the problem of "race relations" can be posed only with respect to Polish-Jewish interactions. But is it a "race" problem at all?

Race, nation and nationalism in Polish sociology

As is well known, popular concepts of race are extremely vague and misleading. Early social and political theories of race, such as those of A. de

Gobineau and J. S. Chamberlain, contributed to further misunderstandings beyond the everyday commonsense level. They confused anthropological classification based on genetically determined somatic traits with the cultural characteristics of human groups.

If then there is any good reason to distinguish racist and national prejudices and attitudes as expressed in current opinions, either "race" should be defined in a way departing from the scientific, anthropological concept or the use of the term "race" by laymen should be disregarded as the indicator of their attitudes. As a third possibility the notion of "quasi-race" and "quasi-racism" could be introduced.

The significance of "popular" quasi-racism lies in the deterministic treatment of ethnic or national differences as sharply delineating human groups, precluding close and friendly contacts and the passing of individuals from one group to the other. A belief in unchangeable (because "natural") ethnic group ascription is the main criterion of "sociological" racism and is often linked with perceptions of race inequality. Always present is the demand for strict "boundary maintenance", i.e. social distance. Somatic indicators of race are not necessarily considered as important in such racist positions. What counts is the concept of ascription, predestination and inseverability of group bonds. Consequently, quasi-racism opposes any form of assimilation. Nationalists do not necessarily share this view; on the contrary, they may advocate forcible assimilation.

Nationalism, on the other hand, entails the over-generalization of group characteristics, an impermeability to empirical evidence contrary to national stereotypes, and, of course, in practice strong preferential attitudes towards one's own group. Only a thin line separates nationalism from quasi-racism in the above defined sense. And the line separating it from patriotism is also difficult to draw in many instances.

"Race" in sociological theory and research in Poland

In the late 1930s, when fascist movements with their racist ideology swept through Europe, Stanislaw Ossowski, a Polish sociologist, wrote a book entitled *Social bonds and the heritage of blood* (1939). The first part contained a refutation of racist social theories in the light of modern genetics and sociology. With rigorous objectivity the author presented the distinction between inherited cultural traditions passed on via the genealogical order, and the genetic causality conditioning some somatic human traits. The second part of the book applied to racism the concept of "humanistic coefficient" devised by Florian Znaniecki, and approximated a pheno-menological analysis. Ossowski examined the sources and functions of the myth of race, and how it impacted on intergroup relations. In this way, he analyzed the characterization of national bonds with deep insight. These bonds, being understood by people as "predestined" and "inseverable" acquired in the public mind a "quasi-racist" character. (Ossowski does not use this term but it fits his interpretation neatly.)

The first edition of Ossowski's work could not reach potential readers because it was destroyed in the first weeks of occupation, but two subse-quent editions (1948, 1956) exerted a strong influence on post-war gen-erations of Polish sociology students. This influence was strengthened by the criticism of racist theories contained in other sociology textbooks (Szczepanski 1961, Szczurkiewicz 1969).

This trend led to an interest in American anthropological studies of "cul-ture and personality". In fact, Polish sociology has been for a long time close to cultural anthropology because of the influence of Bronislaw Malinowski (social and cultural anthropology being not too rigorously distinguished). In the "culture and personality approach" of the F. Boas school and A. Kardiner's group, ample illustrations were found of the mutability of "human nature" under the impact of culture (Kloskowska 1969, Mach 1989a).

In empirical sociological research race was not a prominent object of study, given that "real" inter-racial contacts were very scarce for a long time in post-war Poland. However, in 1960 some data were gathered on the attitudes of Polish children towards Negroes in a research project or-ganized in association with the UNESCO group, headed by Otto Klineberg (Kloskowska 1962).

More recently (in the late 1980s), a survey was conducted involving a country-wide representative sample, in which social distance and race at-titudes were the main issues (de Carvalho 1990, Nowicka (ed.) 1990). The results confirm the degree of confusion in popular consciousness about concepts such as "race" and "nation". Over 80 per cent of respondents thought that Arabs, Negroes and Chinese do not belong to the same race as Poles. But to some extent Jews (47 per cent) and, even, Italians (24 per cent) and the English (24 per cent) were thought to be of different race. Only Slovaks were almost unanimously included in the "racial community" (89 per cent with only seven per cent exclusions). So race was for many people equivalent to nation, and nation was regarded as a cultural category.

Nations, nationalities and ethnic groups as objects of sociological research and theory in Poland

The preoccupation of Polish social sciences with national problems is quite understandable in the light of the previous discussion of historical background. In the 19th and early 20th centuries analysis of nationhood took the form of philosophical or historio-philosphical theories (as illustrated by the work of writers such as M. Mochnacki, J. Supinski, B. Limanowski, A. Gorski and A. Choloniewski). The relationship between nation and state was at that time the primary focus of analysis; this being justified by the prevalence of defensive Polish nationalism and the unfulfilled claims for national independence.

After the First World War "The Polish Peasant in Europe and America" provided a strong impetus to sociological studies of Polish emigration. Economic emigration has been a major national issue in Poland, as millions of Poles and their descendants live in western European countries and elsewhere. The so-called "old emigration", coming mostly from backward rural regions, led in host countries to ethnic communities strongly marked by traditional peasant culture. Problems of adjustment to their new social setting, the growth of new forms of national consciousness and readjustment following eventual re-emigration were the objects of sociological research. Collections of autobiographical material were subjected to analysis, and observational methods were used in various field studies (Chalaskinski 1936b, Duda-Dziewierz 1938, Krzywicki 1939). This type of research continued in the post-war period. A special Institute for Polonia Studies is attached to the Jagellionian University in Cracow; Polonia being the name given to the "old" emigration communities living mainly in the USA, Brazil, a coalmining region of France, and Westfalien (Kubiak 1980, Babinski 1979, Kapiszewski 1984 Markiewicz 1960).

The large number of Polish nationals living within Soviet territory (estimated at about two millions) were excluded from sociological studies for political reasons. Most were victims of deportation from Soviet Ukraine during the period of Stalinist collectivization or, during the Second World War, from the annexed former Polish eastern territory. Only now are they the object of studies emanating from "Eastern Archives" and other research institutions (see, for example, Wyszynski 1990). Interestingly, these studies have discovered persisting national identification, but in a number of different variants.

The post-war, mainly intellectual/political emigration could not be investigated by sociologists for obvious reasons – being politically a taboo subject. In contrast, the new wave of economic emigration prompted by the current situation has demanded considerable attention from sociologists (though the research results are not yet available).

But it is the great migratory movements caused by the war, and postwar, period which represent the principal object of sociological research on "national problems". Over six million Germans fled, were evacuated by German authorities or, most commonly, expelled by Polish authorities from former German territories within Poland. About 1. 5 million Poles were evicted from the territories of eastern Poland (incorporated into what was until recently the Soviet Union) and over two million Polish displaced persons and re-emigrants from the West were settled in their place (Markiewicz & Rybicki (eds) 1967). This situation, abounding in human tragedies, was a direct result of the war waged by Nazi Germany and the subsequent political decisions of the great powers.

From a sociological point of view this was a vast laboratory of new social forms and processes. The research carried out in 1945 by S. Ossowski with Jan Strzelecki and Stefan Nowakowski focused on the autochthonous Silesian population which had largely preserved its Polish ethnic character. Observation and in-depth interviews were the techniques employed. The resulting monographs were used by Ossowski for the elaboration of two types of social bonds: habitual national bonds related to the local private fatherland ("ojczyzna") corresponding to "la petite patriae" of J. Michelet, and national bonds related to the ideological fatherland, i.e. Michelet's "la grade patrie" (Ossowski 1946, 1947). This cultural theory of nation as mediated by the symbolic universe has played a major rôle in the further development of the sociology of nation in Poland.

He and his assistants' work (S. Nowakowski 1960) may also have had a practical dimension in that he focused attention on the faults and misdemeanours of local administrations. The heroic war-time defensive nationalism shifted during this period towards an acquisitive, aggressive and oppressive nationalism executed by socialist authorities. Soon after, in 1949, all sociological research and associated university studies were suppressed for nearly eight years.

Ossowski's theory of nation came close to the subsequent concepts of nation as a community of communication (Deutsch 1953, 1981) or an imagined community (Anderson 1983). His methodology was rooted in the humanities rather than in empirical quantitative sociology. But when, after the Polish October of 1956, sociological studies could be resumed, mass surveys and quantitative research were also developed in this field. Then again, it was not an exclusive form of approach in that J. Chalasinski continued his reflections based on Znaniecki's concepts and on autobiographical analysis (Chalasinski 1968).

For a long time empirical studies of national problems aroused political suspicions insofar as they threatened to make explicit unfavourable social attitudes towards the eastern neighbour. So it was easier to write about the new nationalisms in Africa (Chalasinski 1962) than about the Polish scene. Indeed, in 1975 the results of a study of the attitudes of students towards foreign nations were prevented from circulation (Wilska 1975). But in the 1980s, with the growing societal disquiet and the advances of the Solidarity movement the scene changed. Freedom to research followed in the wake of more general political change.

Systematic public opinion studies concerning attitudes to their own and to foreign nations have been conducted since 1975 by the Official Centre of Public Opinion Research attached to Polish Radio and Television. However, the results were not released and presented in a comparative format until 1988 (Jasinska-Kania 1988). It is not possible to decide whether such data are fully reliable because distrust, or at least reticence, on the part of respondents facing interviewers from an official institution could not be excluded for most of the time up until the political breakthrough of 1989. But most of the data are congruent with observations from other sources.

The data demonstrate a general tendency towards lower levels of hostility to other nations; for example, in 1987 16 per cent professed a dislike of Jews compared with 38 per cent in 1978. The two most often "liked" nations throughout the period have been Hungarians and the French. Most often disliked were Germans, but here too a considerable reduction in negative evaluations occurred during the decade (from 49 per cent to 35 per cent).

As contended before, surveys using large statistically representative samples and formal, pre-categorized questions leave many doubts as to the more subtle dimensions of national attitudes and relations. My own study of 200 children from Warsaw primary schools (Kloskowska 1988) showed that with each repeated question concerning the image of the Germans there appeared more positive traits than in the first description. The same effect was observed in my study about Negroes (Kloskowska 1962). So there is some lability in the expression of attitudes. and survey results should be analyzed alongside other data and their validity assessed in relation to the specific research context. This does not mean that the persistence of some opinions is to be denied. Stable opinions may be sustained by deep-seated national sentiments, by tradition transmitted through many channels, such as family, school, media, and so on; witness the description of Germans given by the children in answer to the first question: "What do you know about them?" In 1988, 40 per cent of answers related to the German invasion of Poland during the Second World War. In the 1959 research, children's descriptions of Germans concentrated on the traits of aggressiveness, but also on the war-time recollections of their parents. But a study from the Centre of Social Opinion Research (CEBOS 1990) among the adult population found that the most often mentioned characteristics of Germans were "hardworking" and "industrious". According to the opinion poll of 1990, average indices for Germans on the emotional attitude scale (ranging from +50 to -50) were -6 for the FDR and -11 for the DDR (Ziemer 1991). At the same time the dominant opinion was that Poland should intensify economic relations with West Germany.

It is the rôle of more detailed and subtle sociological studies to discover the foundations and functions of such evident cognitive dissonance and, perhaps, to seek a resolution of the dilemma rooted in the ambiguity of attitudes.

The European perspective

As is well known the movement towards European, and even global, unification co-exists in Europe and elsewhere with the revival of "national" aspirations and with the burgeoning political claims of "minority" ethnic groups and nationalities. In Poland, national and religious values and symbols played a major rôle in the struggle against the imposed socialist system and foreign political subordination.

Re-entering the capitalist system in the 1990s Poland is obliged to develop a modern industrial foundation for her society and at the same time to cope with the intellectual and ideological problems of postmodernism. In this situation it is necessary to reconsider many questions arising from the notions of nation, nationalism, "traditional" canonic culture and the challenge of cultural uniformity. This is one important aspect of contemporary sociological research and theoretical reflection (Jawlowska 1991, Kloskowska 1990a, b).

Other important fields, only now fully open to sociological investigation, relate to national minorities, border regions and cases of conflicting national identities. With the post-war change in state frontiers the number of minority populations in Poland was greatly reduced. In addition, the non-existence of minorities was declared official by the State. This made the research of these problems impossible; one of the rare exceptions being the study of the Lemk Ruthenian group (Kwilecki 1974).

Since the end of the 1980s, however, research centres have begun to work in Polish-German ethnic border areas – two Silesian research institutes (in Katowice and Opole), and the reorganized Western Institute in Poznan. There are many forthcoming, and some published, results (Mach 1989b, Sakson 1990). Studying the German minority and – more generally – the German-Polish border areas poses many complex sociological and socio-psychological problems: the motives behind changes of national identification, the multiple functions and Protean character of this identification and the effects of centre-periphery relations resulting from the change of national background due to emigration. (The latter is the case with recent Silesian immigration in Germany, this creating new problems of adjustment.)

A related area of sociological research focuses on Polish minority groups in the old Soviet Union and Baltic republics. Whether cut off by the post-war change of frontiers, or composed of the Polish nationals deported in the 1930s from Ukraine, they lived for a long time in complete isolation from Polish culture. Now they are experiencing a "national revival".

A special case for reflection is the present Polish attitude to the Jews, to Jewish culture and – within the same frame of reference – to anti-Semitism. However, the manifestations of anti-Semitism, though not very dissimilar to events in other countries (France, Germany, and Great Britain included), appear as particularly disturbing in the country which witnessed the holocaust, and they are regarded as such by a section of Polish society. A message from Polish bishops transmitted to the congregations of all Catholic churches in Poland on 20 January 1991, stressing the common sources of Christianity and Judaism, has been just one of the measures aimed at counteracting anti-Semitic attitudes. These appear to be decreasing (as was found in the studies quoted above) but they are revitalized occasionally, as the 1990 Presidential campaign propaganda showed.

For most Poles Jews are no longer "insider" strangers, close yet alien. They are simply foreign people, far removed in history and/or in space, neither liked nor disliked. On the other hand, for some categories of intellectual (mainly Catholic) and for young people (mainly students), Jewish culture and religion represent objects of much greater interest than at any period within recent memory. These interests are satisfied particularly by the Jewish Historical Institute in Warsaw. As to the special significance of some aspects of the Jewish national situation, I shall comment on this below.

As stated before, problems of nationhood take centre stage in the theoretical concerns and empirical research of Polish sociologists. But, at the beginning of the 1990s, the national scene is not free from ambivalence. After a period of national enthusiasm, even euphoria, the trend has been towards a deteriorating national self-image. Expressions of patriotism, or even chauvinism, alternate with self-deprecatory comparisons of their own country with the West.

Other sociological studies place Polish national problems within a broader European perspective. Several research groups are devoted to the question of European unification. They include, for example, a European research group organized by Jan Jershina at Jagiellonian University in Cracow, which has been in operation for several years, the Polish Division of the International Society for Universalism, headed by Janusz Kuczynski from Warsaw University, and the Polish Association for the Club of Rome, Institute for Political Studies at the Polish Academy of Sciences, directed by Edmund Wnuk-Lipinski.

A significant barrier to a European unity encompassing the "East" is presented by Polish-German relations. Poland has preserved, as a society if not a socialist state, her Western orientation and attachment to Latinity, Western Christianity and liberal values inherited from the Enlightenment; but animosity and distrust towards her closest western neighbour was an obstacle to the full opening of this frontier; and needs to be addressed by political and economic measures.

However, also of vital importance is intellectual activity bringing to the level of consciousness the real and imagined dimensions of past conflicts, and exposing existing mutual stereotypes to critical scrutiny. The first is fulfilled by a joint German-Polish commission of historians who have been working since 1972 on the analysis of school textbooks and the elimination of distorted nationalistic descriptions and the misinterpretation of historical facts. The second task falls to sociologists.

Since 1988, Richard Grathoff from the University of Bielefeld and the present author have developed a common research project: "The Neighbourhood of Cultures". The approach of the German group is grounded in phenomenological theory. The Polish group have used culturological, semiotic and anthropological approaches. According to the assumptions underlying our research and debates, symbolic culture which transgresses national borders and forms a common stock of cultural experience may contribute to the moderation of prejudices, and to the promotion of mutual understanding.

In a later phase the project has been broadened to include Poland's eastern neighbours: Lithuania, Byelorussia, Russia and Ukraine. In this context the traditional rôle played by Poland as a bulwark against the East (Tartars, Turks and Moscovites) can be reformulated as that of a bridge linking East and West. Among those conducting research on Polish-German and Polish-Eastern relations are: The Western Institute and the Eastern Institute in Poznan, the Silesian University in Katowice, the Opole Institute, and the Laboratory of Eastern Studies at the Institute of Political Studies (Polish Academy of Sciences). In addition, there are many voluntary societies establishing cordial relations across the frontier lines marking traditional national animosity.

The political dissolution of the Soviet Union in the early 1990s has created a new situation between Poland and her immediate neighbours. Independent Polish diplomacy seeks new regulations governing contacts with the now politically independent countries on both sides. These regulations are to replace the sham of "friendship by decree" imposed by the Soviet leadership on all socialist countries. The treaties with Germany on the one side and with Ukraine on the other signify a particularly radical breakthrough in neighbourly relations at the "official" plane. But changes in attitudes and popular stereotypes will require more time. Sociological research may not only monitor this change but may also contribute to its progress by bringing to the level of popular consciousness existing resentments and helping to seek a mutual understanding between groups harbouring age-old prejudices. The latter is of particular importance in Polish-Ukrainian relations.

In place of a conclusion

Zygunt Bauman in his book "Modernity and Ambivalence" (1991) has presented a penetrating analysis of the spiritual state of Western Jews living under the sway of German culture. They escaped the circumscription and parochialism of Eastern small town dwellers who lived their traditional culture, but they paid for it with the feeling of ambivalence and the state of ambiguity.

This description of the specific Jewish situation may be extended to cover the more general human condition. Intensified migratory movements, accelerated spatial and social mobility, and the intermixing of people accompanied by the propagation of ideas using electronic communications media; the growing number of personnel from international political, social and economic institutions commuting from continent to continent and no longer aware of the language of their thoughts and dreams, all of this poses the question of the rôle of national identification in the formation of personal, individual identity – the self. Should the European, or the world community, obliterate the problem of national identification and eliminate the question "Who Am I?" insofar as this is formulated in terms of an ideological affiliation to the great spiritual "patria" and emotional attachment to the narrow, private "patria"? Or will it be possible to realise Charles de Gaulle's idea of "L'Europe des patries"?

These are some questions to be considered by the sociologist of culture. National culture is a syntagm composed of selected elements from different paradigmatic symbolic systems of general character, such as language, religion, art, literature, and so on (Kloskowska 1992). In developed societies no such syntagm is built exclusively from its own ethnic resources. It is never completely isolated from universalized elements nor exempted from the possibility of individual additions. So, theoretically, it is possible to reconcile a high degree of universalization with the preservation of primordial bonds deriving from national or ethnic culture. Theoretically it certainly is, and the practice should quite properly be an object of sociological observation and investigation.

Epilogue

The victory of Solidarity in 1989 signalled, among other things, a full recognition of the existence of ethnic minorities. By 1992 there were no less than fifty organizations representing all the main ethnic groups.

This has not precluded incidents of ethnic violence or manifestations of nationalism on the part of extreme right-wing parties. But on the plus side there has been an unprecedented level of sympathetic interest in ethnic cultures and movements on the part of intellectuals, notably the so-called Catholic Left, which had paved the way even prior to 1989.

Sociological analyses using biographical material have traced the rebirth of ethnic awareness among the younger generation, uncovering occasional cases of "conversion", e.g. the conversion of Polish students to Judaism. But more characteristic are numerous inter-ethnic organizations and social agencies working towards inter-"national" tolerance and understanding, such as German Community "Understanding and Future", Poland-Ukraine Association, Foundation of the Borderland, "Poland in Europe" Foundation, and many others. Over thirty sociological institutes and groups are conducting research on inter-ethnic and inter-"national" relations. This clearly reflects a conscious paradigm shift in the intellectual and cultural climate in a period of sustained democratic development.

Note on nomenclature

Whereas in the West there has been (since the 1960s) a total rejection by social scientists, as well as by those previously so ascribed, of the term "negro", on the grounds of its linkages with outmoded "race" categorization/theorizing, this is not the case in Poland. The corresponding term "Murzyn", which probably stems from the word "Moor" does not carry with it pejorative connotations. In contrast, the favoured term in the West, "black", which translates into Polish as "Czarny", is seen as offensive.

References

Allport, G. 1954. *The nature of prejudice*. Cambridge, Mass: MIT.

Anderson, B. 1983. *Imagined communities*. London: Verso.

Bartoszewski, W. & Z. Lewinówna 1966. *Ten jest z ojczyzny mojej. (This one is from my Country. Polish help for the Jews 1939–1945)*. Kraków.

Bauman, Z. 1991. *Modernity and ambivalence*. Cambridge: Polity Press.

Babiński, G. (ed.) 1979. *Poles in history and culture of the United States of America*. Wrocław.

Bogardus, E. S. 1947. The measurement of social distance. In *Readings in social psychology*, E. L. Hartley & T. M. Newcombe (eds). New York: H. Holt.

Buchanan, W. & H. Cantril 1953. *How nations see each other*. Urbana: University of Illinois Press.

Bystroń, J. S. 1935. *Megalomania narodowa (National Megalomania)*. Warszawa.

Bystron, J. S. 1976. Szlaki migracyjne na ziemiach polskich (Migration routes on Polish territory). *Przeglad Socjologiczny (Sociological Review)* **XXVIII**.

Carvalho de P. 1990. *Studenci obcokrajowcy w Polsce (Foreign students in Poland)*, Warszawa: University of Warsaw.

Chałasiński, J. 1935a. *Antagonizm polsko-niemiecki w osadzie fabrycznej*

Kopalnia na Górnym Śląsku (Polish-German antagonism in the town Kopalnia in Upper Silesia). Warszawa: Dom Książki Polskiej.

Chałasiński, J. 1935b. *Parafia i szkoła parafialna wśród emigracji polskiej w Ameryce (The parish and the parish school of Polish emigrants in USA).* Warszawa: Dom Książki Polskiej.

Chałasiński, J. 1968. *Narod i kultura (Nation and culture).* Warszawa: Książki i Wiedza.

Chałasiński, J. & K. Chałasińska 1962. *Bliżej Afryki (Approaching Africa).* Warszawa.

Chlebowczyk, J. 1980. *On small and young nations in Europe.* Wrocław: Ossolineum.

Deutsch, K. W. 1966. *Nationalism and social communication.* Cambridge, Mass.: MIT.

Deutsch, K. W. 1981. On Nationalism, world regions and the nature of the West. In *Mobilization, centre-periphery structures and nation building*, P. Torvik (ed.), Bergen: Universitetsforlaget.

Dmitrow, E. 1987. *Niemcy i okupacja hitlerowska w oczach Polaków (The Germans and German occupation seen by the Poles).* Warszawa.

Duda-Dziewierz, K. 1938. *Wieś małopolska a emigracja amerykańska (A village in Southern Poland and the emigration to America).* Warszawa.

Dulczewski, Z. 1971. *Społeczeństwo ziem zachodnich (The Society of Western Territories).* Poznan.

Encyclopedia Judaica 1972, vol. 7, Jerusalem.

Geertz, C. 1975. *The interpretation of cultures.* New York: Basic Books.

Gellner, E. 1983. *Nations and nationalism.* Oxford: Basil Blackwell.

Goldberg, L. 1986. The changes in the attitude of Polish society toward the Jews in the 18th Century. *Polin* 1.

Hertz, A. 1961, 1988. *Żydzi w kulturze polskiej (The Jews in Polish culture).* Paris/Warszawa.

Jasińska-Kania, A. 1988. *Osobowość, orientacje moralne i postawy potilyczne (Personality, Moral Orientations and Political Attitudes).* Warszawa.

Jawłowska, A. 1991. Kontrkultura. *W Encyklopedia kultury polskiej XX w (Counterculture. In The Encyclopedia of Polish culture in the 20th Century).* Wrocław: Wiedza o Kulturze.

Kapiszewski, A. 1984. *Asymilacja i konflikty (Assimilation and conflict).* Wrocław: Ossolineum.

Kłoskowska, A. 1961. National concepts and attitudes of children in a middle-sized city in Polish Western Territories. *The Polish Sociological Bulletin* 1-2.

Kłoskowska, A. 1962. The Negroes as seen by Polish children. *International Journal of Sociology* III (2).

Kłoskowska, A. 1969. Koncepcje typu osobowści we współczesnej antropologii amerykańskiej (The concepts of personality types in contemporary American anthropology) *W Z historii i socjologii kultury (in The history and sociology of culture).* PWN.

Kłoskowska, A. 1989. Values against the holocaust. *Dialectics and Humanism* 1.

Kłoskowska, A. 1990. *Oblicza polskości, ed. (Images of Polishness)*. Warszawa: Uniwersytet Warszawski.

Kloskowska, A. 1992. Neighbourhood cultures: some aspects of difficult historical neighbourhoods. *International Sociology* 7 (1).

Kubiak, H. 1982. *The Polish national Catholic Church in the United States of America*. Warszawa.

Kula, M. (ed.) 1989. *Narody, jak powstawały, jak wybijały się na niepodległość, (Nations, their origin and fight for independence)*. Warszawa.

Krzywicki, L. 1939. *Pamiętniki emigrantow. Przedmowa (The memoirs of emigrants. Forward)*. Warszawa.

Klineberg, O. & W. E. Lambert 1959. A Pilot study of the origin and development of national stereotypes. *International Social Science Journal* 11 (2).

Mach, Z. 1989a. *Kultura i osobowość w antropologii amerykańskiej (Culture and personality in American anthropology)*. Kraków.

Mach, Z. 1989b. *Symbols, conflicts and identity*. Kraków.

Markiewicz, W. 1960. *Przeobrażenia spolecznej świadomośći reemigrantów polskich z Francji (Social change among Polish re-emigrants from France)*. Poznań.

Markiewicz, W. & P. Rybicki (eds) 1967. *Przemiany społeczne na ziemiach zachodnich (Social change in Western Territories)*. Poznan.

Merton, R. 1949. *Social theory and social structure*. Glencoe: Free Press.

Nowakowski, S. 1957. *Adaptacja ludności na śląsku Opolskim (Adaptation of the population in Opole Silesia)*. Warszawa.

Nowakowski, S. 1960. *Przeobrażenia społeczne wsi opolskiej (The social transformations of a village in the Opole Region)*. Warszawa.

Nowicka, E. (ed.) 1990. *Swoi i obcy ("We" and the strangers)*. Warszawa: Uniwersytet Warszawski.

(Opole) 1985. *Społeczeństwo Śląska Opolskiego (The society of Opole Silesia)*.

(Opole) 1950. *Górny Śląsk jako pomost między Polakami i Niemcami (Upper Silesia as a bridge between the Poles and the Germans)*.

Ossowski, S. 1948. *Więź społeczna i dziedzictwo krwi (Social bonds and the heritage of blood)*. Warszawa.

Ossowski, S. 1946. Analiza socjologiczna pojecia ojczyzny (Sociological analysis of the concept "Fatherland"). *Myśl Współczesna* 4.

Ossowski, S. 1947. Zagadnienia wiezi regionalnej i więzi narodowej na Śląsku Opolskim (The problems of regional and national bonds in Opole Silesiza). *Przegląd Socjologiczny* 9.

Sakson, A. 1990. *Mazurzy: Społeczność pogranicza (The Mazurs: a borderland collectivity)*, Poznań.

Singer, I. B. 1986. *In my father's court*. New York.

Szarota, T. 1988. *Niemiecki Michel (The German Michel)*. Warszawa.

Szczepański, J. 1961. *Socjologia (Sociology)*. Warszawa.

Szczurkiewicz 1969. *Studia socjologiczne (Sociological studies)*. Warszawa.

Thomas, W. I. & F. Znaniecki 1918-1920. *The Polish peasant in Europe and America*. Boston.

Tiryakian, E. A. & N. Nevitte 1985. Nationalism and modernity. In *New nationalisms of the developed West*, E. A. Tiryakian & R. Rogowski (eds). Boston: Allen & Unwin.

Tomaszewski, J. 1985. *Rzeczpospolita wielu narodów (The republic of many nations)*. Warszawa.

Tomaszewski, J. 1990. *Zarys dziejów Żydów polskich w latach 1918-1939 (An outline of the history of Polish Jews in the years 1918-1939)*. Warszawa.

Wilska-Duszyńska, B. 1975. *Postawy etniczne a niektóre elementy studenckiego systemu wartości (Ethnic attitudes and some elements of students' value systems)*. Warszawa.

Wiatr, J. 1973. *Naród i państwo (The Nation and the State)*. Warszawa.

Wyszyński, R. 1990. *Zapomniani Polacy (The Forgotten Poles)*. Unpublished MA at the Institute of Sociology, University of Warsaw (under the direction of A. Kłoskowska).

Żebrowski, R. & Z. Borzyminska (forthcoming) *Kultura Żydów polskich w XX wieku (The culture of Polish Jews in the 20th century)*. Warszawa.

Ziemer, K. 1991. Können Polen und Deutsche Freunde Sein? In *Die hässlichen Deutschen*, G. Trautmann (ed.). Darmstadt.

Znaniecki, F. 1952. *Modern nationalities*. Urbana: University of Illinois Press.

Chapter 12

Between west and east:
Tartars in the former USSR

Vasil Ziatdinov & Sviatoslav Grigoriev

Introduction

The historical development of any multinational, multicultural society is almost inevitably beset with conflict; conflict grounded in disputes about anything from linguistic autonomy to religious observance, from areas of settlement to more general social inequalities. But the resolution of the "national question" during a process of transition from a totalitarian to a democratic society in the former USSR, and indeed elsewhere in central and eastern Europe, is not only complex but has major implications both for those within the borders of former member states and for those outside them. The first phase of the democratization process served to stimulate ethnic consciousness among the many peoples of the former Soviet Union, and gave an impetus to the formation of popular movements openly demanding greater cultural, social, economic and political autonomy (and even total independence for their "nation").

There are many problems to be overcome, notably the weakness of contemporary democratic institutions, the lack of appropriate civic programmes and, on a more psychological plane, the mental "hangover" which is an inevitable part of a post-totalitarian society in a state of flux. The task now is to face the inevitably difficult task of building a viable democracy that retains the best aspects of traditional values while avoiding the mistakes of history. This will involve drawing on the experience of established democracies in the West, but not the slavish adherence to an overarching Western paradigm. Hitherto few of these potential lessons (in terms of "good practice") had been incorporated into the country's political life and social programmes; but now there is growing interest in

222

the question of poly-ethnic and poly-centric socialization, as well as in the development of a multicultural education strategy geared to the demands of a multinational society.

To undertake an analysis of the complex, shifting relations between ethnic and national minorities and the (now fractured) state would clearly be overambitious. What we propose to do in this chapter, therefore, is to focus primarily on the position of one major "nation" of the former Soviet Union, the Tartars. We begin with a somewhat brief historical account to provide the necessary context to the dynamics of underlying contemporary conflicts; conflicts which, we would argue, both here and in all central and east European countries, have roots deeply embedded in the social and political fabric of their respective milieu.

It is clear that one of the major concerns of the totalitarian system was the problem of "national relations". Ironically it was the central feature of the system, the forced unification of social life, which gave rise to conflict, and a potential "time-bomb" awaiting the removal of the cementing effect of state control. For this reason what might be seen as two historically positive tendencies, namely "democratization" and the growth of "ethnic consciousness", can actually lead to profoundly negative consequences, as is evidenced by the armed conflict and bloodshed in many states over the recent past. Furthermore, the forces of reaction can then use the latter as signalling the need for a return of the status quo ante.

At the same time there are positive developments among some groups, including Tartars living in the former territory of the autonomous republic (TASSR). This Republic recently declared its new political status – TSSR or Tartarstan ("The Republic of Tartarstan"). Although this will be the main focus of the chapter it is also important to reflect on the experiences of nearly five million Tartars dispersed throughout the territory of the former Union (mainly in Russia), over a million in the Republics of Central Asia, and yet others living further afield.

In our view these issues are not only of contemporary interest and significance; it is likely that they will become much more so in the near future, for the following reasons. At the intra-Republic level there is the issue of how, in the light of a long history of conflict, Tartar-Russian relations will develop. On a wider level, there is the possibility of deeper links between Tartars and the Eastern nations who share a common Islamic faith; notably peoples from the banks of the Volga, the Urals, Central Asia and Siberia. (And there are of course broader issues still: relating, for example, to the interaction between Eastern and Western cultures, and between

Christian and Muslim traditions, especially in the light of the significant Muslim presence in Europe.)

The chapter is set out in three parts. First, as noted above, there is a brief account of Tartar history, acknowledging significantly that there are many competing versions. Focusing in particular on the formation and development of Tartar–Russian interactions, we analyze the cultural, religious, political and military struggles up to 1916. In doing so, we also look closely at the implications of these for the process of ethnogenesis in relation to the Tartar people. Part two then traces these events from 1917 up to the present day.

The third section traces changes in the ethnic composition of the Tartar Republic, Siberia and other areas of Tartar settlement. This relates closely to the arguments of the previous section, and focuses in particular on the delicate balance to be struck between the desire for democratization and the achievement of equal rights for all on the one hand, and rising "national" self-awareness on the other.

Tartar history and the process of ethnogenesis.

In the multinational complex which was the former Soviet Union, the word "Tartar" conjured up numerous conflicting images, many of them deeply mistaken. Typical of these is the identification of its origin with the Mongolian invasion in the 13th century.

At the present time "Tartar" represents the "national" identification of around seven million people worldwide. In fact, there is a common saying that "In every Russian flows at least one drop of Tartar blood". In one sense we could draw a parallel between the development of this term and (among others) the word "Slav"; but it is important for us to analyze changes in meaning over time, and the use of ethnonyms such as "Turk", "Tartar" and "Mongol". Leo Gumilev talks about the "camouflage" of identity, for example the "transformation" of the "Turk" into the "Tartar". Referring to Altai he says:

In the sixth century AD a small people living on the eastern slopes of the Altai and Khangai mountains were called Turks. Through several wars they managed to subordinate the whole steppe from Hingan to the Sea of Azov. The subjects of the Great Kaghanate, who preserved their own ethnonyms for internal use, also began to be called Turks, since they were subject to the Turkish Khan. When the Arabs conquered Sogdiana and clashed with the nomads "les Tartars", and in the 19th century when linguistic classification became fashionable, the name "Turk" was arrogated to a definite group of languages.

The following modification of the ethnonym "Tartar" could be interpreted as a further example of this "camouflage".

> Up to the 20th century this was the ethnic name of a group of 30 big clans inhabiting the banks of the Korulen. In the twelfth century this nationality increased in numbers, and Chinese geographers began to call all the Central Asian nomads (Turkish-speaking, Tungus-speaking, and Mongol-speaking), including the Mongols, Tartars. And even when, in 1206, Genghis Khan officially called all his subjects Mongols, neighbours continued for some time from habit to call them Tartars. In this form the word "Tartar" reached Eastern Europe as a synonym of the word "Mongol", and became acclimatized in the Volga Valley where the local population began, as a mark of respect to the Khan of the Golden Horde, to call themselves Tartars. But the original bearers of the name (Kereites, Naimans, Oirats, and Tartars) began to call themselves Mongols. The names thus changed places. Since that time a scientific terminology arose in which the Tartar anthropological type began to be called "Mongoloid", and the language of the Volga Kipchak-Turks, Tartar. In other words we even employ an obviously camouflaged terminology in science (1990: 82).

Although in general accepting this analysis, there is one point of detail with which we would take issue; where he talks of "loyalty" to the Khan. There is much historical evidence to demonstrate the resistance of the people of the Volga Kama region to the invasion, and the especially fierce opposition to it on the part of the Volga Bulgars. Their state "Bolgarlend" – or, the country of towns, "Gardarica" – was well known in Europe (and especially in Scandinavia) as early as the 11th century. Its first treaty with the Rus (the former Russia) was signed at the end of the 10th century. It was a state with high culture and a written language. And it was the staunch resistance of the Volga Bulgars which first prevented the attempts to invade Rus. It took the Mongols a few years before they could continue the invasion (Khalikov 1989: 90-9). The "Bulgar" identity was so strong that it continues to this day; indeed there is a move among a section of the population to readopt this ethnonym.

Because this period of history is so crucial for understanding ethnic formations and the complexities of "Tartar" identity it is necessary to develop these arguments a little further. According to the academic literature, the rebels who lived in the steppes west of the Urals began to call themselves Nogai and those who lived on the banks of the Irtysh became ancestors to the Kazakhs. The ancestors of the Nogai, who adopted Islam, were the Polovtsy, Steppe Alans, Central Asian Turks, and the inhabitants of the Southern frontier of the Rus. Islam at that time and in these areas became a symbol of ethnic consolidation. As for the Tartars, they included Kama Bulgars, Khazars, and Burtasy, and also some of the Polovtsy and Ugric Mishari (Gumilev 1990: 82) [A very detailed and stimulating discussion of the close relations and mutual influences between the Rus and Steppe peoples is contained in Suleimenov (1975).]

According to traditional accounts from both Russian history and literary fiction of the time, "Tartars" were all those who participated in the invasion. But, as D. S. Lichachev has argued, present day Tartars feel this linkage is misleading. The conquerors, he notes, were gradually dissipated amidst the Kipchak steppe. In addition, it is unlikely that " . . . the Volga Bulgars – future Kazanians" were involved in the final intervention of the Mamai army in 1380. Defending this view Lichachev (1983) points to the increased level of agitation by the Golden Horde in 1360, and as a result of rebellions many regions had been liberated, among them "Volga Bulgars – the region of the future Kazanian Khan area . . . " (ibid.: 236-7). The fact that these arguments come from a respected Russian scholar, and a non-Tartar, is significant for two reasons. First, it provides confirmation of the existence of the Bulgar state on the banks of the Volga, and, secondly, it clearly characterizes the Golden Horde as its enemy.

In the 12th and 13th centuries the Bulgars and Khazars belonged, according to Gumilev (1990: 141), to the Levantine or Muslim superethnos.

> They did not differ from their neighbours in their mode of adaptation to their country. But Bulgar's systematic trade and cultural relations with Iran were more effective than the influence of the geographical environment, and it was they which made Great Bulgar an outpost of the "Muslim" superethnos . . .

There was a tradition of close contact between the Bulgars and Arab-Persian peoples and to some extent the broader Muslim East, despite various historical hiccoughs. The significance of this is clear, in that it tells us a great deal about the formation of a "national" culture and collective consciousness.

The rising "ethnic potential" was to be severely tested by a savage history. There were, as we have seen, Mongolian invasions and armed struggles against the Golden Horde by among others the Volga Bulgars. But a new independent state was formed in the area of Kazan's Khan. And despite the presence of descendants of different branches of Genghis Khan's clan, it thrived as a strong and powerful entity. Its population largely consisted of Bulgars, whose rich social and cultural traditions facilitated the rapid development of a viable state. Unfortunately, however, it lacked the military organization to back up its economic muscle (Khudiakov 1990: 20–21, 242).

During a period of more than a century (1438–1556), relations between the new state and Rus fluctuated wildly, including a period of subordination of the latter by the former and, following a shift in the balance of power, a period in which Rus provided protection for the Kazanian State. For the most part, however, relations were on the basis of equality, regulated by treaty. The two states as neighbours along the great Volga river could not in fact have existed without mutual contacts and influence. Khudiakov, for example, points to the wide-ranging and positive influence of Tartar culture on that of the Russians. Evidence of this ranges from state organization to diplomacy, to the use of data gathering procedures such as the census. Interestingly also he argued (in 1923) that these issues were largely ignored (ibid.: 232–44). In fact we could extend this point by arguing that until very recently they were very definitely "off the research agenda".

One thing is clear; it is inconceivable to imagine the life of Kazan's population as one of barbarism. Schools were widespread and the general level of literacy high. Mosques, which were to be found in many villages, were often linked to schools; thereby combining an educative rôle with one which helped to protect religious and ethnic identity. Kazan's people had a literature, poetry and music which was both distinctive and exclusive to their country. At the same time economic, diplomatic and cultural links were maintained with Turkestan, Persia, Turkia and Arabia. In the light of this who would recognize the common Russian stereotype of the "poor and dark" Tartars? But it does of course provide an insight into the reasons why the former totalitarian state did not wish to sanction the study of "nations" such as the Tartars.

The second invasion, in the sixteenth century, came from a rather different source, the Russian state. It was the second tragedy to befall this people, and the second blow to its natural ethnogenesis. In retrospect it had an even more devastating effect than the first because of the collision with the opposing superethnos, i.e. the collision between Christianity and Islam. The Russian Orthodox Church was seen to be fully behind the expansionist policy and to support the idea of revenge against Muslims. By 1552 Russia was a politically united entity, and was in a much more powerful position than Kazan, given that it could draw upon Western military expertise and artillery. It also had a much larger military force, and although relations between the states were formally governed by treaty, expansionism was clearly the key policy of the Russian ruling elite. The latter also planned the subordination of the independent state. There followed a life-and-death struggle, the people having rejected "voluntary subordination". The aspiration to achieve national freedom at whatever cost, led many to die for the cause. After a terrible struggle Kazan was occupied but the people were never subordinated as all males, and indeed the majority of the civil population, were murdered and the town destroyed. No one from the original population could live within 45 kilometres; and the town, and especially all symbols of Eastern Muslim cultures (including mosques) were targeted for destruction. Such was the beginning of the "Christianization" process. But the furious struggle of the people against Russian military might continued for around six years in every village and every part of the country (ibid.: 148–66).

The impact of this aggression on the Volga Tartars was felt in the interruption of its national development for many years, the death of a major part of its population, the forced resettlement of many who survived, and the degradation of the native culture. Moreover, it represented an attempt to annihilate one superethnos, either through genocide or the violent imposition of Christianity. It must not be forgotten that Russia gained much by this policy.

Reflections on the development of ethnic identity

The following centuries were difficult for those who wished to overthrow the existing order; but a strong ethnic identity was maintained through the memory of their Bulgar roots and Muslim traditions, and the ultimate aspiration of a free national state remained. For many years, though, the name "Tartar" disappeared from common usage, to be replaced by "Bulgar" or "Muslim" (Khalikov 1989: 163).

There were national liberation movements, of course, one of the most recent being formed in the second half of the 19th century, and known by the name of its leader, Waisov. Lasting from 1862 until 1922 this movement came to prominence through the activities of the first Muslim party, "Firkai Najia" (The Party of Deliverance), and the movement of Volga Bulgar's Muslims. The principal demands included the creation of a Bulgar state, an end to the negative treatment of Bulgarians, the introduction of "people's power", and the freedom of religion. In other words it was much more than a religious movement; its goals were those of national liberation.

It represents a very interesting page in the history of national-liberation movements, and one which is almost completely ignored in "official" Soviet literature. Much fundamental research remains to be done. As to the importance of the movement for the strengthening of ethnic ties one should note that in its base in Kazan was founded the "Muslim Academy" – the first cultural and political centre for Bulgars in Soviet history. Contained here were important resources such as the middle school (mekteb) and high school (medrese) printing house.

All members of the movement used the Bulgar ethnonym – al-Bulgari – which was not recognized officially. They were involved in the revolution of 1917 on the grounds that the struggle for Volga Muslims was geared to national and social liberation, based on the principles of "Muslim socialism" (Nurutdinov 1990). At the same time, even before the revolution, there were official Muslim services and local administrations loyal to the tsarist regime. But in general all avenues for the advancement of Tartars were closed, the only option essentially being the preservation of identity through the tradition of study in their mosques. But what was the impact of the "official" suppression of ethnic identity, and the consequent unrest?

According to information presented in Russian newspapers at the end of the 19th century, there were significant disparities in the educational attainments of Russians and Tartars living in the regions of Kazan and Ufa. In 1879, at least 60 per cent of Tartars were literate compared with only 10 per cent of Russians. As far as the Tartars are concerned this was largely due to self-help and rising national consciousness geared to survival as a people. The concerns of the state were those of Russian literacy levels, and little assistance was available for non-Russians, and especially non-Christians.

As for the Soviet period, it could be argued that the first twenty years promised much in terms of the liberation of national minorities throughout the country. This was the period which witnessed an explosion of national aspirations. In 1917, the idea of creating free Volga-Ural States or a Tartar-Bashkir Republic as part of an also free Russia, was born. In the opinion of many experts, there was at this time a real chance of creating either a united Tartar-Bashkir Republic or two independent republics based on a common principle. The Muslim Socialist Committee, which provided an effective base for democratic forces within the national liberation movement, was organised in the Kazan region. Sultan-Galeev, one of its most prominent leaders argued forcefully, at the highest levels of Party and State, that aspirations of the Eastern peoples to self-determination were rising markedly. At this time, too, he ranked second only to Stalin in the State Committee of Nationalities. But these arguments did not carry sufficient sway with some government leaders. In addition, he disagreed with Stalin's conception of the rôle of national republics, demanding instead equal rights for autonomous and union republics, ("Tatarinform" 1990a) – uncannily similar to contemporary demands in fact.

The October revolution provided a major creative impetus to Tartar aspirations for an independent cultural and spiritual life, and the aftermath saw the first financial help from the government to back Tartar periodicals. Over the years 1917–18 the number of newspapers in the Tartar language grew to over 60. (It should perhaps be added that official permission to run its own press was finally given to the Volga Tartars in 1905, much later than other non-Christian peoples, and was not only a great distance from Kazan (in Petersburg) but also was an "official" press loyal to the Tsarist government.) Prior to the revolution there had been a total of 58 newspapers and 37 magazines (in Tartar), though the number in production at any particular time was very much smaller ("Tatarinform" 1990b).

Within a short space of time at the beginning of the present century Volga Tartars regained their position of importance among East Muslim peoples. By the latter part of the 19th century Kazan State University had gained pre-eminence in Russia for the excellence and uniqueness of its typography. Concentrated here were facilities for printing in all the world's languages, past and present, Western and Eastern. In fact, after 1917 it was the only place in the Soviet Union with the technical capability of printing in the languages of the Muslim East. The University therefore fulfilled a vital rôle in providing for the cultural needs of Muslim peoples, and had particularly significant dealings with the Turkestan Republic. Quite how important it was is demonstrated in a letter to the All-Russian Trade Union's Central Council in 1920 from Lunacharski, who at that time was the Soviet government official responsible for education. In it he argued that cultural and educational work among the Muslim population of Turkestan was quite impossible due to the absence of the relevant printed materials, and "according to unofficial information, such print there is only in English and Kazan" (Karimullin 1989). Around 10 million Tartar books, involving 2400 different titles (ibid.: 268), were produced between 1917 and 1932, and these were widely distributed among Khazah, Bashkir, Uzbek, Turkmen, Krymean Tartar, Kumyk and Balkar readers.

In spite of the often turbulent history of the area, and the increased rôle played by Tartars in the eastern region of the Soviet Union, relations between Russians and Tartars remained stable and for the most part friendly. This was so because there was a widespread perception of the revolution as predicated on the desire for social and national liberation on the part of all peoples. Following this of course was the collective awareness that the imposed unification of the society would potentially lead to the destruction of ethnic identity, religious practices, popular traditions, and of the right to free cultural and spiritual expression. In the wake of Stalin's repressions, for example, the number of Tartar newspapers fell from a peak of 66 to, by 1927, a mere 16 ("Tatarinform" 1990b). The simultaneous collectivization of the peasantry dealt a further, savage blow against any attempt to preserve a distinctive ethnic identity. The violent deportation of rural populations led in turn to an even wider dispersion of the Tartars. People simply could not comprehend the reality of their treatment. But even such ordeals did not lead to conflict between Tartars and Russians, owing to an adherence to the ideals underpinning the revolution; namely social liberation.

A good illustration of this came with the Second World War, when fascists wanted to employ on a grand scale the model (noted earlier) involving the creation of a Volga-Ural Republic. They began to organize army groups from Tartar-Bashkir prisoners of war. According to their scheme these were to form the national army, but fighting against the Soviet Union, and therefore against Russians, to obtain their own nation-state. This plan was not without its appeal, of course, given the level of suppressed nationalist sentiment, but the dangers of fascism were generally recognized, in that true freedom had to involve the freedom of Russians, and other peoples. One prominent champion of this cause was Musa Jalil. A well known Tartar poet, he became the leader of the wide scale rebellion among Muslim prisoners of war.

The war and its immediate aftermath was accompanied by a rise in national aspirations and new hopes of liberation. The year 1946 saw the high point of Tartar press activity; the number of newspapers rising to 116 (ibid.). As is well known, this new wave of optimism soon foundered on old barriers.

Empirical evidence of social and political inequality

Prior to the Soviet period, the image of the Tartar which was embedded in the consciousness of Russians was overlaid with fear and suspicion; fear of retribution for years of marginalization enshrined in the policies of the Tsarist regime. But where would the threat emerge, and from whom? The roots of this vision of "Tartars" as "the enemy" are to be found in the Mongolian invasions discussed earlier. This symbolism was then transferred to those who acquired the ethnic label, despite many years of peaceable co-existence. Further, Russian power was constantly used to undermine their ethnic identity.

The creation of distinct republics (with only limited rights of autonomy) and the provision of free access to education for non-Russian peoples, were clearly of value to Soviet society. But with the exception of a few, if very productive, years the development of the different nationalities did not materialize. That it failed to do so can be attributed essentially to the policy of enforced unification of the lives of many disparate peoples. Multilingualism in education was rejected, meaning that Russian was imposed on the Tartar population.

If we look at the ethnic composition of the Tartar Soviet Socialist Republic (TSSR) we see that, as a result of the historical factors noted earlier, it reflects the level of diversity commonly seen elsewhere in the country. Out of a population of almost 4 million there are in excess of 70 nationalities. Most are either Tartars (48.5 per cent) or Russians (43.2 per cent); Chuvashes (3.7 per cent), Ukrainians (0.9 per cent) and others making up the total. As illustrated by the data in Table 12.1, despite being in a numerical minority Russians form the major part of the urban population. The consequences of this historically entrenched imbalance could, of course, be grave.

Any resulting conflict would probably be long drawn-out and bloody. But thus far the Republic has avoided a drift towards a situation of this kind. Current evidence suggests that, despite problems such as high levels of criminal behaviour among young people, the dialogue between different forces and socio-political movements is constructive.

Table 12.1   Urban–rural distribution by nationality.

	Urban (%)	Rural (%)
Russians	51.7	20.5
Tartars	41.8	66.3
Others	6.5	13.2
Total	100.0	100.0

Source: *Communist Tatarii* 1990. No 7.: 11.

To see how the current situation has come about we turn to the first ethno-sociological study of the whole population of the TSSR. According to this study, undertaken in 1960 by Yu. V. Arutyunyan and his colleagues, there were social inequalities between Russians and Tartars but these were relatively small, and were narrowing over time. However, to put these results into perspective it is necessary to present some historical detail.

Tartars were traditionally employed in many disparate trades; handicrafts, ferrous and non-ferrous metallurgy, glass manufacture, pottery, tanning, jewellery, and so on. Particularly popular were trades which were viable on an international scale (Davletshin 1990: 7). However, during a period roughly spanning the sixteenth to eighteenth centuries, Russian powers imposed a ban on many of these activities, and especially those which might lend themselves to the production of arms. As a result of occupation in the sixteenth century, many of the original inhabitants lost the right to live in the towns.

Inequalities are in many ways grounded in past eras of national deprivation. The dispersal of native populations and the denial of a (public) religious identity were clearly important. At the beginning of the last century Russians and Tartars lived in separate villages. In 1920, for example, 42.2 per cent were solely inhabited by Tartars and 43.7 per cent by Russians. By the mid-1920s only 3 per cent of Tartars lived in towns in the TSSR; in doing so they comprised 17 per cent of the urban population compared with the Russian figure of 77.3 per cent. As a result of increasing levels of migration Tartars constituted almost a quarter of the population of the Republic's capital Kazan by 1926. Despite evidence of a shift in residential patterns differences remained substantial; but the key question relates to broader social inequalities based on "nation" and ethnic identity.

The transformation of the alphabet first from Arabic to Roman and then from Roman to Cyrillic, the extermination of nationalist intellectuals and other free-thinking persons, and the collectivization of the peasantry, re-

233

duced the majority of Tartars from a literate people to one cut off from their historical, cultural and religious traditions. Given little option they were "prepared" for Russification, but nevertheless started from a very lowly disadvantaged position compared with Russians. Political control from the Party at the Centre also inhibited "national" development, for Tartars and other non-Russian peoples. "Origins" were deemed to be unimportant; to be Soviet meant to be Russian. Ironically, however, Russians also lost their clear identity, becoming "Homo Soveticus".

This situation led to differentials, particularly in employment, as the medium of teaching and training was mainly Russian. Theoretically, Party rule should have led to an equalization of recruitment to senior posts, but until recently (see below) the Centre could never quite bring themselves to trust non-Russians in senior local posts. In spite of these negative influences, however, Tartars continued to strive for high educational attainment and an active social and cultural life. Whereas in 1926 the Republic's entire Tartar population could boast only 3 engineers, 76 artists and 1680 teachers, by 1959 in Kazan alone there were more than 1200 engineers, 500 artists and 4400 teachers. According to Arutyunyan's research the proportion of Tartar workers with low qualifications was, at almost 10 per cent, above average; and among highly qualified (scientific/technical) labour they lagged behind Russians by around 17 per cent. More disturbing was the marked disparity at the level of decision-makers. No less than 71 per cent of "leaders" in Kazan were Russian, compared with 19.3 per cent Tartar. In the middle-sized industrial town of Almeteivsk, the figures were 53.9 per cent and 33.3 per cent respectively. The situation was reversed only in a small town (with figures of 36.4 per cent Russian and 54.5 per cent Tartar) (Socialnoe i Nacionalnoe 1972: 15–25). However, the marked change hinted at above comes in some recently published figures (Narodnoie. khoziaistwo RSFSR v 1989 g 1990: 118), which suggest that the proportion of senior posts in the TSSR held by Tartars may now be as high as 61.1 per cent.

As for levels of literacy, even as early as 1960 Tartars had achieved parity. And by the end of the sixties this position seems to apply to educational achievements in general. Figures recently released for the 1989/90 academic year (ibid.: 268) also suggest that around 41 per cent of pupils in TSSR's higher schools are Tartars. All is not well in the school system, however, and ongoing research is revealing increasing conflict between national, regional and general models of education.

Tartars are in the main bilingual, especially urban dwellers. Even by

1960 almost nine out of every ten Tartars in Kazan knew Russian. The same cannot be said for Russians, with only 2 per cent of the urban, and 3.2 per cent of the rural, populations being bilingual (Socialnoe i Nacionalnoe op. cit.: 122, 235). As to whether Tartars are becoming predominantly Russified the evidence is mixed. Certainly, given the general levels of dispersal and the dominance of Russian in the entire educational process, Russification is inevitable, especially among non-believers and converts to Christianity. However, recent research by Anderson and Silver (1990) suggests that of all nationalities the Tartars exhibit the lowest estimated rate of ethnic re-identification, and belong to the category of peoples with little net change in "ethnic self-identification" between 1959 and 1970.

Much the same could be said about Tartars living outside the TSSR. This was certainly the conclusion of Tomilev (1983) writing about those in the Tomsk region of Siberia. It was here that in 1919 the Turk-Tartar pedagogical seminary (later to become the Turk-Tartar Institute) was founded. During the 1920s all high schools in Tomsk opened Turk-Tartar facilities for anyone who wished to use them, including simple labouring people. There were a few major concentrations of Tartars in Tomsk, Tumen and Tobol, but by the 1970s living standards, community development and educational levels could be seen to vary markedly. Indeed, although the census gave a literacy figure of 100 per cent, academic research indicated illiteracy rates of as much as 8 per cent among rural Tartars in the Tomsk area (ibid.). Many would argue, ourselves included, that one of the main reasons for this was the cessation during the 1950s of school teaching in native languages.

It has to be said that expressions of Tartar self-identification vary considerably, with levels in Siberia, for example, being much lower than those in the Volga-Kama region. What we observe essentially is a fusion of ancient Turk roots, East Muslim traditions, and a distinctive Tartar component concretized by the single national language. Clearly the precise form it takes is influenced by the sort of migration processes already discussed, in particular the repeated waves of emigrants from the "core" Volga-Kama region. Interestingly, however, we are now witnessing a reversal of this process; a return to the principal centre of Tartar national culture, and also a return of Crimean Tartars to their native land. (Unfortunately, there is insufficient space in the current chapter to develop the rather complex Crimean case.)

The desire to return appears to be greater among urban Tartars. Research from scholars in Volgograd found that the majority of urban Tartars and a section of those in rural communities wish to re-emigrate. What this suggests of course is that in the future there may be a significant imbalance in the population distribution, and this would have implications not only for the Republic of Tartarstan but throughout the former Union. The position of widely dispersed minorities could become tenuous.

This is clearly a major problem, and one whose solution will have implications for the positive democratic transformation of the former Soviet society. After the long period of suppression of the reality of different nationalities, any readjustments will have to take into account both internal relations and those with the outside world. The position of Tartars, for example, will need to be assessed in terms of a multi-ethnic, multinational complex internally, as part of a rapidly evolving and (in some senses) unifying Europe, and as part of the more general East-West and Christian-Muslim debate. To complicate matters even further it should be stressed that, although the majority of Tartars live in the European part of the former Union, a substantial minority are settled in Asia.

The development of aspirations towards self-determination on the part of nations resulted in rising tensions between the Centre and republics, but at the same time emotional association with the Centre also revealed rising tensions between Russians and non-Russians. On a further level, there was evidence of heightened conflict between different peoples within republics. For this reason Tartar-Russian relations, currently being subjected to the severest of tests, have to be seen on a number of different planes.

Tartars are aware that threats to their autonomy may also come from those who have traditionally been seen as allies and neighbours. The earlier example referring to the Bashkirs is a case in point. Their aspirations to self-determination and the proclaimed priority of the Bashkir language (in a republic where the majority of the population were Tartars) illustrates the escalating tensions. The Central Asian Republics, despite the community of Muslim traditions, may also add to the clamour of competing interests.

At the end of 1990 and the beginning of the following year there were popular slogans at demonstrations such as "Russians – to Riazan: Tartars – to Kazan" (Riazan being an old Russian town, Kazan of course being the symbol of the Tartar Motherland). This imperative of "Go home to where you belong" served to fuel tensions further (and would, ironically, create major problems for Tartars wishing to conform to it). As we have seen, migration was already underway from those unable to find the deep sense of "Motherland" in many areas of the vast superstate, and especially the drab, grey and monotonous towns with their anomic social life.

The paradox of an autonomous status for Tartarstan is more than evident. Because of the rapid rate of industrialization, it is capable of an output greater than that of all the Baltic States taken together. It is an important region for oil and gas production, and has a massive motor car plant, known as "Kamaz", on the banks of the Kama. Furthermore, in spite of general economic difficulties, there were in 1990 around 20,000 job vacancies at all skill levels, and investment in plant and machinery was increasing. All of this seems to provide the ideal conditions for returning "exiles", but in the whole of 1990 according to official figures a mere 414 arrived, and of these only half were of Tartar nationality. (These were people who came by way of the usual procedure whereby large industrial concerns would offer work plus general financial, including re-location, assistance.) The overall position is nevertheless unclear, as there is unregistered migration, and under Soviet law at that time there was no scope for the creation of "priority treatment" on the basis of national origin.

There is evidence now, however, of a network of self-help organizations geared to assist potential returners. The independent Tartar publication "Tatarinform" (1990b) gives the addresses of more than 60 regional departments, clubs and societies throughout the former Soviet Union, including most major towns. But the key questions are as follows:- How can one estimate the real national potential, the real strength of the "new" ethnic consciousness given the past history of brutal suppressions of its natural development? And in the light of many grave and bloody conflicts, is it possible to control this new ethnic fervour by socio-political means?

According to figures from the All-Union Public Opinion Research Centre in December 1990, 51 per cent of the population of Tartarstan supported the idea that the Republic should remain within the then Russian Federation. However, among Russians the figure was around 76 per cent as against 46 per cent among Tartars; and significantly, 24 per cent of the latter argued for an independent state. In support of the general idea of sovereignty for republics were 75 per cent of Tartars and 39.5 per cent of Russians, though the authors of the report claim that one should be wary of reading too much into these figures given the lack of comparative data.

In order to interpret the data and to determine the factors which lead to the adoption of certain political positions, one needs to take on board the political situation across the country at that time and the social structural position of the different population groups. The body which invoked the highest level of confidence was the Supreme Council of Russia (with 30 per cent completely in support and only 12 per cent opposed to it). All other institutions of power, from the highest body in the land to the most local, were viewed with suspicion and distrust. At the same time the general opinion was that the real power in Tartarstan belonged to the Union's structures and to the authorities of the TSSR, and not at all to the Russian Parliament ("Komsomolskaia pravda" 7 February 1991).

Such a situation leads to public pressure for the creation of organizations which are independent of the formal power-brokers. Out of the various bodies dealing with national, social and general political issues one of the most important to emerge over the last few years has been the Tartar Public Centre (TPC). This broadly-based movement projects the national aspirations of Tartars. As with all such bodies there have been a variety of internal conflicts, but owing to the strong "nucleus" extreme elements appear to have been effectively marginalized.

As was argued earlier, the development of educational institutions and general scientific knowledge in the Kazan area was largely due to the presence of Kazan State University. It was one of the most prestigious at the time of its founding (1804) and remains in the leading group. At present, most of the active participants in the Republic's national-democratic movement are drawn from the ranks of the university's professors and students, along with intellectuals from other institutions, and (importantly) other nationalities. In our view this accounts for the predominantly democratic slant of public opinion, and the powerful cultural and intellectual basis of the dialogue with other national, social and political forces.

A major focus of contemporary aspirations is the strengthening and democratic development of the national republic as a free and independent state within its existing borders, becoming at the same time the world centre of Tartar culture and national traditions. The TPC then sees its rôle as that of actively helping Tartars living outside the TSSR towards the realization of cultural autonomy. The Second Congress of the movement held in Kazan from 15–17 February 1991, looked back on its first two years and saw itself as having achieved one of its central aims; this being the adoption by the republican power of the "Declaration Concerning State Sovereignty of the TSSR and the Transition to a Market Economy".

For the coming period it set itself a series of broad goals, and identified the key political forces in the Republic at that time as three-fold:

(a) The TPC,
(b) The Official Authorities, along with the Communist Party of the Soviet Union (CPSU), and

(c) A heterogeneous stream of activity, but centred around the newspaper "Vecherniais Kazan" (*Evening Kazan*)

The core strategy of the national-democratic movement was then defined as the attainment of equal human rights as the basis for *free development of the whole population of the TSSR.*

As far as relations between Tartarstan and Russia were concerned the TPC had to tread warily, in the knowledge that the majority of Tartars live in Russia, among Russians. Any agreement governing such relations would need to be based on a bilateral treaty covering economic and political matters, involving a partnership of equals and precluding any element of deference to the Russian Federation. This was the position taken in early 1991 by the national democratic movement, and appeared to conform to the views of the mass of public opinion. Similarly the position in relation to the All-Union Treaty was clear; participation should be on the basis of equality and independence. From the Tartar side, however, it was always seen that this was going to be very difficult to achieve, given that the major part of industry was controlled by the Treaty.

In such a brief chapter it is not possible to develop these arguments further. But one should perhaps comment on the general significance of these political processes. It is essentially a question of re-establishing the position of the Tartar nation in history. Traditionally it had a mediatory rôle in the relations between peoples and in particular between Russia and Central Asia: it was an intermediate point between East and West. It had a central rôle in trading, in diplomacy and as a military "buffer", in addition to the dissemination of culture via the written word.

It may well be that the intermediary rôle will be even more crucial in the near future owing to the rising aspirations for self-determination among nations in Central Asia; the consequences of which will include a re-orientation towards Eastern culture and "traditions", the adoption of native languages and a sharp reduction in the use of Russian. In this context one should perhaps note the creation of an Association of Turkish Peoples and the involvement of Tartars in this consolidation of Turkish cultures (*Millet* January 1991. This is a publication from the TPC.) A key element of the dialogue with the West is likely to be the recognition that there is much knowledge to be shared in matters as diverse as economics, politics, and social and cultural traditions.

Conclusion

The history and culture of the Tartar nation, an extremely broad ethnic community, have deep roots in the East-Muslim world and especially that of the Turkish peoples. At the same time there are a number of "branches", one being intimately linked to the Volga-Kama region (the Bulgar – and later, Kazan – state). The current Republic of Tartarstan covers roughly the same territory, explaining its deep significance for Tartars. But it is important to recognize that the common self-identification is rather differentiated at the level of sub-ethnos. The ancient Bulgar identity is quite distinct from that of the Tartar and, as argued earlier, this has led to a great deal of historical confusion.

In light of the recent upsurge of national consciousness in the former USSR, the relations between Tartars and Russians take on a new significance. This is so for two major reasons:

1. In the "historical consciousness" of the two peoples there are memories of long and bitter struggles. On the part of Russians, these include an awareness of the indignity rained upon them by the Mongolian invasion – this being encapsulated by the very term "Tartar". Among Tartars, there are memories of an ancient high culture, a strong independent state, and a period of superiority over the Russian state. Mixed with this is knowledge of the aftermath; the destruction of their state, the annihilation of many of their people, and the period of subjugation prior to the revolution of 1917.

2. As for the Soviet period, social distance was reduced as a matter of policy, inevitably increasing the chance of ethnic conflict. The overall effect of Russification was the denial of national identity, and a growing resentment of the "Centre" and of Russians. This in turn created the potential for a massive conflagration spreading throughout Soviet society, given the dispersion of Tartars and the geo-political position of the Republic.

The concept of ethnogenesis, as employed by Gumilev, helps us to estimate the potential of the re-emerging "ethnos" and to understand why it has occurred at the present time. The deep significance of ethnic identity to societal development has finally been recognized, in such a way as to complement existing social theories, for example those based on class struggle. In this way we can come to understand the struggle, confrontation, collaboration and co-existence of Russians and Tartars as representatives of Turkish language and Slav ethnos at the frontiers of Europe and

Asia. It throws light on the desire for a conservation of ethnic identity, and to the new rapprochement with its increasing levels of mutual interaction. In the Republic of Tartarstan, the creation of a common cultural and intellectual base is seen as a way of improving relations between Russians and Tartars, and thus reducing the chances of future confrontation.

Our conclusion therefore would be that, although the situation in the former Union is at the same time both complex and potentially grave in its implications for all its peoples, there are some positive signs. Although bitter struggles have torn apart much of Armenia, Georgia and Azerbaijan, other conflicts based on the quest for independent recognition of nationhood may be settled without such bloodshed. (Ending on a personal note, it should perhaps be pointed out that this chapter was prepared jointly by two scholars, one of Tartar and one of Russian origin.)

Postscript: aftermath of the attempted coup of August 1991

In the wake of the failed coup, moves to attain equal status between Tartarstan and the other republics of the former Union have undergone a process of transformation. The rising level of conflict between the RSFSR and TSSR in the light of the new political situation, involving both current realities and future aspirations, explained the somewhat cool response of the Republic to the events in Moscow. The only clear protest came from the national Party "Ittifak", and a handful of students. No military action was taken and the situation remained calm. In spite of waves of protest, both the powers of the President and the current incumbent (elected in the summer of 1991 following the elections for the Russian Presidency) remained in place.

The position regarding food and accommodation was better than in many other regions, and dialogue between different parties continued despite the demise of the CPSU. On the other hand, there were political tensions stemming from a rise in nationalist sentiment. There remained the possibility of conflict while nationalist groups on both sides expressed increasingly radical, and often extremist views. As one might expect there were very different conceptions of what a "new" republic might look like. Visions varied from those concerned with the primacy of "nation", to those who supported the idea of a broad liberal democracy, to those who wanted nothing less than a fully-fledged independent Islamic state.

The vision from Moscow, however, was of a single, indivisible Russian state. Now, while this position was widely condemned, the idea of a resort to military action was unpopular. There were memories of the last such attempt, by Chechen's nationalist movement. This provoked the retrenchment of all non-Russian peoples and especially those with Islamic traditions.

Given the state of flux which currently (mid-1992) engulfs all parties to the former Union there are undoubtedly widespread fears as to the nature of the ultimate political resolution of the competing claims of nations. On the other hand, in Tartarstan there are positive signs. There is evidence to suggest that useful progress is being made on an economic treaty to govern internal affairs, and its former international trading rôle is being restored.

Despite geo-political tensions, academic and quasi-academic research has continued. In October 1991, for example, a public opinion survey on the socio-political situation in Tartarstan was conducted by the Information Service of the Supreme Council of the TSSR. This was based on a representative sample of 1505 people from rural areas and a number of major towns, including Kazan. Bearing in mind the usual caveats in relation to survey data, and the possible unwillingness of respondents to completely "open up" to official interviewers, a few tentative conclusions may nevertheless be put forward.

Russians appear to be less confident than Tartars that political developments in the Republic will lead in the direction of democracy. They are also less sure (34 per cent as against 54.7 per cent) about the desirability of signing the new treaty between Tartarstan and the RSFSR, which would confer equal sovereign status. Russians are for limited sovereignty in economic matters (61.6 per cent), but opposed to the idea of an independent state, only 18.9 per cent expressing support (the figures for Tartars being 37.1 per cent and 28 per cent respectively). And, additional data from the survey shows that while around half of the general population are concerned with the state of relations between "nations", the sense of rising tension is much more common among Russians. Our conclusion would be that the latter are suffering the insecurity of a nation whose claim on the land on which they have settled is being challenged by force of historical argument.

References

Anderson, B. A. & B. D. Silver 1990. Some factors in the linguistic and ethnic Russification of Soviet nationalities: Is everyone becoming Russian? In *The Nationalities Factor in Soviet Politics and Society*. L. Hajda & M. Beissinger (eds), 117-9. Boulder, San Francisco and Oxford: Westview Press.

"Communist Tatarii" (The Communist of Tartaria) 1990. 7 (11).

Davletshin, G. M. 1990. *Voljskaia Bulgaria: duhovnaya kultura*. Kazan: Tatknigizdat.

Gumilev, L. 1990. *Ethnogenesis and the Biosphere*. Moscow: Progress Publishers.

Karimullin, A. 1989. *Stanovlenie i razvitie tatarskoi sovetskoe knigi*. Kazan: Tatarskoie knijnoie (Tartars' Book Publishers).

Khalikov, A. K. 1989. *Tartarskii narod i eigo predki*. Kazan: Tatarskoe knijnoe izdatelstvo.

Khudiakov, M. 1990. *Ocherki po istorii Kazanskogo khanstva* (Essays on the history of Kazan's Khanate). Kazan: Fond tatarskogo iazyka i literatury (The Tartar's Language and Literature Foundation Publishers). (Reprint of work first published in 1923)

Likhachev, D. S. 1983. *Zemlia rodnaia*. Moskva: Prosveshchnie.

"*Narodnoie khoziaistvo RSFSR v 1989 g*" (The National Economy of the RSFSR in 1989). 1990. Moskow: Goskomstat (Publishers for the State Committee of the RSFSR).

Nurutdinov, F. G. 1990. Jizn Sardara, *Bolgar Ile* ("Bulgar Land"), Istoriko-kulturnaia gazeta kluba "Bulgar al Djadid" (Monthly newspaper of the cultural organization, "New Bulgar").: Kazan-Orenburg, aprel 1990.

"*Socialnoe i Nacionalnoe: Opyt etnosociologicheskogo issledovania po materialam Tatarskoe ASSR*" ("Social and National: the findings of ethno-sociological research into data from the Tartarstan ASSR") 1972. Moskow: izdatelstvo "Nauka" (Science Publishers).

Suleimenov, O. 1975. *AZ i IA*. Alma-Ata: izdatelstvo "Jazuiny".

Tatarinform 1990a. (New Edition) Nezavicimaia gazeta informationnogo agentstva "Tatarinform" (New edition of the independent newspaper of the information agency, "Tartarinform"), Kazan: December.

Tatarinform 1990b. First edition. Kazan.

Tomilev, N. A. 1983. *Ocherki etnograii turkskogo naselenia Tomskogo Probia* (Essays on the ethnography of the Turkish population of the Tomsk region on the river Ob). Tomsk: Izdatelstvo TGU (Tomsk State University Publisher).

Index

Printed in the United Kingdom
by Lightning Source UK Ltd.
103170UKS00001B/9